THE SUFI BROTHERHOODS IN THE SUDAN

The Sufi Brotherhoods in the Sudan

ALI SALIH KARRAR

الطرق الصوفية في السودان

علي صالح كرار

NORTHWESTERN UNIVERSITY PRESS
EVANSTON, ILLINOIS

Northwestern University Press
Evanston, Illinois 60201-2807

Printed in Hong Kong

ISBN 0-8101-1045-8

Library of Congress Cataloging-in-Publication Data

Karrar, Ali Salih.
The Sufi brotherhoods in the Sudan / by Ali Salih Karrar.
p. cm. — (Series in Islam and society in Africa)
Includes bibliographical references and index.
ISBN 0-8101-1045-8 (cloth : alk. paper)
1. Sufism—Sudan—History. I. Title II. Series.
BP188.8.S8K36 1992
297'.65—dc20 91-41037
CIP

The paper used in this publication meets the minimum requirements of American National Standard for Information Sciences—Permanence of Paper for Printed Library Materials, ANSI Z39.48-1984.

To My Daughters Fadwa and Marwa

CONTENTS

DIAGRAMS

FOREWORD

by R.S. O'Fahey

Conventionally the modern history of the Sudan is considered to start with the Turco-Egyptian invasion of 1821. The new colonial power began a process of modernization that mirrored, however feebly, what Muḥammad ᶜAlī Pasha and his successors were to attempt in Egypt; cash crops and taxation in money were introduced, a rudimentary but uniform system of administration was imposed, some schools were opened, maps were drawn and later telegraph lines were laid. Northern Sudanese society experienced a quasi-European form of colonialism.

An alternative view might suggest that the decision in 1815 by the Moroccan mystic, Aḥmad ibn Idrīs, to allow his young student, Muḥammad ᶜUthmān al-Mīrghanī, to undertake a missionary journey through the northern Sudan was as much a turning-point as the southward march of Muḥammad ᶜAlī's army a few years later. If the latter were to bring the structures of a colonial state, al-Mīrghanī and others like him were to bring about profound changes in the spiritual life and loyalties of the northern Sudanese. The coming together of these two processes was to culminate in the Mahdist revolution (1881-5).

Dr. Karrar's study is an "insider's" account and analysis of the history of the Sufi brotherhoods in the northern Sudan generally, but with a particular focus on his own homeland, the Shāyqiyya country. The Sufi character of Sudanese Islam is a cliché in that country's historiography. Since the survey of J.S. Trimingham, *Islam in the Sudan* (London, 1949), much detailed research has been done, which Dr. Karrar has been able to build upon and to extend. The result is a comprehensive study based on internal written and oral sources.

The earliest Sufi affiliations in the Sudan, Qādiriyya and Shādhiliyya, were localized and lineage-based. The holy man, teacher, mediator, medical practitioner, lived in uneasy harmony with the local rulers. Son followed father or nephew succeeded uncle. Compromises with pre-Islamic customs were common and there was relatively little contact with the outside Islamic world.

For reasons that are still not completely clear, change came in the late eighteenth and early nineteenth centuries. As in Southeast Asia, India, North and West Africa, a new style of Sufi organization was brought to the Sudan between about 1780 and 1830 that marked a significant break with the past. The coming of the new orders,

Sammāniyya, Khatmiyya, Rashīdiyya and others, was to lead to profound changes in the lives of most Sudanese Muslims. The local holy families were incorporated into mass supra-tribal organizations that gave their allegiance to families, like the Mīrghanī and Idrīsī, whose links were pan-Islamic. Many more Sudanese lived and studied in Cairo or the holy cities; there was an upsurge in both popular devotional poetry and scholarly writing, which played their part in raising Sudanese Islamic consciousness. It is this process that Dr. Karrar documents in detail and where he provides a case study that will serve as a valuable contribution to future comparative studies.

These new Sufi orders have been frequently discussed under the rubric "neo-Sufism" with the suggestion that they brought with them new doctrines that were in part Wahhābī-inspired. More recent research suggests that such generalizations are premature if not inaccurate, that what was new, as Dr. Karrar makes clear, were organizational and devotional innovations.

Dr. Karrar concludes his study by emphasizing the continuity between the work of the new brotherhoods and the upsurge of the Mahdist revolution. Here he provides a new perspective on one of the great cataclysms in nineteenth-century Islam.

PREFACE AND ACKNOWLEDGEMENTS

The present study attempts to trace the historical development and the impact of the Sufi brotherhoods on the Sudan until the end of the nineteenth century, with special reference to the Shāyqiyya region. For the sake of brevity and without intending any disrespect, honorific titles such as shaykh, *sayyid* and *ustādh* have been kept to a minimum.

As will be shown, during the period when the central Sudan was under the influence of the ancient brotherhoods, the Qādiriyya and Shādhiliyya, the Shāyqiyya region was dominated by a number of religious teachers who were either not Sufis or who adopted an unaffiliated form of Sufism. By the mid-seventeenth century, however, the Qādiriyya and Shādhiliyya began to infiltrate into the Shāyqiyya region, but it seems that these orders did not gain much ground.

By contrast, the nineteenth century saw the domination of the region by a number of centralized new brotherhoods, mainly connected with the school of Aḥmad b. Idrīs, one of the key figures of Islam in that century.

The shift in the Shāyqiyya region from what may be termed a "Sudanic belt" pattern of Islam, dominated by individual holy men, to a Middle Eastern one with organized Sufi brotherhoods is discussed within its political and socio-economic context.

The present book is a revised version of my Ph.D. thesis, "The Sufi Brotherhoods in the Sudan until 1900, with special reference to the Shāyqiyya region", submitted to the Faculty of Arts, University of Bergen in 1985. I have benefited from the critical comments and valuable suggestions offered by my examiners: Professor J.O. Hunwick, Northwestern University, who acted as my First Opponent, Professor R.S. O'Fahey and Dr. Anders Bjørkelo, University of Bergen.

During my four years of research at the Department of History, University of Bergen, Norway, I have acquired debts of gratitude to many people and several institutions. Although it is impossible to list all of them here, mention should be made of some of them. First of all, thanks must go to the Sudan Government and the Norwegian Agency for International Development (NORAD) for providing the financial support which made this study possible. I am also indebted to my superior, Dr. M.I. Abu Salim, the Director of the National Records Office, Khartoum, for releasing me from my duties there for over four years. He, together with Professor Yūsuf Faḍl Ḥasan and Professor

Muhammed Omer Beshir of the University of Khartoum, has set me on the "path" of research. To all of them I am most grateful.

Thanks are also due to my old teachers at the University of Khartoum, namely Professor Tāj al-Sirr Ḥarrān, Professor Ḥasan Aḥmad Ibrāhīm, the late Dr. Aḥmad ᶜUthmān Ibrāhīm and Dr. Bashīr Ibrāhīm Bashīr, for their valuable comments and encouragement. Mention should also be made of my friends, Drs. ᶜAlī Osman Moḥammad Ṣāliḥ, Ibrāhīm Karsanī, ᶜAlī al-Tijānī al-Māhī, Amīn Ḥāmid Zein al-ᶜĀbdīn, ᶜAwaḍ al-Sīd Karsanī and Maḥmūd ᶜAbdalla Ibrāhīm.

I owe a longstanding debt of gratitude to the members of the Adārisa family of Omdurman and Dongola with whom my ties of friendship go back nearly ten years. The same is true of the descendants of *sayyid* Ibrāhīm al-Rashīd and their senior representative, *khalīfa* Muḥammad al-Tuhāmī al-Ḥasan.

I would also like to express my deepest gratitude to all my informants from the various orders, whose names are given at the end of the book under "Sources and Bibliography". Special mention, however, should be made of *khalīfa* Muḥammad ᶜAbd al-Ḥamīd al-ᶜIrāqī, *khalīfa* ᶜAlī Muḥammad al-Shaykh Jiqaydī and *ustādh* Muḥammad Aḥmad ᶜAbd al-Raḥmān al-Nāṭiq.

I am grateful too to my colleagues in the National Records Office, Khartoum, and to my friends at the Sudan Library and Institute of the African and Asian Studies, both at the University of Khartoum, for being so helpful. To my friend and former colleague, ᶜAbd al-ᶜĀl Aḥmad ᶜUthmān, who acted as my research assistant in the Shāyqiyya region, I will always remain indebted. I wish also to thank my friends, *ustādha* Sawsan ᶜAbd al-Ghanī and *ustādh* Hāshim of the Egyptian National Archives, Cairo, for their valuable help.

I would also like to express my thanks to Professor R.H. Pierce of the Classics Department, University of Bergen, for his constructive criticism and for giving me much of his time. I am indebted as well to Professor P.M. Holt, the "Shaykh" of the historians of the Sudan, for his valuable comments and suggestions and for providing me with copies of some of his articles and certain manuscripts.

My thanks are also owed to Professors J.N. Bell, J.O. Hunwick, F. de Jong and J.L. Spaulding, and to Drs. Lidwien Kapteijns, Anders Bjørkelo, Einar Thomassen, Aḥmad al-Shāhī, Neil McHugh, and to Knut S. Vikør, Albrecht Hofheinz, Leif Manger, Linda Sørbø, and Daniel Wolk.

I am indebted to the Department of History, University of Bergen, for creating very stimulating working conditions and for placing all their facilities at my disposal. I should thank too the staff of the University Library for the help that they have given.

To my Sudanese friends in Bergen, Sharīf Ḥarīr, Anwar M. Osman, ᶜAbd al-Ḥamīd M. Osman and Āmāl Abū ᶜAfān, I am also indebted in many ways. My Norwegian, African, Arab and Asian friends have made my stay with my little family in Norway very pleasant.

Special thanks are due to Sunniva Bjørkelo for her superb typing of this study. My deepest appreciation and gratitude go to my parents and members of my family in the Sudan for their support. This gratefulness, indeed, should be extended to my wife Zaynab and my daughter Fadwa who lived with me in Norway for three years. Their understanding and patience were an indispensable aid to me, especially in moments of frustration.

Last but not least, mention should be made of my painstaking supervisor, Professor R.S. O'Fahey. For his help and encouragement, without which the present study would have not reached its present form, I am most grateful.

ABBREVIATIONS AND SHORT TITLES

Al-A^{c}lām	Khayr al-Dīn al-Ziriklī, *al-A^{c}lām: qāmūs tarājim li-ashhar al-rijāl wa'l-nisā' min al-^{c}arab wa'l-musta^{c}ribīn wa'l-mustashriqīn*, n.p. (Beirut?), n.d. (c. 1979)
b.	*ibn*: "son"
Bergen	Literary manuscripts and other documents in the Photographic Collection, Department of History, University of Bergen
BSOAS	Bulletin of the School of Oriental and African Studies
bt.	*bint*: "daughter".
EI^2	*Encyclopaedia of Islam*, new edn., Leiden, 1969 (in progress)
ENA	Egyptian National Archives, Cairo
ERE	*Encyclopedia of Religion and Ethics*
GAL	Carl Brockelmann, *Geschichte der arabischen Literatur*, 2nd. edn., 2 vols., Leiden, 1943-9
GAL S	*ibid.*, Supplementbanden, I-III, Leiden, 1937-42
k.	*kitāb*: "book"
K. al-ibāna	Aḥmad b. Idrīs b. al-Naṣayḥ, *Kitāb al-ibāna al-nūriyya fī sha'n ṣāḥib al-ṭarīqa al-Khatmiyya*, ms. (see Sources and Bibliography, B.2). Unless otherwise indicated, references are given to the Bergen photocopy, accession no. 240.
IJAHS	*International Journal of African Historical Studies*
IJMES	*International Journal of Middle East Studies*
Makhṭūṭa	*Makhṭūṭa kātib al-shūna fī ta'rīkh al-salṭana Sinnāriyya wa'l-idāra al-Miṣriyya*, ed. al-Shāṭir Buṣaylī ^{c}Abd al-Jalīl, Cairo 1963
MDS	*Majallat al-dirāsāt al-Sūdāniyya* (Khartoum)
NRO	National Records Office, Khartoum
r	*Risāla*: "letter, treatise"

SAD	Sudan Archive, School of Oriental Studies, University of Durham
SNR	*Sudan Notes and Records*

A NOTE ON TRANSLITERATION

Arabic personal names have generally been transliterated according to the system used by the *Encyclopaedia of Islam*, but with the omission of the subscript ligatures and the substitution of "j" for "dj" and "q" for "ḳ". In some instances, I have preferred "ō" to "ū", e.g. Khōjalī for Khūjalī, and have written ^{c}Abdullāhi and ^{c}Abdallāhi instead of ^{c}Abd Allāh, e.g. ^{c}Abdullāhi al-Dufārī and ^{c}Abdallāhi, the Khalīfa. Nor have I always been consistent in the grammatical form of ethnic names, e.g. Ja^{c}aliyyūn, but Ḥalawiyyīn.

Most place names have been spelt as written, except for Khartoum (al-Khartoum), Omdurman (Ummdurmān) and Shendi (Shandī).

I have chosen to spell Shāyqiyya thus to avoid giving the impression that the name coming from our eponymous father, Shāyq, contains a medial *hamza*.

1

THE LAND, ITS HISTORY AND THE COMING OF ISLAM

Introduction

Trimingham traces the development of the Sufi orders in Islam through three stages: the *khānqāh* stage, the *ṭarīqa* stage and the *ṭāʾifa* stage.[1] This threefold typology, however, is not applicable to the Sudan. The *khānaqāh*, which originated in Persia and gained popularity in Iraq, Syria and Egypt during the twelfth century, did not exist in the Sudan. As Professor De Jong notes, Trimingham uses the term *ṭāʾifa* inconsistently, replacing it in several passages with *ṭarīqa*. Furthermore, the term *ṭāʾifa* is not used in Sudanese sources to denote *ṭarīqa*.[2]

As is shown in the present study, Sufism was the most fundamental characteristic of Islam in the Sudan. Its development may be traced through two main stages, the pre-*ṭarīqa* stage and the *ṭarīqa* stage. The first stage was dominated by the activities of religious men who adopted an unaffiliated form of Sufism, that is a Sufism not bound to a particular organizational pattern. The second stage in its turn may be divided into two phases. The first began in the sixteenth century with the coming of the decentralized Sufi affiliations, namely the Qādiriyya and Shādhiliyya. This coincided with the foundation of the Funj Sultanate that ruled the country until it was destroyed by the Turco-Egyptian invasion in 1820-1. The second phase took place in the eighteenth and nineteenth centuries when the country came to be dominated by a number of centralized or semi-centralized *ṭarīqas*, namely the Sammāniyya, Tijāniyya, Khatmiyya and Idrīsiyya. With the exception of the Sammāniyya and Tijāniyya, all these orders derived ultimately from the teachings of the Moroccan Sufi and scholar Aḥmad b. Idrīs (d. 1837).

1 J.S. Trimingham, *The Sufi Orders in Islam*, Oxford 1971, 1-104.
2 In a review of Trimingham, *Sufi Orders*, in *Journal of Semitic Studies*, 17/2, 1972, 279.

The Sufi "Way" is a long and arduous journey marked by a number of spiritual attainments (*maqāmāt*) that reflect the adherent's progress. Through its chain of spiritual authority (*silsila*) deriving from the founder and, in several cases, from the Prophet and his cousin ᶜAlī, a *ṭarīqa* gave its members a sense of legitimation. All *ṭarīqas* were agreed that an aspirant who desired a safe journey and arrival at his destination (i.e. perfect knowledge of God) should put himself under the guidance of a shaykh. One of the early Sufi teachers, Abū Yazīd al-Bisṭāmī (d. 260/874-5), is frequently quoted in this respect:

He who has no Shaykh, his Shaykh is Satan.

The Sufi orders in the Sudan, as in the rest of the Muslim world, never constituted a world of their own. In the view of most Sufi shaykhs and followers, Sufism and Sharia were entirely interlocking manifestations of faith. Muḥammad ᶜUthmān al-Mīrghanī, the founder of the Khatmiyya, confirmed this when he gave the metaphor:

The Sharia is a root, *ṭarīqa* is a branch and the *ḥaqīqa* ["Reality" or "Truth"- metonymy for the Sufi way] is the fruit.[3]

There were, however, some religious figures who did not give equal weight to the exoteric sciences (represented by *fiqh* and Sharia) and esoteric (*taṣawwuf*). A *ṭarīqa* shaykh had absolute authority and expected the total submission of his followers. He was believed to be divinely-guided and incapable of sin. Whatever his actions, even if they were in open contravention of Sharia, they had to be understood within the context of his infallibility. Some Sufi shaykhs were not concerned to suppress local non-Islamic practices. This tolerance was presumably why some pious and learned figures were unwilling to join the *ṭarīqas*.

The Sufi orders in the Sudan, as elsewhere in the Muslim world, played significant social, economic, cultural and political roles. In these organizations the ties of brotherhood were to supersede the old bonds of kinship. The present book reveals the close connexion between the brotherhoods, trade and traders. This association was, indeed, not unique to the Sudan. In Northwest Africa, for example, the Kunta-Qādiriyya, Nāṣiriyya, Sanūsiyya and Tijāniyya played important roles in the trans-Saharan trade. Furthermore, the late nineteenth century saw the

3 Aḥmad b. ᶜAbd al-Raḥmān al-Raṭbī, *Minḥat al-aṣḥāb li-man arāda sulūk ṭarīq al-aṣfiyā' wa'l-aḥbāb*, in, *al-Rasā'il al-Mīrghaniyya*, 99 and Ahmad al-Shahi, *Themes from Northern Sudan*, London 1986, 25.

economic activity of the Murīdiyya order founded by Aḥmad Bamba in Senegal.[4]

There are several examples of Sufi orders throughout the Muslim world that transformed themselves into political forces. In Africa, for instance, the fifteenth century saw a *jihād* movement by the adherents of the Jazūliyya branch of the Shādhiliyya order in Morocco against the Portuguese who were establishing enclaves on the Atlantic coast. Further examples may be seen in the *jihād* of the Amīr ᶜAbd al-Qādir against the French in western Algeria in the 1830s and 1840s and the movement of Muḥammad ᶜAbd Allāh Ḥasan, the so-called "Mad Mullah", in Somalia against the British and Italians in the period 1899-1920. Finally, mention should be made of the *jihāds* of the Qādirī shaykh ᶜUthmān b. Fūdī (Usuman dan Fodio) in northwestern Nigeria and the Tijāniyya representative *al-ḥājj* ᶜUmar Tall in Mali in the nineteenth century.[5] As Professor Hunwick has pointed out, in contrast to the former movements, these *jihāds* were waged against internal enemies.[6] The present book shows that a Sufi *ṭarīqa* may serve as a tool for foreign or local political authorities, or at least co-operate with them. In this sense the militancy of the Qādiriyya under ᶜAbd al-Qādir in Algeria contrasts sharply with the Nāṣiriyya in Morocco, who capitulated without resistance to the French and co-operated with them.[7] Although the present book traces the evolution of the *ṭarīqas* in the Sudan in the approximate period from 1600 to 1900, it concentrates mainly on the period of colonial rule. The Turco-Egyptian invasion of 1820-1 led to major political, economic and religious changes. Despite the fact that the new regime established an official hierarchy of *ᶜulamāʾ* on the Egyptian pattern and encouraged the Sudanese to study at al-Azhar, there is no evidence of a conscious religious policy, parallel to that adopted for Egypt, seeking to control the Sudanese religious institutions. At the local level, the religious life in the Sudan continued to be much the same as it had been during the Funj period. The religious teachers

4 R.G. Jenkins, "The evolution of religious brotherhoods in North and Northwest Africa, 1523-1900", in *Studies in West African Islamic History*, ed. J.R. Willis, i, London 1979, 61. On the Murīdiyya see D. Cruise O'Brien, *The Mourids of Senegal*, Oxford 1971.

5 Jenkins (1979), 62.

6 Personal communication.

7 Jenkins (1979), 62.

continued to play their traditional role and their centres of learning were subsidized by the government.

The present study, however, suggests that the relations between the invaders and the Sudanese religious class should be understood within the general framework of those who supported and those who opposed the regime.

As will be shown, in 1881 the Turco-Egyptian regime was overthrown by a religious revolution, the Mahdiyya. Muḥammad Aḥmad, the Mahdi, believed in the universality of his movement and thus sought to unify all Muslims. Muḥammad Aḥmad was a Sufi shaykh before manifesting himself as a Mahdi. He made use of the general Sufi atmosphere and networks in the Sudan to preach his cause. Thus his earliest contacts were with influential Sufi figures.

The Geographical Setting

The name Shāyqiyya, describing one of the most prominent riverain ethnic groups of the northern Sudan, appears not to have existed before the penetration of the Arabs into the Sudan during the fourteenth to the sixteenth centuries.[8] However, the region which was later to become the Shāyqiyya homeland was, for example, the administrative and, by about the middle of the third century BC., the religious centre of the Kingdom of Kush (c. 750 BC. - 350 AD.), whose influence was felt as far as Asia Minor.[9] The region also saw the rise of the Christian Kingdom of Maqurra during the sixth century AD. After the coming of the Arabs the northern Sudan came to be divided into regions, each known as *dār* (pl. *diyār*, lit. "homeland"). Although each of these *dārs* was dominated by one descent group which had pre-eminent domain over the land, water and other resources, they were never exclusive and other ethnic groups were to be found in them.

According to Crawford, the Shāyqiyya region or *dār al-Shāyqiyya* extended from Bartī Island, ten miles above the Fourth Cataract, to Jabal

8 R.S. O'Fahey and J.L. Spaulding, *Kingdoms of the Sudan*, London 1974, 28, refer to an account by an Italian visitor to Upper Egypt in 1529, "Who was correctly informed that pyramids could be found south of Egypt in the land of the 'Xiogeia'".

9 W.Y. Adams, *Nubia. Corridor to Africa*, Princeton 1977, 245-93.

al-Ḍayqa, on the west bank of the Nile near Jabal ibn ᶜAwf in the Arāk area.[10] Gleichen, however, says that the Shāyqiyya region extended from al-Dabba, forty-five miles west of Kūrtī at the southern end of the great bend of the Nile, upstream to Bartī.[11] An indecisive battle which took place in 1812 between the Mamluks who had escaped massacre in 1811 by Muḥammad ᶜAlī Pasha, the ruler of Egypt, and established their camp at Dongola al-ᶜUrdī (Dongola "the camp"), and the Shāyqiyya, resulted in a compromise (*ṣulḥ*) according to which the latter's northern frontier was moved back to the village of al-Ghurayba, just south of Kūrtī, where it remained until the time of the Turco-Egyptian invasion in 1820.[12]

Giving precise geographical limits for the Shāyqiyya region is difficult. Hayder Ibrahim attributes this to the warlike and predatory nature of the Shāyqiyya, who continuously raided their neighbours, causing the territory under their control to fluctuate.[13]

The Land and the People

The dominant ethnic group in *dār al-Shāyqiyya* was, of course, the Shāyqiyya. According to MacMichael, all those who claimed Arab descent in the Sudan may be divided into two groups: the Jaᶜaliyyūn and the Juhayna, the latter being mainly nomads.[14] The term Jaᶜaliyyūn in its wider sense denotes all the sedentary groups which claim descent from al-ᶜAbbās, the Prophet's uncle, through their eponymous founder Ibrāhīm Jaᶜal. Two of the latter's descendants, ᶜArmān and Abū Kham-

10 O.G.S. Crawford, *The Fung Kingdom of Sennar*, Gloucester, 1951, 43.

11 See A.E.W., Gleichen, *The Anglo-Egyptian Sudan*, i, London 1905, 83.

12 Muḥammad ᶜAbd al-Raḥīm, *Al-Nidāʾ fī dafᶜ al-iftirāʾ*, Cairo 1952, 27, and ᶜAwaḍ ᶜAbd al-Hādī al-Awaḍ, "al-Shāyqiyya taʾrīkhuhum wa-thaqāfatuhum ḥattā al-fatḥ al-turkī", *MDS*, 1971, 21.

13 Hayder Ibrahim, *The Shaiqiya. The cultural and social change of a Northern Sudanese riverain people*, Wiesbaden 1979, 10.

14 H.A. MacMichael, *A History of the Arabs in the Sudan*, Cambridge 1922, i, 197-306.

sīn, were the "founding fathers" of the Jaᶜaliyyūn proper of the Shendi area.[15]

The Shāyqiyya, the descendants of Shāyq, like other northern riverain ethnic groups, claim ᶜAbbāsid ancestry.[16] This claim has been interpreted by several historians to mean that they are Arabized Nubians, the result of the Arabs intermarrying with the indigenous people, the Nubians.[17]

The origin of the Shāyqiyya, which is still a controversial issue in Sudanese history, lies beyond the scope of this study.[18]

Although the Shāyqiyya claim to descend from a common ancestor, they never formed a unified kingdom under one king or *malik*.[19] The Shāyqiyya consisted of numerous sub-divisions.[20]

At the time of the Turco-Egyptian invasion in November 1820, their region was divided into four separate kingdoms: the Ḥannikāb, which extended for sixteen miles between Jabal al-Ḍayqa and the village of al-Zūma[21] and was under the rule of *malik* Ṣubayr; the Kajabī, which was under *malik* Madanī; the ᶜAdlānāb, which was ruled from Marawī by *malik* Shāwīsh;[22] and finally, the ᶜUmārāb, which was under the rule of Ḥamad w. ᶜAsalā.[23]

Although relations between the Shāyqiyya kingdoms were often hostile, a common enemy always brought them together. Thus, when the Turco-Egyptians invaded in 1820, the four kingdoms united under the leadership of *malik* Shāwīsh to resist the invaders.[24] They, indeed, were

15 P.M. Holt, "Djaᶜaliyyūn" in *EI* ², ii, 351.
16 MacMichael (1922), ii, 337-8.
17 Holt, "Djaᶜaliyyūn" in *EI*², ii, 351.
18 See MacMichael (1922), i, 213-4, and Ibrahim (1979), 8-15.
19 R. Hill, *On the Frontiers of Islam*, Oxford, 1970, 70, 73 and 74, and J.L. Spaulding, "Kings of Sun and Shadow: a History of the ᶜAbdallāb Provinces of the Northern Sinnār Sultanate, 1500-1800 A.D", Ph.D. thesis, Columbia University 1971, 220. The Shāyqiyya were the only northern riverain group who did not adopt the title *makk* for their rulers. This has been explained by their desire to be distinct from others.
20 See W. Nicholls, *The Shaikia*, Dublin 1913, 46-51, and MacMichael (1922), ii, 339-40.
21 Crawford (1951), 46.
22 See G.B. English, *A Narrative of the Expedition to Dongola and Senaar*, London 1822, 82; Crawford (1951), 48, and MacMichael (1922), ii, 218.
23 Crawford (1951), 48.
24 English (1822), 82; see also Nicholls (1913), 8.

the only riverain group to resist the Turco-Egyptian expedition from the outset.

The Shāyqiyya possessed great wealth in corn and cattle, resulting from the fertility of their region. English, who visited the region in 1820, found its land better cultivated than any of the areas south of Egypt that he had so far seen:

> the waterwheels [Ar.sing. *sāqiya*], so far as we have passed their country, being frequently within half a stone's throw of each other.[25]

Another writer has observed that the Nile:

> has cut for itself a much broader trench, and fairly broad flanking terraces may be found on one side, though rarely on both.[26]

Rainfall alone in the area is insufficient to support either agriculture or nomadic life. The Shāyqiyya, like other northern riverain groups, are primarily sedentary farmers who cultivate by irrigation the narrow strip of land along the banks of the Nile as well as the islands formed by the river. To the Shāyqiyya, as for most Sudanese ethnic groups, land is not only the fundamental basis of their economy but also a symbol of social status and security against life's vicissitudes.

Before the Shāyqiyya revolt against the Funj kingdom at the end of the seventeenth century, their region was crossed by several trade-routes which followed the Nile to Upper Egypt. But as one consequence of the revolt, caravans tended to avoid Shāyqiyya raiding by travelling across the Bayūḍa desert in a northwesterly direction to meet the Nile at Kūrtī away from *dār* Shāyqiyya.[27]

The Shāyqiyya were already well-known as horse-traders in the seventeenth century.[28] Horses were always of great importance in Shāyqiyya society. According to Burckhardt,

25 English (1822), 64-5.

26 K.N. Barbour, *The Republic of the Sudan: A Regional Geography*, London 1961, 133.

27 P.M.Holt and M. Daly, *The History of the Sudan*, London 1979, 9.

28 Muḥammad al-Nūr b. Ḍayf Allāh, *K. al-ṭabaqāt fī khuṣūṣ al-awliyāʾ wa'l-ṣāliḥīn wa'l-ʿulamāʾ wa'l-shuʿarāʾ fī'l-Sūdān*, ed. Yūsuf Faḍl Ḥasan, 2nd edn, Khartoum 1974, 228; see also MacMichael (1922), ii, 266.

They [the Shāyqiyya] all fight on horseback, in coats of mail which are sold to them by merchants from Suakin and Sennar. Fire-arms are not common among them, their only weapons being a lance, target and sabre.[29]

The Shāyqiyya region was, and still is, inhabited by people of diverse ethnic origin. Although most of these groups have been assimilated into the Shāyqiyya through intermarriage, they still claim, by virtue of patrilineal descent, a non-Shāyqī origin. Since it is not my intention to give here an historical ethnography of the region, I shall confine my account to those ethnic groups who have been influential in the religious life of the region.

The Shāyqiyya region was well-known for its religious schools which attracted students from both within and outside the Sudan.[30] In turn, the Shāyqiyya were known for their hospitality and the respect given to their learned men.[31] It was presumably because of this and the wealth of the region that holy men moved in to settle among the Shāyqiyya. Like most holy men in the Sudan and elsewhere in the Muslim world, these religious figures claimed Sharifian descent (i.e. descent from the Prophet), which was a way of legitimizing their religious role.[32]

One of the non-Shāyqī families who contributed to the religious life of the Shāyqiyya region during the Funj period was the Ḥamadtūiyāb (or Ḥamatūiyāb), who settled in the village of Nūrī. Their "founding father", Ḥamadtū al-Khaṭīb, is said to have been a member of the Bakriyya ethnic group of Upper Egypt, that is a descendant of Abū Bakr al-Ṣiddīq, the first Caliph after the Prophet.[33] He settled in the region during the fifteenth century and died and was buried in al-Arkī in the Jilās area.[34] It was, however, his son ᶜAbd al-Raḥmān, known as Abū

29 J.L. Burckhardt, *Travels in Nubia*, London 1822, 64.

30 See, for example, Ibn Ḍayf Allāh (1974), 224 and 359-60; see also Burckhardt (1822), 65.

31 Burckhardt (1822), 65.

32 P. M. Holt, *Studies in the History of the Near East*, London 1973b, 126.

33 *Nasab al-Ḥamadtūiyāb*, in the possession of Ṣiddīq Shaykh, a descendant of ᶜAbd al-Raḥmān w. Ḥamadtū, Nūrī; see also MacMichael (1922), ii, 93, and al-Shahi (1986), 61.

34 Ahmad al-Shahi, "An Anthropological Study of a Sudanese Shaigiyya Village", Ph.D. thesis, Oxford University 1971, 303, and interview 19.

Shawārib, and his descendants who established the Ḥamadtūiyāb religious centre of Nūrī (see pp. 29-30).

Another non-Shāyqī religious clan is the ᶜIrāqāb (or ᶜUrāqāb) of Nūrī. Their ancestor, al-ᶜIrāqī, is said to have come from Iraq.[35] One of his descendants, *al-ḥājj* Abū'l-Qāsim, was the first member of the family to come in the seventeenth century and settle in the Shāyqiyya region. He lived and died on al-Gharīb Island in the Nūrī area. His sons were to play a significant religious and educational role in different parts of the Sudan.

Our concern here is mainly with his son, ᶜAbd al-Ḥamīd al-Aḥmar, the founder of the ᶜIrāqāb of Nūrī. He, like other holy men, received gifts of land and married into the Shāyqiyya.[36] His grandsons and their descendants were to become prominent religious teachers and among the senior local representatives of the Khatmiyya brotherhood.

A third religious family whose founder came from outside the Shāyqiyya region is the Kawārīr of Nūrī. Their pedigree shows that they are Jummūᶜiyya and that they share a common ancestry with Aḥmad al-Ṭayyib w. al-Bashīr, the founder of the Sammāniyya *ṭarīqa* in the Sudan (see pp. 44-7).[37]

Mention should also be made of the Duwayḥiyya, who belong to the Juhayna group. Although most of the Duwaḥiyya were nomads living mainly in Kordofān, they also produced religious men who influenced the northern parts of the Sudan and the Blue Nile area.[38] Among those who influenced the Shāyqiyya region were ᶜAbd al-Raḥmān w. Ḥājj al-Duwayḥī and his grandson Ibrāhīm al-Rashīd (see below pp. 102-3). A descendant of ᶜAbd al-Raḥmān, Warāq, also founded a religious subclan known as al-Warārīq.[39]

Members of the Rikābiyya holy clan, descendants of the famous religious teacher Ghulām Allāh b. ᶜĀ'id, settled among the Shāyqiyya too. The Shāyqiyya region also saw the activities of some religious figures of Maḥas and Ṣawārda origin. Finally, mention should be made of the Ṭirayfiyya, who influenced not only the religious but also the economic life of the region. The rise of the Shāyqiyya confederation in the seven-

35 MacMichael (1922), ii, 338.
36 Al-Shahi, thesis (1971), 301, and interview 18.
37 Interview 7, and al-Shahi (1986), 62.
38 Ibn Ḍayf Allāh (1974), 87, 205 and 286; see also MacMichael (1922), ii, 338.
39 Al-ᶜAwaḍ (1971), 32.

teenth century forced many members of these groups to emigrate to Kordofan and Dār Fūr.[40]

A Brief Political History

Politically, the Shāyqiyya region was part of Dongola province, which in turn was tributary to the ᶜAbdallāb, the governors of the north on behalf of the Funj, who ruled over most of the central and northern Sudan from about 1504 until 1821. At the end of the seventeenth century, the Shāyqiyya successfully revolted against Funj rule and thus became independent of the ᶜAbdallāb until 1821.Their period of independence saw their war against the fugitive Mamluks, who were supported by the King of Arqū.[41]

The Turco-Egyptian invasion of 1820, which was motivated by the desire of Muḥammad ᶜAlī Pasha, the Viceroy of Egypt, to seize control of the wealth of the Sudan,[42] led to major political, social, economic and religious change. It put an end to the declining Funj state and to the political autonomy of the local ethnic groups, bringing them under a highly centralized government.[43]

After the defeat of the Shāyqiyya by the invaders in November 1820, *malik* Shāwīsh fled to the Shendi area. Later, however, he submitted and was given a military title and his troops were enlisted as irregular cavalry (*bāshī-būzuq*).[44]

Although many people of Shāyqī origin co-operated with the new regime, serving it as soldiers and tax collectors, stigmatizing all the Shāyqiyya as collaborators is inaccurate. A fair appraisal of the attitude of the Shāyqiyya towards both the Turco-Egyptian regime and the Mahdiyya has to distinguish between those who did and those who did not support the regimes. Most of the Shāyqiyya who moved from their homeland after the defeat in 1820, and settled in the Shendi area, co-operated with the invaders and received privileges, including exemption

40 Holt, "Djaᶜaliyyūn" in *EI*², ii, 351, and R.S. O'Fahey, *State and Society in Dār Fūr*, London 1980, 141.

41 Burckhardt (1822), 66-7.

42 See further, R. Hill, *Egypt in the Sudan*, London 1959, 7-8, and Ḥasan Aḥmad Ibrāhīm, *Muḥammad ᶜAlī fī'l-Sūdān*, Khartoum n.d., 23-40.

43 See Hill (1959), *passim*.

44 *Ibid.*, 10, and Holt and Daly (1979), 51.

from taxes. Thus Khūrshīd Pasha, Governor-general of the Sudan (1826-38), exempted those Shāyqiyya who collaborated from taxes and provided them with a free monthly ration for their horses.[45] By contrast, most of the Shāyqiyya who remained in their homeland paid taxes like the rest of the Sudanese.[46]

Relations between the Turco-Egyptian regime and its supporters, however, were not always easy. Aḥmad Pasha Abū Wīdān, Khūrshīd's successor as Governor-general of the Sudan, abolished the privileges of the Shāyqiyya and ordered them to pay taxes.[47]

Muḥammad ᶜAlī Pasha had sent three jurists, Aḥmad al-Salāwī al-Maghribī al-Mālikī, Aḥmad al-Baqlī al-Shāfiᶜī and Muḥammad al-Asyūṭī al-Ḥanafī, with the invading army in 1820. Their duty was to convince the Sudanese that the invasion was being undertaken on behalf of the Ottoman Sultan in his capacity as "Commander of the Faithful", *amīr al-muʾminīn*.[48] The sending of these three *ᶜulamāʾ* has been interpreted by some scholars as part of a plan by the Egyptian regime to encourage Islamic orthodoxy in the Sudan and thus to undermine the status of the Sudanese traditional religious leadership.[49] Although the new regime did establish an official hierarchy of *ᶜulamāʾ* on the Egyptian pattern and encouraged the Sudanese to study at al-Azhar,[50] there is no evidence of a conscious religious policy seeking to undermine the Sudanese religious class. Again, the attitude of the invaders towards the holy men should be understood within the general framework of collaboration. As will be shown, those Sudanese holy men who were willing to collaborate enjoyed monthly subventions and their religious centres were subsidized.

The colonial regime also encouraged a number of Egyptian Sufi *ṭarīqas*, namely the Rifāᶜiyya, Aḥmadiyya (Badawiyya), Bayyūmiyya

45 Hill (1970), 69.

46 A letter from the Turkiyya period; see NRO, Misc. 1/27/386.

47 Hill (1959), 70.

48 Naᶜūm Shuqayr, *Taʾrīkh al-Sūdān al-qadīm wa'l-ḥadīth wa-jughrāfiyatuhu*, Cairo 1903, iii, 3-4.

49 See, for example, Hill (1959), 125-6; G. Warburg, "Religious policy in the northern Sudan: ᶜulamāʾ and Ṣufism, 1899-1918", *Asian and African Studies* (Jerusalem), vii, 1971, 90, and Holt (1973b), 127 and 139-40.

50 Holt (1973b), 127.

and the Naqshbandiyya, to move into the Sudan.[51] Aḥmad al-Salāwī, who was appointed first as Mālikī *muftī* and later as the grand *qāḍī* of the Sudan (*qāḍī ᶜumūm bilād al-Sūdān*),[52] was also a Sufi (see p. 46).

Although the Turco-Egyptian regime imposed heavy taxes upon the Sudanese and caused considerable disruption, it brought some elements of modernization. These came to include better communications, steamers on the Nile and an expanding telegraph network. Trade-routes and public security also improved considerably.[53] These facilities were to be used by the Sufi orders to centralize and administer their networks of local representatives (see Chapters Five and Six).

In 1881 the Turco-Egyptian regime was overthrown by a religious revolution, the Mahdiyya. The Mahdist state ruled the Sudan until it was in turn destroyed by an Anglo-Egyptian force in 1898. It is beyond the scope of this study to discuss the complex causes of the Sudanese Mahdiyya, but harsh economic measures and maladministration are among the main reasons for the revolt.[54] Although the Mahdī, who believed in the universality of his movement and thus sought to unify all Muslims, in theory abolished the *madhhabs* and *ṭarīqas*, in practice his policy towards the latter was much more complex.

The Coming of Islam

In the centuries known in Europe as Middle Ages the northern region of the present Republic of the Sudan was divided into three kingdoms; Maris or Nobatia, between the First and Third Nile Cataracts, Maqurra, above the Third Cataract (these two kingdoms were soon united into one kingdom called Nubia with its capital at Old Dongola on the Nile), and ᶜAlwa or Alodia with its capital at Soba on the Blue Nile.

51 NRO, Intel. 2/32/270, p. 59, and J.S. Trimingham, *Islam in the Sudan*, London 1949, 241.

52 Hill (1959), 43, and R.S. O'Fahey, "A colonial servant. Al-Salāwī and the Sudan", *Der Islam* (forthcoming).

53 *Ibid.*, 130-1, 157-60, and Holt (1973b), 139.

54 See P.M. Holt, *The Mahdist State in the Sudan, 1881-1898*, 2nd edn, Oxford 1970, 32-44.

By the middle of the sixth century, Christianity was firmly established as the state religion in all three kingdoms.[55] The Sudan enjoyed a period of cultural and economic prosperity.[56]

According to Muslim historians, the Nubians were Jacobites, that is Monophysites.[57] But, despite the active missionary campaigns in Nubia, Christianity remained the religion of the state and appears not to have gained much ground among the ordinary population.

The turning-point in the history of the northern part of the Sudan, and indeed in the Sudan as a whole, was the penetration of the Arabs, and thus the spread of Islam and Arab culture.

The Islamization of the Sudan, which was a result of cultural, political, socio-economic and military factors, was a gradual and continuing process. However, it may be divided roughly into two broad stages: superficial or primary Islamization which preceded the beginning of the sixteenth century, and real or secondary Islamization which began with the emergence of the Funj kingdom in about 1504.

During the first stage Islam was spread in two main ways; the first was through cultural influences coming in as a result of peaceful trade between Muslims and the local population. This phenomenon of combining trade with proselytization is a common theme in Islamic history. But the role of traders in Nubia was strengthened by the *Baqṭ* treaty resulting from the military campaign of the Arab governor of Upper Egypt, ᶜAbd Allāh b. Saᶜd b. Abī Sarḥ, against Nubia in 651-2. The treaty also paved the way for Arab penetration in Nubia.[58]

By the middle of the tenth century the Rabīᶜa Arabs had already settled among the local people of eastern Sudan, the Beja. Eventually, intermarriage resulted in the emergence of the Arabized Nubian Kingdom of the Banū'l-Kanz near Aswan, which extended its authority over the northern parts of Sudanese Nubia. The chief of the Banū'l-Kanz was rewarded by the Fāṭimids, the rulers of Egypt, with the title of *Kanz al-Dawla* ("The treasure of the state") for his help in arresting an Arab rebel.[59]

55 Adams (1977), 443.

56 P.L. Shinnie, "The culture of medieval Nubia and its impact on Africa", in *Sudan in Africa*, ed. Hasan, Khartoum 1971, 42-50.

57 Yūsuf Faḍl Hasan, *The Arabs and the Sudan*, Edinburgh 1967, 8.

58 *Ibid.*, 20-4.

59 *Ibid.*, 59.

The second wave of Islamization was due to the influx of Arab nomads, who had already been settled in Upper Egypt, during the period from the early fourteenth to the end of the fifteenth centuries, a period known as the Dark Ages of Sudanese history. The Nubian Kingdom of Maqurra was unable to withstand the continuous waves of Arab tribes. They thus tried to cultivate peaceful relations with them and allowed them to settle.

This influx from Upper Egypt was speeded up by the hostile policies of the successive rulers of Egypt, the Fāṭimids, Ayyūbids and Mamluks, towards the nomads. By contrast the Fāṭimids and Ayyūbids were on good terms with the Nubians, a policy that was to change drastically under the Mamluks (1250-1517). The latter set out first to interfere politically in Nubia and then to undertake military conquest.[60] This change in policy, together with a process of intermarriage and assimilation between Arabs and Nubians, resulted in the disintegration of Christian Nubia.[61] Ibn Khaldūn explains this process of disintegration paradigmatically:

> Thus it was that their kingdom fell to pieces, for it passed to the sons of the Juhayna from their Nubian mothers ...[62]

With the fall of Christian Nubia, a powerful barrier in the way of the Arab tribes disappeared. Consequently new waves came to the Sudan; most were nomads driven by the search for pastures.[63] In short, regardless of the motives of these imperfectly Islamized nomads, they were initially responsible for the Islamization and Arabization of the Sudan.[64]

The First Holy Men

The initial spread of Islamic teaching owed its impetus to holy men, often also adherents of Sufi orders, who came from the Islamic heartlands of Egypt, the Ḥijāz, the Yemen and, at a later stage, Morocco.

60 *Ibid.*, 47, 90-123.
61 Adams (1977), 525.
62 ᶜAbd al-Raḥmān b. Khaldūn, *al-ᶜIbar wa-dīwān al-mubtadāʾ wa'l-khabar*, Beirut 1958, v, 922-3.
63 B. Lewis, *The Arabs in History*, London 1960, 23.
64 Hasan (1967), 177.

Most of these holy men were to come after the rise of the Funj kingdom in about 1504.

The main difficulty in the study of the pre-Funj period is the lack of written sources. Oral traditions, however, mention the arrival of two holy men in the Sudan during the period from the early fourteenth to the beginning of the sixteenth centuries. The first was Ghulām Allāh b. ᶜĀʾid; his father came from the Yemen and he himself moved south with his sons, possibly in the second half of the fourteenth century, to Dongola, which he found:

> In extreme perplexity and confusion for lack of learned men. When he settled there he built the mosques and taught the Qurān and religious sciences ...[65]

Ghulām Allāh is described as a *ᶜālim*, that is a scholar primarily concerned with the Sharia, as well as the possessor of *baraka.*[66] His possession of *baraka* may, perhaps, be attributed to his claim to descend from the Prophet.

The second learned man was Ḥamad Abū Dunāna, who also claimed to descend from the Prophet. Abū Dunāna, unlike Ghulām Allāh, was primarily a Sufi who is said to have propagated the Shādhiliyya order in the Sudan.

The settlement of the Arabs and their intermarriage with the indigenous peoples led to the emergence of a quasi-tribal group known as the Jaᶜaliyyūn inhabiting the region between the confluence of the Atbara and Sabalūqa Gorge. The territory further south around the confluence of the Blue and the White Niles was under the control of the ᶜAbdallāb, who were themselves soon to be subjected to a new power, the Funj.

The Funj kingdom, also known as the Sinnār Sultanate after its capital Sinnār, was established by its first ruler, ᶜAmāra Dunqas. The Funj were at some stage formally converted to Islam. Although, as elsewhere in the Sudanic belt, African rituals, especially at the installation of a new sultan, were maintained.[67] The Funj rulers, however, welcomed *ᶜulamāʾ* and Sufi teachers to their country. These holy men were usually granted

65 Holt (1973b), 89; see also MacMichael (1922), ii, 35.

66 Holt (1973b), 89-90 and 122.

67 P.M. Holt, "Islamization of the Sudan", in M. Brett, ed., *Northern Africa: Islam and Modernization*, London 1973a, 15; see also M. Hiskett, "The Development of Islam in Hausaland", in *ibid.*, 59.

land and exemption from taxes and dues. The early Funj period saw a great increase in the number of these religious figures.[68]

When the Funj came to power in about 1504, there flourished in these lands neither schools of learning nor of the Quran; it is said that a man might divorce his wife and she be married by another the same day without any period of probation [*ᶜidda*], until *shaykh* Maḥmūd al-ᶜArakī came from Egypt and taught the people to observe the laws of *ᶜidda*. He lived in the White Nile area where he built a *qaṣr* [lit. palace; stronghold] known now as Maḥmūd's *qaṣr*. In the second half of the tenth [sixteenth AD.] century A.H. Sultan ᶜAmāra Abū Sikaykīn [965/1557-976/1568-9] appointed *shaykh* ᶜAjīb al-Mānjilūk. Early in his rule, *shaykh* Ibrāhīm al-Būlād came from Egypt to the Shāyqiyya region where he taught *Khalīl* [i.e. the *Mukhtaṣar* of Khalīl b. Isḥāq] and the *Risāla* [the *Risāla* of Ibn Abī Zayd al-Qayrawānī], from where knowledge of *fiqh* [jurisprudence] spread to the Gezīra. Then, after a short time, *shaykh* Tāj al-Dīn al-Bahārī came from Baghdad and introduced the path of the Sufis [i.e. the Qādiriyya] into the Funj country.[69]

This picture of the state of Islam in the pre-Funj period is, however, disputed by the author of the Funj Chronicle on the grounds that several schools flourished in the pre-Funj period in, for example, Ḥalfāyat al-Mulūk and al-Ṣabābī, in the present-day area of Khartoum North. He adds that the author of the *Ṭabaqāt* must have meant the White Nile area in the central Sudan.[70]

The most eminent religious teachers in the Shāyqiyya region during the second half of the sixteenth century were the Awlād Jābir, the "sons of Jābir", the descendants of the Ghulām Allāh b. ᶜĀʾid referred to above. Their respective qualities were described thus:

The four sons of Jābir were like the four elements; each one had his own virtue. The most learned of them was Ibrāhīm, the most worthy ᶜAbd al-Raḥmān, the most pious ᶜAbd al-Raḥīm, and their sister, Fāṭima, was their equal in learning and faith.[71]

The Awlād Jābir's fame in the field of Islamic learning was due mainly to Ibrāhīm al-Būlād.[72] He was born on the island of Turunj near

68 *Makhṭūṭa Kātib al-Shūna*, ed. al-Shāṭir Buṣaylī ᶜAbd al-Jalīl, Cairo 1963, 4-6; Muṣṭafā Musᶜad, "The Downfall of the Christian Nubian Kingdoms", *SNR*, xl, 1959, 124-7.

69 Ibn Ḍayf Allāh (1974), 41.

70 *Makhṭūṭa*, 124.

71 Ibn Ḍayf Allāh (1974), 47.

72 *Ibid.*

the present town of Karīma in the Shāyqiyya area and went to Cairo, where he studied law and grammar under a Mālikī jurist, Muḥammad al-Banūfarī (d. between 967/1559-60 and 1000/1591-2). He returned to his homeland in about 1570 and established a school at Turunj where he taught two standard textbooks of Mālikī law, the *Mukhtaṣar* of Khalīl b. Isḥāq (known simply in the Sudan as *Khalīl*) and the *Risāla* of Ibn Abī Zayd al-Qayrawānī. Ibrāhīm was, according to Ibn Ḍayf Allāh, the first to teach *Khalīl* in Funj territory. He taught for only seven years, but nevertheless had numerous pupils.

The school continued under Ibrāhīm's brother, ᶜAbd al-Raḥmān,[73] who studied under Ibrāhīm and under al-Banūfarī in Egypt. He established two other mosque-schools in the Shāyqiyya region, at Kūrtī and al-Dufār, and divided the year among the three of them. ᶜAbd al-Raḥmān was the first in his family to combine *ᶜilm* with Sufism. The two sides of his teaching are shown in that he wrote both a treatise on judicial opinions and rulings (*risāla fī'l-fatāwī wa'l-aḥkām*) and a work on Sufism (*murshid al-murīdīn fī ᶜilm al-taṣawwuf*).[74] After ᶜAbd al-Raḥmān's death, his schools passed to his third brother, Ismāᶜīl, who had studied under both ᶜAbd al-Raḥmān and al-Banūfarī.[75]

The fourth son of Jābir, ᶜAbd al-Raḥīm, seems to have taken no part in the activities of his brothers.[76] Upon Ismāᶜīl's death, his position passed to his nephew, Idrīs b. ᶜAbd al-Raḥmān. Idrīs, who was a famous scholar, consolidated his ties with the Shāyqiyya ruling class by marrying the queen of the Kingdom of Kajabī and moving his school to her residence. This, however, allegedly led to the school's decline since his students, who feared the corruption of their religion by the queen's beautiful serving women, abandoned him for the schools of ᶜAbd al-Raḥmān w. Ḥamadtū and shaykh Ṣughayrūn.[77] After Idrīs, the importance of the male line of Jābir declined. Later generations descended through his daughter Fāṭima who married Sirḥān b. Muḥammad b. Sirḥān, known as Ṣirhān al-ᶜŪdī.[78]

The early phase of effective Islamization was dominated by foreign Sufi and other scholars who came from the old established Muslim

73 *Ibid.*, 252.
74 *Ibid.*
75 *Ibid.*, 47.
76 Holt (1973b), 92.
77 Ibn Ḍayf Allāh (1974), 48-9.
78 *Ibid.*, 48.

countries. However, Sudanese who had studied abroad, mainly in the Ḥijāz and at al-Azhar, then began to dominate the scene. Among these, in addition to the Awlād Jābir, was ᶜAbd al-Raḥmān w. Ḥamadtū, founder of the Ḥamadtūiyāb of Nūrī. He studied under Ismāᶜīl w. Jābir and then travelled with Ṣughayrūn to Cairo, where they were both taught by al-Banūfarī. Having completed their studies, they returned to the Sudan where ᶜAbd al-Raḥmān's fame as a jurist and *muftī* began to grow.[79] ᶜAbd al-Raḥmān mastered not only the Mālikī but also the Shāfiᶜī *madhhab*, which he studied with Muḥammad b. ᶜAlī Qaram al-Miṣrī, probably in Berber.[80]

ᶜAbd al-Raḥmān had three wives; the first was the mother of his sons Madanī al-Nāṭiq and al-Aᶜsar; the second, Umm Jiddayn, was the mother of Muḥammad and another Madanī (their descendants are known as the Awlād Umm Jidayn). The third wife was the mother of Mālik, who became influential in the Zawara area of the Manāṣīr region, and Abū Diqin.[81]

The schools of the Ḥamadtūiyāb in Nūrī, Umm Bakōl and al-Zawara attracted students from various parts of the Sudan. One of ᶜAbd al-Raḥmān's b. Ḥamadtū's sons, al-Aᶜsar, promised victory to ᶜUthmān w. Ḥamad, a leader of the Shāyqiyya in the mid or late seventeenth century, in his revolt against the Funj. The fulfilment of al-Aᶜsar's prophecy and the liberation of the Shāyqiyya from the ᶜAbdallāb strengthened his links with the Shāyqiyya leadership.[82]

The flourishing of the Shāyqiyya schools in the early Funj period may be attributed to the unity and political stability imposed by the early rulers of the Funj Sultanate. These schools, however, began to decline and to be overshadowed by schools in other areas such as Muqrāt, Berber, al-Dāmar, and al-Qōz and al-Fijayja south of Shendi.[83] But our

79 *Ibid.*, 257.

80 A manuscript of a work by al-Miṣrī on Shāfiᶜī *fiqh* in the possession of the present shaykh of the Tijāniyya in the Sudan has recently been photographed by the NRO.

81 *Ibid.*

82 *Ibid.*, 228. See also O'Fahey and Spaulding (1974), 66-7.

83 Ibn Ḍayf Allāh (1974), 358-9 for the schools of al-Ghubush in Berber; see also Burckhardt (1822), 209.

evidence is too scanty to trace the development of the schools of the Shāyqiyya region in any great detail.[84]

When the Arabs migrated to the Sudan, they brought with them the simple tenets of the Mālikī *madhhab* which was predominant in Upper Egypt.[85] With the emergence of the Funj Sultanate, a number of Egyptian scholars were attracted to the Sudan. They included a Mālikī teacher, Muḥammad al-Qināwī, who came in the first half of the sixteenth century.[86] The latter half of the same century also saw the introduction of the Shāfiᶜī *madhhab* by another Egyptian jurist, Muḥammad b. ᶜAlī Qaram, referred to above; he taught a number of Sudanese, including ᶜAbd al-Raḥmān w. Ḥamadtū, ᶜAbd Allāh al-ᶜArakī and *qāḍī* Dushayn. The latter two functioned as judges in the Funj state.[87] However, the Mālikī *madhhab* became predominant in the Shāyqiyya region and in the Sudan generally.

84 A real decline appears to have occurred immediately after the Turco-Egyptian invasion; G.A. Hoskins, *Travels in Ethiopia*, London 1835, 169, who visited the area in 1835 states, "But his account [i.e. Burckhardt (1822), 70, of the Shāyqiyya schools and learning] would scarcely be applicable to the Shaygeea of the present-day".

85 P.M. Holt, *A Modern History of the Sudan*, 2nd edn, London 1963, 220-21, n. 17, and Yūsuf Faḍl Ḥasan (1971a), "External Islamic influences and the progress of Islamization in the Eastern Sudan between the fifteenth and the ninteenth centuries", in Ḥasan, *Sudan in Africa*, Khartoum 1971, 78.

86 Ibn Ḍayf Allāh (1974), 101-2.

87 *Ibid.*, 213 and 354-5.

2

THE ANCIENT BROTHERHOODS: THE QĀDIRIYYA AND THE SHĀDHILIYYA

Introduction

The previous chapter has established that the first phase of Islam in the Shāyqiyya region was dominated by the activities of individual *fuqarā*ᵓ. However, a gradual transition from what may be described as a "Sudanic belt" pattern of individualistic *fuqarā*ᵓ to a Middle Eastern and North African one with organized Sufi brotherhoods was beginning to take place.

The coming of the *ṭarīqas* into the Shāyqiyya region may conveniently be divided into two stages. The first, which may be dated from about the mid-seventeenth century, began with the attachment of some *fuqarā*ᵓ to the decentralized "ancient" *ṭarīqas*, the Qādiriyya and Shādhiliyya. The second stage saw the recruitment of a much greater number into the centralized "reformist" *ṭarīqas* founded in the early nineteenth century.

Since the internal organization of the *ṭarīqas* is discussed in Chapter Seven, it is sufficient here to note that the "ancient" *ṭarīqas* were autonomous branches, each with its independent shaykh and its particular chain of spiritual authority, *silsila*. The meeting ground for these sometimes rival branches was the common respect they paid to the founder of the order. As is shown in Chapter Six, none of these geographically defined "units" seems to have established a proper hierarchy during the Funj period. By contrast, the centralized new *ṭarīqas* each had a shaykh at the head of its hierarchy who enjoyed absolute authority and who was assisted by a number of *khulafā*ᵓ, "deputies", and local representatives. And in the new *ṭarīqas*, in contrast to the decentralized ones, the members shared a common devotional life.

Although the main theme of this chapter is the introduction and the spread of the ancient *ṭarīqas* in the Shāyqiyya region, this requires a survey of their introduction into the Sudan.

The Qādiriyya

The coming of the Qādiriyya. This *ṭarīqa*, known also as the Jīlāniyya, was the most popular and widespread *ṭarīqa* in the Muslim world. It is named after ᶜAbd al-Qādir al-Jīlānī, who was born in Persia in 1077 and died and was buried at Baghdad in 1166.

ᶜAbd al-Qādir was an *ᶜālim* before becoming a Sufi. He began his career as a Ḥanbalī jurist and preacher. Nothing is known of the reasons that led him to attach himself to the Sufi way. ᶜAbd al-Qādir studied Sufism with Abū'l-Khayr Muḥammad b. Muslim al-Dabbās (d. 521/1131). After he had demonstrated his seriousness he received the *khirqat al-taṣawwuf*, the Sufi livery or dress, which was given to him by the *qāḍī* Abū Saᶜd Mubārak al-Mukharrimī, the head of a Ḥanbalī school in Baghdad which ᶜAbd al-Qādir appears to have attended. He then began his life as a public preacher, establishing a Ḥanbalī *madrasa* or school and a Sufi *ribāṭ* or devotional centre in Baghdad. His doctrine was strictly orthodox, being based solely on the Quran and the *sunna*. Large audiences attended his lessons on Sufism, in which he repeatedly emphasized the struggle against the self, *jihād al-nafs*, and the need for submission only to God and His will. Al-Jīlānī exercised great spiritual influence, being considered one of the four *quṭbs* (lit. "pole", or head of the hierarchy of saints) of the Sufis. He was also known as the *sulṭān al-awliyāʾ*, "the ruler of the saints".

Although the Qādiriyya is always traced back to ᶜAbd al-Qādir al-Jīlānī, there is no evidence that he himself founded a *ṭarīqa*. His sons and his numerous pupils simply called themselves Qādiriyya in his memory.[1]

ᶜAbd al-Qādir's teachings were propagated by his pupils in various parts of the Muslim world. It was through one of these missionaries, Tāj al-Dīn al-Bahārī, that the Qādiriyya came to the Sudan in the mid-sixteenth century. The *Ṭabaqāt* asserts that Tāj al-Dīn was a *khalīfa* of ᶜAbd al-Qādir al-Jīlānī but does not give his *sanad*, or chain of spiritual authority.[2] While on the pilgrimage in Mecca, al-Bahārī was invited to

1 Trimingham (1971), 42 n. 3 and p. 43.

2 The primary references to al-Bahārī are Ibn Ḍayf Allāh (1974), 4, 109-10 and 128-9, and *Makhṭūṭa*, 5. Secondary references include Trimingham (1949), 115; Ḥasan Muḥammad al-Fātiḥ Qarīb Allāh, *"al-Taṣawwuf fī'-Sūdān*

the Sudan by Dā'ūd b. ᶜAbd al-Jalīl, a Sudanese merchant from Arbajī. He married into the local people and resided with his host at Wādī Shaᶜīr in the Gezira for seven years. There is a popular story that describes how he chose those who were worthy of initiation. He hid some rams in a storeroom and then told those present that he was going to initiate, guide and slaughter them; they would thus die in the faith. The people were so frightened that all fled, except three who volunteered to be initiated. These were Muḥammad al-Hamīm, Bān al-Naqā al-Ḍarīr and ᶜAjīb al-Manjilūk, the ᶜAbdallāb ruler. Al-Bahārī took them one by one into the storeroom, initiated them and slaughtered the rams. When those waiting saw the blood flowing from the storeroom, they thought he had indeed slaughtered his initiates.[3]

Al-Bahārī is said to have travelled to Taqalī in southern Kordofan where he initiated ᶜAbd Allāh al-Ḥammāl, the grandfather of Shaykh Ḥamad al-Naḥlān b. Muḥammad al-Bidayrī, known as Wad al-Turābī. The *Ṭabaqāt* records that al-Bahārī said that he came from Baghdad because of Muḥammad al-Hamīm, to whom he taught the names and attributes of God, various spiritual exercises and how to enter into retreat.[4]

It was perhaps the severe requirements which al-Bahārī laid down and the harsh methods which he adopted in recruiting his followers that prevented him from winning a greater number of adherents. Thus the Qādirī branch of Muḥammad al-Hamīm, al-Bahārī's *khalīfa,* was not as popular as the other Qādirī branches, especially the one which was founded by ᶜAbd Allāh al-ᶜArakī.[5]

The ᶜArakiyyūn Tradition. Al-Bahārī tried unsuccessfully to initiate ᶜAbd Allāh b. Dafᶜ Allāh al-ᶜArakī, later appointed as *qāḍī* at the court of Shaykh ᶜAjīb al-Manjilūk. He was a member of the ᶜArakiyyūn holy family of al-Hillāliyya who later moved to Abū Ḥarāz in the Gezira. His father was Dafᶜ Allāh b. Muqbil and his mother was Hadiyya bt. ᶜĀṭif,

---

ilā nihāyat ᶜaṣr al-Funj", MA thesis, University of Khartoum 1965, 94; Ḥasan (1967), 180 and *idem* (1971a), 79, and Holt and Daly (1979), 34.

3 Ibn Ḍayf Allāh (1974), 109-10, 128, and 317-8.

4 *Ibid.,* 129. Trimingham (1949), 219, states that al-Bahārī came to the Sudan for the sake of ᶜAbd Allāh al-Ḥammāl. Yūsuf Faḍl Ḥasan, the editor of the *Ṭabaqāt* of Ibn Ḍayf Allāh (1974), however, says that al-Bahārī came because of al-Hamīm. This disagreement is caused by the ambiguity of the language of the *Ṭabaqāt.*

5 On the Qādiriyya branches, see Qarīb Allāh, thesis (1965), 131.

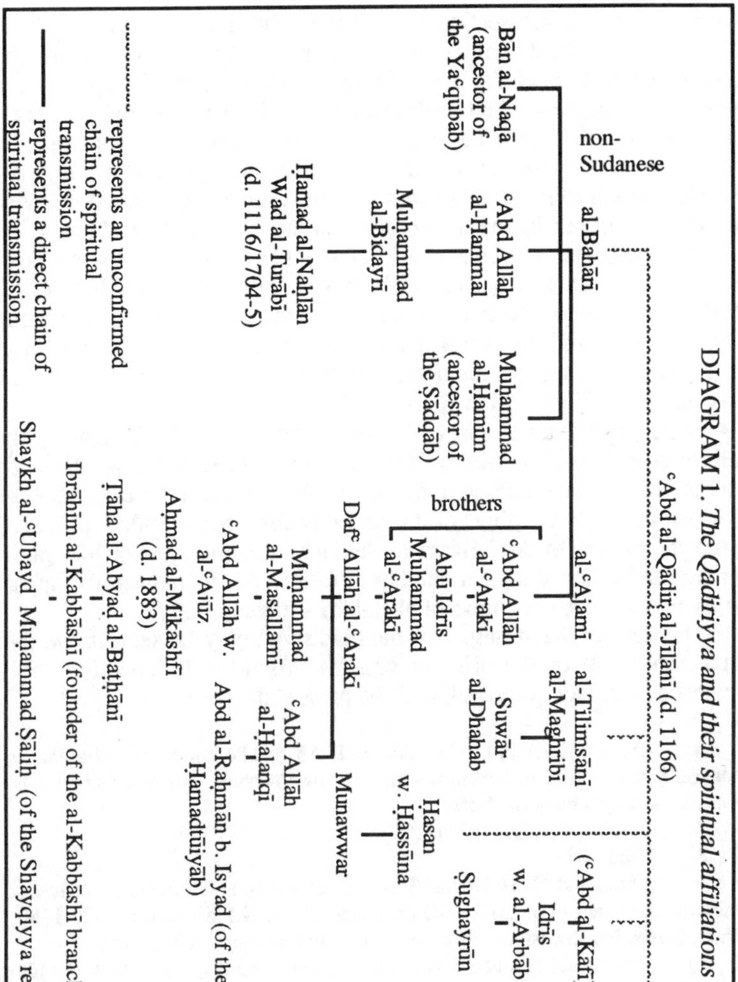

DIAGRAM 1. *The Qādiriyya and their spiritual affiliations*

from the Jimiᶜāb sub-section of the Jaᶜaliyyūn. He was born at Abyaḍ Dīrī, memorized the Quran with his father, and then travelled with ᶜAbd al-Raḥmān al-Nuwayrī to the Shāyqiyya region where they spent seven years studying with ᶜAbd al-Raḥmān w. Jābir. It is said that al-ᶜArakī was taught the *ism Allāh al-aᶜẓam*, "the most exalted name of God", by his teacher, who also gave him four pupils to study under him.[6] Al-ᶜArakī refused to join the Qādiriyya on the grounds that he did not wish to involve himself in anything other than the *ᶜilm* that he had learnt.[7]

Al-ᶜArakī later regretted his decision when he realized that his position as an *ᶜālim* had been overshadowed by the Sufi *khalīfas* of al-Bahārī, who began to enjoy great social status and influence among both the Funj and the Arabs. He thus decided to go to Mecca to meet al-Bahārī; learning that the latter had died, he agreed to be initiated by his successor, Ḥabīb Allāh al-ᶜAjamī.[8]

ᶜAbd Allāh al-ᶜArakī was a frequent visitor to the Ḥijāz, making the pilgrimage twenty-four times. He was renowned for his knowledge even in the Ḥijāz, where he taught at the *maqām* (a small building near the Kaᶜbah used for teaching) of the *imām* Mālik. In the Sudan, al-ᶜArakī used the village of Abū Ḥarāz in the Gezira as the seat for his Qādirī branch and initiated a great number of followers. His branch was apparently more active than those of al-Bahārī's direct pupils.[9]

The decentralized nature of the Qādiriyya may be seen in the fact that almost all of the original *khalīfas* founded independent holy dynasties that have survived until the present day.[10]

6 Ibn Ḍayf Allāh (1974), 206 and 255-6. The *ism Allāh al-aᶜẓam* is generally considered to be known only to the Prophets. But such knowledge was also claimed by some Sufis.

7 Ibn Ḍayf Allāh (1974), 253.

8 *Ibid.*, 254.

9 *Ibid.*, and N. McHugh, "Holymen of the Blue Nile: Religious leadership and the genes of an Arab Islamic society in the Nilotic Sudan, 1500-1850," Ph.D. thesis, Northwestern University 1986 (publication forthcoming).

10 On these branches, see Trimingham (1949), 219,ᶜAbd al-Qādir Maḥmūd, *al-Ṭawāʾif al-ṣūfiyya fīʾl-Sūdān. Ansābuhum wa-uṣūl turāthihim wa-falsafatihim,* Khartoum 1971, 6; Holt (1973b), 121-2; Khadiga Karrar Osman, "Aspects of Sufism in the Sudan", MA thesis, University of Durham 1975, 67 and Abdullahi Mohamed Osman, "The Mikashfiyya: a study of a Religious Ṭarīqa in the Sudan", MSc. thesis, University of Khartoum 1978, 6-8.

The Qādiriyya in the Shāyqiyya region. The Shāyqiyya region was influenced by the teachings of al-ᶜArakī through al-Fijayja near Shendi at an early stage and at al-Kabbāshī village, north of Khartoum North, later. The teachings of al-ᶜArakī (a middle way between mysticism and *ᶜilm*) appealed to a number of *fuqarāʾ* of the Shāyqiyya area.[11]

The Shāyqiyya region was also influenced by several Qādiriyya branches which emerged and flourished independently of al-Bahārī and his *khalīfas.* The first of these was founded in Dongola during the seventeenth century by Muḥammad b. ᶜĪsā b. Ṣāliḥ, known as *suwār al-dhahab* (lit., "the bracelet of gold"). Muḥammad came from the Bidayriyya and studied the *Mukhtaṣar* of Khalīl b. Isḥāq and part of the *Risāla* of al-Qayrawānī under his father. After the latter's death he continued his studies under Muḥammad b. ᶜAlī Qaram al-Miṣrī al-Shāfiᶜī, who had settled in Berber in the early period of the Funj rule. It is also said he was initiated by him into Sufism.[12] Muḥammad Suwār al-Dhahab also joined the "path" of the Sufis and learnt theology and the sciences of the Quran at the hands of a teacher known only as al-Tilimsānī al-Maghribī.[13] The *Ṭabaqāt* does not mention any specific *ṭarīqa* with reference to either of his teachers, but some scholars suggest that al-Tilimsānī initiated him into the Qādiriyya.[14]

Suwār al-Dhahab's centre of learning in Dongola played a considerable role in spreading the Qādiriyya throughout the area.[15] The Suwār al-Dhahab family was to become important in the Shāyqiyya region when it transferred its allegiance from the Qādiriyya to the Khatmiyya in the first half of the nineteenth century.

Another independent Qādirī branch was founded by Idrīs b. Muḥammad al-Arbāb, of Maḥasī origin. He was born, died and was buried at al-ᶜAylafūn, southeast of Khartoum, where his tomb is still a place of pilgrimage. Idrīs studied in two different religious schools, first at al-Ṣabābī (in Khartoum North) where he studied under Ḥamad w. Zarrūq, whom he greatly impressed; he was later taught by al-

11 Ibn Ḍayf Allāh (1974), 253.

12 *Ibid.*, 348 and 354-5.

13 *Ibid.*, 42; see also MacMichael (1922), ii, 220.

14 R. Hill, *A Biographical Dictionary of the Sudan*, 2nd edn, London 1967, 259; Ḥasan (1971a), 80; Holt and Daly (1979), 34, and Abū Salīm, in NRO, 7/1/10 *Majmūᶜat Abī Salīm*, p. 2.

15 *Ibid.*

Bandārī at Ḥalfāyat al-Mulūk.[16] Gradually, Idrīs' reputation began to grow. He is said to have cured the mother of Sultan ᶜAmāra b. Nāyil, known as Abū Sikaykīn (965/1557-8 to 976/1568-9), after the famous shaykh Bān al-Naqā al-Ḍarīr had failed to do so. This incident undoubtedly enhanced his fame as a holy man.[17]

The *Ṭabaqāt* gives several versions as to the source of Idrīs' spiritual authority and knowledge; the most exalted are that it came directly from God, *al-ᶜilm al-rabbānī*,[18] that it was revealed to him by the Prophet,[19] or that a mysterious stranger from the West (*al-maghrib*), ᶜAbd al-Kāfī, came to him *bi'l-khaṭwa*, "by the step", and initiated him.[20] According to Khōjalī b. ᶜAbd al-Raḥmān, Idrīs was "The first to light the fire of ᶜAbd al-Qādir al-Jīlānī" in the Sudan, i.e. propagate the Qādiriyya.[21]

Idrīs possessed considerable political influence and throughout his life was consulted by various Funj sultans and ᶜAbdallāb rulers.[22] He was famous for his role as a mediator in a number of political disputes; for example, he mediated between the Funj Sultan, ᶜAdlān b. Ūnsā (deposed 1020/1611-2), and the sons of ᶜAjīb the Great after the latter's defeat by the Funj in 1607-8 at Karkōj. ᶜAjīb's sons fled and took refuge in Dongola and it was Shaykh Idrīs who persuaded them to come back.[23] This successful mediation may be attributed to the learning and charisma of Shaykh Idrīs as well as to the attachment of members of the Funj ruling class to his branch of the Qādiriyya; one example was Sultan Bādī b. Rubāṭ, who died in 1680.[24]

16 Ibn Ḍayf Allāh (1974), 51; see also Trimingham (1949), 220.

17 Ibn Ḍayf Allāh (1974), 41 and 51.

18 *Ibid.*, 52.

19 *Ibid.*

20 *Ibid.*, 42; see n. 20, where the editor interprets *al-khaṭwa* as the ability of a holy man to cover vast distances in the twinkling of an eye. Trimingham (1949), 220, simply translates it as "saintship".

21 Ibn Ḍayf Allāh (1974), 57; see also Yūsuf Faḍl Ḥasan, *Muqaddima fī taʾrīkh al-mamālik al-Islāmiyya fī'l-Sūdān al-sharqī 1450-1821*, Cairo 1971b, 133 and *idem*, *Dirāsāt fī taʾrīkh al-Sūdān*, vol. i, Khartoum 1975, 76.

22 Ibn Ḍayf Allāh (1974), 51-2 and 61; see also H.C. Jackson, "The Mahas of ᶜEilafun", *SNR*, 1919, ii, 288, and R.A. Lobban, "Social Networks in the Urban Sudan", Ph.D. thesis, Northwestern University 1973, 43.

23 Ibn Ḍayf Allāh (1974), 65; see also O'Fahey and Spaulding (1974), 37-8.

24 Ibn Ḍayf Allāh (1974), 65.

There was another Qādirī centre which influenced the whole Dongola Reach, that of Shaykh Ḥasan w. Ḥassūna (d. 1975/1664-5), the grandson of a Maghribī immigrant, probably from Tunisia.[25] Ḥasan established the village known as Wad Ḥassūna, twenty-seven miles west of Abū Dilayq, from which he propagated his own branch of the Qādiriyya.[26] Like Idrīs w. al-Arbāb, Ḥasan was regarded as a saint without a shaykhly intermediary. His sainthood was manifested shortly after that of Shaykh Idrīs. The *Ṭabaqāt* reports that he was instructed in the Qādiriyya by the Prophet himself.[27]

Ḥasan w. Ḥassūna initiated a number of *fuqarāʾ* from Dongola, among them Munawwar, who was a holy man of Mirayfābī origin. His father, Idrīs b. Muḥammad nicknamed Mirayf, is said to have settled in the sixteenth century at Karabah village, west of Arqū. He married a local woman by whom he had Munawwar. Munawwar's mother was famous for her learning and piety; she died and was buried at Karabah, where a domed tomb (*qubba*) was erected over her grave.[28] Munawwar was not only a Sufi but also an *ᶜālim* who studied in the *masīd* (religious school) of Wad ᶜĪsā on the Blue Nile.[29] After returning home, he established his own centre on Bilnārtī Island near Arqū, taught many persons *ᶜilm* and initiated them into the Qādiriyya.[30]

The *Ṭabaqāt* shows that the *ṭarīqas*, especially the Qādiriyya, began to gain ground in the Shāyqiyya region even among the *ᶜulamāʾ*. For example, Muḥammad b. Sirḥān al-ᶜAwdī, commonly known by his nickname Ṣughayrūn, the eldest son of Fāṭima bt. Jābir, followed the Qādirī Shaykh Idrīs w. al-Arbāb. Ṣughayrūn, the most famous teacher in the generation that followed his maternal uncles, the Awlād Jābir,

25 See *ibid.*, 65, for his biography. See also Holt (1973b), 124.

26 Ḥasan (1975), 76. Abū Dilayq, the centre of the Baṭāḥīn, lies about 90 miles east of Khartoum, halfway between the capital and the River Atbara.

27 Ibn Ḍayf Allāh (1974), 42 and 135.

28 *Ibid.*, 143, and Muḥammad Saᶜīd Aḥmad ᶜAbd Allāh, *"Min taʾrīkh manṭaqa Dundulā"*, mimeograph, Khartoum 1978, 86. On the Mirayfāb, see MacMichael (1922), i, 209-11.

29 ᶜIzz al-Dīn al-Amīn, *Qariyat Kutrānj wa-atharuhā al-ᶜilmī fī'l-Sūdān*, Khartoum 1395/1975, 21; al-Amīn's work is a study of the *masīd* of the Āl ᶜĪsā at Kutrānj, halfway between al-Kāmlīn and al-ᶜAylafūn on the Blue Nile. See also ᶜAbd al-ᶜAzīz Amīn ᶜAbd al-Majīd, *al-Tarbiyya fī'l-Sūdān wa'l-usus al-nafsiyya wa'l-ijtimāᶜiyya allatī qāmat ᶜalayhā min awwal al-qarn al-sādis ᶜashar ilā nihāyat al-qarn al-thāmin ᶜashar*, Cairo 1949, iii, 18-9.

30 ᶜAbd Allāh (1978), 87.

was born on Turunj Island in the Shāyqiyya area. He studied the *Mukhtaṣar* with Muḥammad al-Banūfarī in Cairo, who was impressed with his learning and predicted that he would become a successful teacher.[31]

Upon his return, Ṣughayrūn, who combined "*ᶜilm*, *ᶜamal* [lit. practice], *fiqh* and Sufism", taught in the school of his maternal uncles, the Awlād Jābir. But he suffered from the envy of his maternal cousins; so at the invitation of the Funj Sultan Bādī I (1020/1611-2 to 1025/1616-7), Ṣughayrūn, together with his family, left the Shāyqiyya region for Dār al-Abwāb near Shendi. After hours of disagreement between his pupils as to where to settle, he was said to have been guided by al-Khaḍir (see p. 50, n. 31) to settle in Qōz al-Muṭraq, south of Shendi, which was then an area of bush. Settling there, he made a small clearing (Sudanese Ar. *fijayja*) and prophesied that al-Fijayja would one day be the residence of the brothers of ᶜAbd al-Raḥmān w. Ḥamadtū. Sultan Bādī I confirmed the grant of land, upon which he established his school which "succeeded that of the sons of Jābir as a principal centre of religious and legal education in the northern Funj territories".[32]

Ṣughayrūn travelled with some of his pupils from the Dār al-Abwāb to the Gezira. They found the people divided between supporters and opponents of the teachings of Idrīs w. al-Arbāb and decided to visit him. Ṣughayrūn and his pupils are said to have put seventeen complicated questions on various religious matters to Idrīs, intending to test his learning. Ṣughayrūn and his pupils were so impressed with his answers that they decided that his learning came directly from God, from *al-lawḥ al-maḥfūz*, that is "The Guarded Tablet" preserved in Heaven, and thus agreed to be initiated by him into the Qādiriyya.[33]

Ṣughayrūn became a Qādirī missionary as well as a Quran and *fiqh* teacher. After his death, the school continued under his son al-Zayn, who taught there for about fifty years. At al-Zayn's death in 1086/1675-6, his pupils were said to number about a thousand, most of whom became jurists and judges over a vast area that extended as far as Wadai (Dār Ṣulayḥ) in modern Chad.[34] Al-Zayn was succeeded by his son

31 The following is based on his biography in Ibn Ḍayf Allāh (1974), 235-8.

32 Holt (1973b), 94.

33 Ibn Ḍayf Allāh (1974), 56.

34 *Ibid.*, 74-5.

Muḥammad al-Azraq, who ran the school until his death in 1108/1696-7).[35]

In 1107/1695 ᶜAbd al-Raḥmān b. Isayd of the Ḥamadtūiyāb holy family, together with his maternal uncles, the Awlād Umm Jidayn, moved to al-Fijayja.[36] Isayd memorized the Quran under a shaykh from Arbajī and was taught the *Mukhtaṣar* by his maternal uncle, Muḥammad b. Madanī w. Umm Jidayn. He studied the rules of Quranic recitation (*tajwīd*) under ᶜAbd al-Raḥmān al-Aghbash in Berber.[37] It was through these links and contacts between the descendants of Ṣughayrūn and the Awlād Umm Jidayn section of the Ḥamadtūiyāb family that the Qādiriyya began to penetrate into the Shāyqiyya region.

An oral tradition among some of the Ḥamadtūiyāb family of Nūrī records that their ancestor ᶜAbd al-Raḥmān b. Ḥamadtū al-Khaṭīb, known as Abū Shawārib, was initiated into the Qādiriyya by ᶜAbd al-Raḥmān w. Jābir.[38] But examining the *Ṭabaqāt* and other sources, one may dispute the Ḥamadtūiyāb claim on three grounds. ᶜAbd al-Raḥmān w. Jābir, although he was influenced by Sufism in general, was not associated with any particular *ṭarīqa*.[39] Furthermore, ᶜAbd al-Raḥmān w. Ḥamadtū was not taught by ᶜAbd al-Raḥmān w. Jābir, but by his brother and successor, Ismāᶜīl.[40] Finally, there is no record that ᶜAbd al-Raḥmān w. Ḥamadtū was initiated by any of the Awlād Jābir into the Qādiriyya or any other *ṭarīqa*.[41]

The school of the Awlād Umm Jidayn in al-Fijayja began to flourish under Muḥammad b. Madanī w. Umm Jidayn bt. ᶜAbd al-Raḥmān w. Ḥamadtū.[42] His brother, Madanī, continued it after his death entrusting, ᶜAbd al-Raḥmān b. Isayd with teaching the *Mukhtaṣar*. Ibn Isayd also began to teach the Quran and a range of other subjects.

Ibn Isayd was to play an important role in propagating the Qādiriyya in the Shāyqiyya region in the eighteenth century. According to the

35 *Ibid.*, 357-8.

36 *Ibid.*, 282-5.

37 *Ibid.*, 353-4; MacMichael (1922), ii, 225.

38 Interviews 19 and 23.

39 Ibd Ḍayf Allāh (1974), 252. See also ᶜAbd al-Majīd (1949), i, 66; Qarīb Allāh, thesis (1965), 56-8, and Sirr al-Khatim ᶜUthmān, *Awlād Jābir*, Khartoum 1975, 16-17.

40 Ibn Ḍayf Allāh (1974), 47 and 257, and ᶜUthmān (1975), 18.

41 Ibn Ḍayf Allāh (1974), 257, and Qarīb Allāh, thesis (1965), 56.

42 Ibn Ḍayf Allāh (1974), 353-4.

Ṭabaqāt, he travelled south to Abū Ḥarāz in the Gezira to be initiated by *al-ḥājj* ᶜAbd Allāh al-Ḥalanqī, from a section of the Beja people of the eastern Sudan. He was born at al-Tāka, near Kasala and memorized the Quran at Islānj Island, north of Omdurman. He studied *fiqh* and *tawḥīd* under Dafᶜ Allāh b. Muḥammad al-ᶜArakī, who also initiated him into the Qādiriyya and authorized him to initiate others.[43] Ibn Isayd returned to his home in Nūrī where he continued his career as a religious teacher and Qādirī preacher. Among those he taught were Saᶜd al-Karsanī and ᶜAbd al-Raḥmān w. Ḥājj al-Duwayḥī, both of whom were to play important roles in the religious life of the Shāyqiyya.[44]

Upon Ibn Isayd's death in 1715, his Quranic school in Nūrī passed to his favourite pupil, Saᶜd al-Karsanī, who was of Shāyqī origin. His reputation as a successful religious teacher, especially in the Quranic sciences and recitation, attracted pupils from Dār al-Abwāb, Dongola and the Shāyqiyya region.[45]

The Kabbāshī Tradition. One of the most important Qādirī centres to influence the Shāyqiyya region in the nineteenth century lay outside it, namely al-Kabbāshī, just north of Khartoum North. Its founder was Ibrāhīm al-Amīn b. ᶜAlī al-Kabbāshī; although known by his nickname al-Kabbāshī, he was not from the Kabābīsh people, but probably from the ᶜArakiyyūn holy clan of the Gezira. Ibrāhīm was probably nicknamed al-Kabbāshī because his family lived in the Gezira among a Kabābīsh clan known as al-Tamāsīḥ (lit., "the crocodiles"). Perhaps this explains his popularity among the Kabābīsh tribesmen to the present day. But like most holy men in the Sudan and elsewhere, al-Kabbāshī himself claimed Sharīfian descent.[46]

43 *Ibid.*, 210-12, 226, 236, 282 and 353; see also MacMichael (1922), i, 254.

44 Ibn Ḍayf Allāh (1974), 224-5 and 283; MacMichael (1922), ii, 224 and 264, and interview 19.

45 Ibn Ḍayf Allāh (1974), 224 and 266. An oral tradition confirms that al-Karsanī was affiliated to the Qādiriyya, probably through Ibn Isayd; interview 19.

46 Ibrāhīm al-Kabbāshī, *Inshiqāq al-qamar li'l-rasūl sayyid al-bashar*, ed. al-Mikāshfī Ṭāha al-Shaykh Muḥammad ᶜAlī, Khartoum 1971, 11; his pedigree is traced back to al-Ḥusayn b. ᶜAlī, the grandson of the Prophet. Other sources disagree as to his "Sudanese" descent; Hill (1967), 173, calls him a Maḥasī, while al-Fakī al-Ṭāhir al-Faḥl, *Taʾrīkh wa-uṣūl al-ᶜArab bi'l-Sūdān*, Khartoum n.d., 106, calls him a Jaᶜalī.

Al-Kabbāshī was born in 1201/1786-7 in a small village called Abū Qamīṣ near al-Manāqil in the Gezira and died and was buried at al-Kabbāshī in 1286/1869-70. His mother was Umm al-Ḥusayn bt. Muḥammad ᶜAlī b. Maḥmūd, from the Nifīᶜāb clan of the Jaᶜaliyyūn.[47]

Ibrāhīm studied the Quran under ᶜAlī w. al-Fādnī at the village of Wad al-Fādnī, southeast of al-Ḥaṣahayṣa. He then moved to Ṭayyiba, an ᶜArakiyyūn centre in the Gezira, where he perfected his knowledge of the Quran and mastered the various forms of recitation under Shaykh Kalī. He studied *fiqh, tawḥīd* and other Islamic sciences under Ibrāhīm b. Aḥmad ᶜĪsā at the famous *masīd* of Wad ᶜĪsā at Kutrānj.[48] Having studied *fiqh*, al-Kabbāshī felt the need to combine it with Sufism; he was initiated into the Qādiriyya by Ṭāha al-Abyaḍ al-Baṭḥānī.[49] Al-Baṭḥānī had taken the Qādiriyya from Aḥmad al-Mikāshfī (d. 1883), a holy man of the Kawāhla and a descendant of ᶜAbd al-Bāqī al-Nayyal.[50] Al-Mikāshfī himself was initiated into the ᶜArakiyyūn branch of the Qādiriyya by ᶜAbd Allāh w. al-ᶜAjūz,[51] a pupil of Muḥammad ᶜAlī al-

47 Al-Kabbāshī (1971), 11 and 13. Al-Kabbāshī's mother was a cousin of the famous Mahdist *amīr*, ᶜAbd al-Raḥmān w. al-Nujūmī.

48 *Ibid.*, 13-4. Nothing is known of the life of shaykh Kalī.

49 *Ibid.*, 14. Little is recorded of Ṭāha al-Abyaḍ's life; he was said to be from the Baṭāḥīn, who live as nomads around Abū Dilayq, the centre of the descendants of Ḥasan w. Ḥassūna. To the Baṭāḥīn also belonged Faraḥ w. Taktūk who was famous for his gift of prophecy; see Ibn Ḍayf Allāh (1974), 313; S. Hillelson, *Sudan Arabic Texts*, Cambridge 1935, 156-71, and al-Ṭayyib Muḥammad al-Ṭayyib, *Faraḥ wad Taktūk*, Khartoum 1977, 41-50.

50 Al-Mikāshfī claimed Sharifian descent. He was one of the earliest Mahdist leaders in the Gezira; see Holt (1970), 66; Hill (1967), 35 and *idem* ed., *The Sudan Memoirs of Carl Christian Giegler Pasha, 1873-83,* London 1984, 188. His grandfather, ᶜAbd al-Bāqī al-Nayyal (died *c.* 1750) was from the Kawāhla (or Banū Kāhil), who claim descent from al-Zubayr b. al-ᶜAwwām, a companion of the Prophet. The Kawāhla emigrated from Egypt during the fourteenth century, settling among the Beja; some clans later moved to the Buṭāna, Gezira and Kordofān; see Ibn Ḍayf Allāh (1974), 116; H.A. MacMichael, *The Tribes of Northern and Central Kordofan*, Cambridge 1912, 199-205, and Ḥasan (1967), 140 and 162.

51 Al-ᶜAjūz was a Jaᶜalī by origin. He died and was buried at Jabal Saqadī, west of Sinnār. He was a contemporary of a number of leading holy men, among them Badr al-Dīn Umm Bārak (Ibn Ḍayf Allāh [1974], 113-14); Muḥammad b. ᶜAbd Allāh b. al-Ṭirayfī (*ibid.*, 337-9) and Khōjalī b. ᶜAbd al-Raḥmān (d. 1155/1743-4; *ibid.*, 191-202). Ibn Ḍayf Allāh (1974), 271-2, com-

Masallamī w. Abī Winaysa.[52] The *sanad* of this branch of the Qādiriyya (see Diagram 1) shows that Muḥammad al-Masallamī was initiated by Dafᶜ Allāh al-ᶜArakī (d. 1094/1682-3), who had been initiated by his father Shaykh Abū Idrīs, the brother and student of Shaykh ᶜAbd Allāh al-ᶜArakī.[53]

Al-Kabbāshī established his own independent Qādirī branch (*farᶜ*) and travelled widely in the Gezira instructing people in both *fiqh* and Sufism. He is said to have reached as far north as Qarrī, the former capital of the ᶜAbdallāb, where he settled in a large area of wasteland (*ghāba*). The bush was teeming with wild animals which attacked the ᶜAbdallāb livestock; they requested him to pray to God to drive them off. In return for his prayers, al-Kabbāshī was granted the area which came to be known as *al-Farᶜ* (lit., "the branch").[54]

The bush was cleared and the land cultivated by al-Kabbāshī and his followers. He founded a large *masīd,* which served as both a school and as the seat of his branch of the *ṭarīqa.* Al-Kabbāshī's reputation for sanctity and miracle-working attracted great numbers of people; his village, which became known as al-Kabbāshī, began to expand both in size and importance.[55]

Shaykh al-Kabbāshī was the contemporary of a number of prominent holy men; among them were al-Ḥasan al-Mīrghanī, a close friend, Aḥmad al-Jaᶜalī and al-Shaykh al-ᶜUbayd w. Badr. Al-Kabbāshī was openly hostile to the rule of the Turks in the Sudan (1821-85). He urged his followers to resist the Turks and not to pay the heavy taxes imposed upon them by the invaders. While on a visit to Khartoum, he upbraided the Governor, Mūsā Pasha Ḥamdī (1862-5): "Your rule is oppression and injustice." Al-Kabbāshī's words infuriated the Pasha, who decided to imprison him. But al-Kabbāshī is said, by a *karāma,* to have caused the Pasha to faint and change his mind.[56]

---

ments that following the deaths of his generation of holy men the Qādiriyya began to decline.

52 Al-Masallamī studied under ᶜAbd al-Raḥmān w. Jābir, being one of the forty students of the latter who attained the mystical rank of *quṭbiyya*; see Ibn Ḍayf Allāh (1974), 79-80.

53 For the biography of Dafᶜ Allāh b. Muḥammad al-ᶜArakī, see Ibn Ḍayf Allāh (1974), 206-10; for that of his father, *ibid.*, 66-70.

54 Al-Kabbāshī (1971), 14, and interview 12.

55 Al-Kabbāshī (1971), 14. After his death, the village became known as al-Qubba after his domed tomb.

56 *Ibid.*, 15-6. Al-Kabbāshī made the pilgrimage in 1283/1866-7.

Al-Kabbāshī left twenty-two sons and twenty-one daughters, one of whom married the Mahdist *amīr* ᶜAbd al-Raḥmān w. al-Nujūmī. All were to become devoted supporters of the Mahdist cause. His son al-Miṣbāḥ joined the Mahdist army and was killed in a battle at Jabal al-Dāyir in Kordofan in 1884. Three other sons, Muḥammad, Muḥammad Aḥmad and ᶜAbd al-Raḥmān, joined al-Nujūmī's expedition to Egypt. The first died on the way to Egypt and was buried in Dongola. The others were killed with Wad al-Nujūmī in the battle of Tushkī on 3 August 1889.[57] The devotion of al-Kabbāshī's family to the Mahdist cause was probably due to three reasons. First, they inherited their father's tradition of opposition to the colonial regime. Secondly, al-Kabbāshī had through his writings played a role in preparing his followers' minds to accept the idea of the expected Mahdī.[58] Finally, they were related by kin and marriage to Wad al-Nujūmī.

Al-Kabbāshī initiated a number of persons into the Qādiriyya including al-ᶜUbayd Muḥammad Ṣāliḥ al-Nāṣirābī, who spread the Qādiriyya in the Shāyqiyya region.[59] Shaykh al-ᶜUbayd was of Shāyqī origin and was born on the island of Umm Daraq near Marawī. After he had memorized the Quran in a local *khalwa*, he decided to travel, earning his living by building mud houses in the central Sudan. On his way to the Gezira, he heard of the fame of Shaykh al-Kabbāshī and decided to settle at his village. Al-ᶜUbayd studied under al-Kabbāshī, who initiated him into the Qādiriyya. He became known as one of the sixteen superior followers of al-Kabbāshī called *abkār al-Kabbāshī*.[60]

Shaykh al-ᶜUbayd is said to have wandered over the open country of the Gezira (*sāḥa fi'l-kalāʾ*) for about four years before settling at al-Nūba village between Khartoum and Madanī, where he married and founded a *khalwa*. Another tradition says that he left al-Nūba village for Umm Daraq, his birthplace, where he settled, married for the second time and fathered a son, named Ḥabīb Allāh. It was from Umm Daraq that the Kabbāshī-ᶜArakī offshoot of the Qādiriyya began to infiltrate into the Shāyqiyya region. His followers were found mainly, apart from Umm Daraq, in Jilās, in al-Bār on the west bank of the Nile just opposite to Kurtī, and in al-Shaqāʾiq near Jabal al-Barkal.

57 *Ibid.*, 15-6.

58 One of his works now with his family is, *al-Mahdī al-muntaẓar*.

59 The following is based on interview 20 and ᶜAbd Allāh al-Bashīr, ed., *Dīwān al-shāᶜir al-ṣūfī, Wad Nafīsa*, Khartoum 1976, 3-8.

60 The term *abkār* was later used by the Mahdi for his earliest followers: Holt (1970), 133.

Al-ᶜUbayd remained loyal to his teacher, whom he used to visit frequently; he visited his shaykh before the latter's departure for the Ḥijāz in 1283/1866-7 and after his return, and he was present at his death in 1286/1869-70. Al-ᶜUbayd's loyalty to al-Kabbāshī's family continued into the next generation, to Shaykh Ṭāha, son and successor of Ibrāhīm al-Kabbāshī. Al-ᶜUbayd continued his practice of visiting al-Kabbāshī for the various Islamic festivals. It was during one of these visits that he died early in the twentieth century and was buried beside his master's tomb.

The Tradition of Aḥmad al-Jaᶜalī. Another Qādirī centre which influenced the Shāyqiyya area was Kadabās, on the west bank of the Nile near Berber. This centre was established by Shaykh Aḥmad al-Jaᶜalī, a holy man from the Ḥasaballāb section of the Sirayḥāb branch of the Jaᶜaliyyūn.[61] Aḥmad al-Jaᶜalī was born at al-Mikhayrif (the present-day Berber) in 1818. As a youth, he travelled to Nūrī where he memorized the Quran under Muḥammad Aḥmad al-Kārūrī of the Kawārīr holy family and was taught *ᶜilm* and the *Mukhtaṣar* by Muḥammad Ṣāliḥ al-ᶜIrāqī.

After he had finished his studies in the Shāyqiyya region, Aḥmad returned to Berber and lived there for some years mainly as a trader. Upon his father's death, he moved from Berber to the west bank of the Nile where he established the village of Kadabās. He was said to have made the minor pilgrimage (Ar. *ᶜumra*) to Mecca, during which he was ordered by the "Prophet" al-Khaḍir in a vision to detach himself from worldly matters (*al-umūr al-dunyāwiyya*) and devote his time to the worship of God. On his return he entered a retreat (*khalwa*) for seven years in a grotto (*ghār*) which he built for that purpose at Kadabās.

When he emerged from his retreat, he is said to have written to some of the prominent holy men of his day, al-Ḥasan al-Mīrghanī, al-Shaykh al-ᶜUbayd w. Badr and Ibrāhīm al-Kabbāshī, asking them to initiate him into their respective *ṭarīqās*. They are alleged to have replied that they were not authorized to initiate him and that the one who was would come to al-Jaᶜalī in his home area. Soon afterwards, al-

61 On al-Jaᶜalī, see *Manāqib al-shaykh Aḥmad al-Jaᶜalī*, ms in the possession of his family at Kadabās, and *Sudanow* (March 1982). See also al-Faḥl (n.d.), 62, and MacMichael (1922), i, 200 and ii, 340 (on the Sirayḥāb). Al-Jaᶜalī's origin, like that of the Yaᶜqūbāb, can be traced back to the Jaᶜalī section, Umm Sālim, who became assimilated into the Shāyqiyya.

Ja^calī was recruited into the Qādiriyya by a Persian mystic, ᶜAbd al-Raḥmān al-Khurāsānī, who visited Berber in about 1865-70. It was believed among the people of Berber that al-Khurāsānī was divinely guided to the Sudan to initiate al-Jaᶜalī.[62] After the capture of Berber by the Mahdists in 1884, al-Jaᶜalī was summoned to Omdurman by the Khalifa ᶜAbdallāhi; he was kept under surveillance until 1898. Al-Jaᶜalī then returned to his village, where he died and was buried in 1902.

The Qādirī branch of Shaykh al-Jaᶜalī gained many adherents throughout the Sudan, but its followers in the Shāyqiyya region were confined to the area of Amrī on the Shāyqiyya-Manāṣīr border.[63] Al-Jaᶜalī's teachings undoubtedly found their way into the Shāyqiyya region from his *khalīfas* at al-Zawara in the Manāṣīr region. There have always been close links between the Shāyqiyya and Manāṣīr; for example, in the mid-seventeenth century, Mālik b. ᶜAbd al-Raḥmān w. Ḥamadtū settled in al-Zawara and built a mosque in which he taught the *Mukthaṣar*.[64] Mālik married into the Manāṣīr, and his descendants, who live there at the present day (1982), have maintained relations with their relatives among the Shāyqiyya.[65]

In the other direction, the Manāṣīr were accustomed to travel through the Shāyqiyya region working as hired labourers during the date-harvesting season; some of these migrant workers probably propagated Qādiriyya teachings among the Shāyqiyya.[66]

Shādhiliyya

Introduction. The Shādhiliyya, whose foundation is ascribed to the blind Shaykh Abū'l-Ḥasan al-Shādhilī (1196-1258) may be described as a Sufi affiliation rather than a formal *ṭariqa,* since al-Shādhilī did not initiate his followers into any formal set of rules or rituals.[67] The lack of an organized *ṭarīqa* resulted in the growth of various Shādhilī-in-

62 *Manāqib ... al-Jaᶜalī,* and Hill (1967), 17 and 34.
63 NRO, Intel. 2/32/266.
64 Ibn Ḍayf Allāh (1974), 351-2.
65 Interview 19.
66 Ibn Ḍayf Allāh (1974), 352, n. 7.
67 Trimingham (1971), 48-51 and *passim.*

spired branches among his followers. This why the Shādhiliyya is found in most of the Muslim world as localized orders.[68]

The Shādhiliyya seems to have appeared in some parts of the Sudan before the Qādiriyya. Its diffusion in the Sudan was the work of a number of independent individuals and its teachings were to become more widespread than those of the Qādiriyya. The Shādhiliyya, like the Qādiriyya, was represented in the Sudan by a number of independent branches, each with its distinctive *sanad* and *silsila* and with little connection with each other. According to the *Ṭabaqāt*, it was the first *ṭarīqa* to enter the Sudan, being introduced by a Sharīf called Ḥamad Abū Dunāna, who settled in Saqādī Gharb, west of the present-day Maḥmiyya, in 1445.[69] Abū Dunāna is described as the son-in-law of Abū ᶜAbd Allāh Muḥammad b. Sulaymān al-Jazūlī, the propagator of the Jazūliyya Shādhiliyya in Morocco.[70] One of Abū Dunāna's daughters is said to have married Muḥammad w. al-Arbāb and been the mother of Idrīs w. al-Arbāb; another daughter married ᶜAbd Allāh Jammāᶜ and became the mother of ᶜAjīb al-Mānjilūk. According to a tradition of the ᶜArakiyyūn clan, their ancestors, before the initiation of ᶜAbd Allāh al-ᶜArakī into the Qādiriyya, were adherents of the Shādhiliyya.[71]

Despite the absence of written evidence to support the traditions summarized above, it seems reasonable to suggest that before the introduction of the Qādiriyya during the sixteenth century the northern Sudan may have already been familiar with the doctrine of the Shādhiliyya. This suggestion may be supported by an earlier written tradition which asserts that Abū'l-Ḥasan al-Shādhilī died and was buried at Ḥummaythrā near ᶜAydhāb, about twelve miles north of Ḥalayb in the

68 See further, E. Montet, "Religious orders (Muslim)", *ERE*, x, 1967, 724-5; Muḥammad b. ᶜAlī al-Sanūsī, *al-Manhal al-rawī al-rāʾiq fī asānīd al-ᶜulūm wa-uṣūl al-ṭarāʾiq*, n.p. 1968, 83; Trimingham (1971), 276-9, and Jenkins in Willis (1979), i, 44.

69 Ibn Ḍayf Allāh (1974), 4 and 9; see also ᶜAbd al-Majīd ᶜĀbdīn, *Taʾrīkh al-thaqāfa al-ᶜarabiyya fī'l-Sūdān,* 2nd edn, Beirut 1967, 64, and Holt and Daly (1979), 28.

70 Ibn Ḍayf Allāh (1974), 10; on al-Jazūlī see Khayr al-Dīn al-Ziriklī, *al-Aᶜlām. Qāmūs tarājim li-ashhar al-rijāl wa'l-nisāʾ min al-ᶜarab wa'l-mustaᶜribīn wa'l-mustashriqīn,* n.p. (Beirut) n.d. (c. 1979), vii, 22.

71 Muḥammad al-Fātiḥ Maḥmūd al-Maghribī, "Taʾrīkh al-ṭuruq al-Ṣūfiyya fī'l-Sūdān. Al-ṭarīqa al-Qādiriyya", *Majallat al-taṣawwuf al-Islāmī*, Cairo 1982, 57.

eastern Sudan.[72] ᶜAydhāb was in its heyday one of the most important ports of the Middle East; from the beginning of the twelfth century it was not only an important trading port, but also the main pilgrimage port of Africa. In part this was caused by the Crusades, which threatened the route via Sinai. Consequently, the pilgrim traffic to the Ḥijāz from Egypt and West Africa tended to shift to ᶜAydhāb. ᶜAydhāb continued to flourish until it was destroyed during the reign of the Mamluk Sultan Barsbay (1422-38) and its place taken by Sawākin.[73] ᶜAydhāb apparently served in the pilgrimage season as a centre for public lectures in religion. Abū'l-Ḥasan al-Shādhilī, who made the pilgrimage to Mecca annually, gave public lectures in ᶜAydhāb[74] and these, one may hypothesize, may well have been attended by pilgrims from the future Shāyqiyya region, who in their turn propagated his ideas and teachings among their kin.

Shaykh Khōjalī. One of the first to propagate the Shādhiliyya in the Funj period was Khōjalī ᶜAbd al-Raḥmān b. Ibrāhīm (d. 1155/1743). He was of Maḥasī origin, his mother being Ḍawwa bt. Khōjalī and his father ᶜAbd al-Raḥmān, who was from the Kabānī Maḥas.[75] Khōjalī's grandfather, Ibrāhīm, had studied in the Shāyqiyya region under Ibrāhīm al-Būlād of the Awlād Jābir. Khōjalī was born on Tūtī Island at the confluence of the Blue and White Niles near Khartoum. He began his education at the Quranic school of ᶜĀʾisha *al-faqīra* bt. Qaddāl and studied theology and Sufism under Arbāb b. ᶜAlī (d. 1102/1690-1). He then moved to al-Qōz, near Shendi, to study the *Mukhtaṣar* under al-Zayn w. Ṣughayrūn.

72 Abū ᶜAbd Allāh Muḥammad b. Baṭṭūṭa, *Tuḥfat al-nuẓẓār fī gharāʾib al-amṣār wa-ᶜajāʾib al-asfār*, Cairo n.d., i, 30.

73 On ᶜAydhāb, see A. Paul, "Aidhab: A Medieval Red Sea Port", *SNR*, xxxvi/1 (1955), 64-5; Muhammad Muṣṭafā Musᶜad, *al-Maktaba al-ᶜArabiyya al-Sūdāniyya,* Cairo 1972, 15-6; Bashīr Ibrāhīm Bashīr, "ᶜAydhāb, ḥayātuhā al-dīniyya wa'l-adabiyya", *MDS*, 1979, 53-84 and H.A.R. Gibb, "ᶜAydhab", *EI* 2,, i, 782.

74 Ibn Baṭṭūṭa (n.d.), i, 30; Jamāl al-Dīn al-Shayyāl, *Aᶜlām al-Iskandariyya fī'l-ᶜaṣr al-Islāmī*, Cairo 1965, 189; Bashīr (1979), 67.

75 What follows is based on Ibn Ḍayf Allāh (1974), 80-4, 100-1, 191 and 196, and interview 3. Khōjalī's pedigree is usually traced back to Muḥammad Kabānī, ancestor of the Maḥas, but al-Faḥl (n.d.), 32, claims he was not Maḥasī but Dahmashī Bidayrī.

Shaykh Khōjalī was originally a follower of the Qādiriyya, but nothing is known of the circumstances of his initiation. It was while on the pilgrimage in Mecca that he was initiated into the Nāṣiriyya branch of the Shādhiliyya by Aḥmad al-Timbuktāwī al-Fallātī, a student of Muḥammad al-Nāṣiri al-Shādhilī.[76]

Upon his return from the Ḥijāz, Khōjalī began to propagate the teachings of the Nāṣiriyya Shādhiliyya. He claimed, however, that while the foundation (*asās*) of his *ṭarīqa* was Qādirī, its litanies (*awrād*; sing. *wird*) and rules of personal conduct (*qawāʿid al-sulūk*) were Shādhilī. This tactic may have been adopted by him to gain followers without incurring the hostility of the Qādiriyya. Despite this, Khōjalī apparently had several confrontations with one prominent Qādiriyya *shaykh*, Ṣāliḥ b. Bān al-Naqā al-Ḍarīr (1092/1681-2 to 1167/1753-4).[77] Khōjalī exercised considerable influence and succeeded, before his death in 1155/1743-4, in attracting a number of followers. But in the time of his son and his successor, Aḥmad, their branch of the Shādhiliyya lost adherents to the other *ṭarīqas*, namely the Sammāniyya in the Gezira and the Majdhūbiyya and Khatmiyya in the northern Sudan.[78]

The Early Majdhūbiyya. Another offshoot of the Nāṣiriyya Shādhiliyya in the Sudan is the Majdhūbiyya. This began as a local *ṭarīqa* founded by Ḥamad b. Muḥammad al-Majdhūb early in the eighteenth century in al-Dāmir in northern Sudan. The Majādhīb holy family claim to descend from a certain ᶜAbd al-ᶜĀl, a son of ᶜArmān, the common ancestor of the Jaᶜaliyyūn. ᶜArmān fathered two sons; Shāᶜ al-Dīn, ancestor of the Shāᶜ al-Dīnāb, and ᶜAbd al-ᶜĀl, ancestor of the ᶜUmarāb, the Majādhīb and the Judalāb. According to oral tradition, ᶜAbd al-ᶜĀl himself had two sons, Ḥamad and Qindīl, the latter being the father of *al-ḥājj* ᶜĪsā who was initiated into the Qādiriyya by Tāj al-Dīn al-Bahārī.[79] The Majādhīb were established in al-Dāmir by Muḥammad b. ᶜAlī, known as *al-Majdhūb al-kabīr*, "the elder" (*fl.* 1720). Before his time, the family had been known as al-Qindīlāb after their ancestor,

76 Ibn Ḍayf Allāh (1974), 191; nothing further is known about al-Timbuktāwī.

77 Ibn Ḍayf Allāh (1974), 239-45. See also Qarīb Allāh, thesis (1965), 226, and Hill (1967), 327.

78 Trimingham (1949), 223.

79 *Ibid.*, 224, and Qarīb Allāh, thesis (1965), 228-9. On ᶜArmān, see MacMichael (1922), i, 200 and ii, 85.

Qindīl b. ᶜAbd al-ᶜĀl. The Majādhīb family continued, up to the time of al-Majdhūb *al-kabīr's* death, to be loyal adherents of the Qādiriyya.

It was Ḥamad b. Muḥammad al-Majdhūb *al-kabīr* (1105/1693-4 to 1190/1776-7) who strayed from the "path" of his forefathers and joined the Shādhiliyya. Ḥamad was a Qādirī in his early life, but after studying in Nūrī with a member of the Ḥamadtūiyāb family, Madanī b. Muḥammad al-Nāṭiq, he is said to have abandoned the Qādiriyya because he felt that some of its practices were not in conformity with Islam. While on the pilgrimage, Ḥamad was initiated into the Nāṣiriyya Shādhiliyya by ᶜAlī al-Darāwī.[80] Ḥamad was succeeded by his son Aḥmad Qamar al-Dīn (b. 1159/1746-7); the Majādhīb and the Nāṣiriyya-Shādhiliyya *ṭarīqa* continued to flourish.

Other Branches of the Shādhiliyya. There were others who brought the Shādhiliyya to the Sudan; for example, ᶜAbd Allāh al-Sharīf, who was born in Fez in Morocco. He was initiated into the Nāṣiriyya Shādhiliyya by Muḥammad (or Aḥmad) b. al-Nāṣir and came to settle in Ḥalfāyat al-Mulūk.[81]

There is another tradition which attributes the propagation of the Shādhiliyya in the Sudan to Abū Jārid Ādam ᶜAbd Allāh, who lived in the Gezira during the sixteenth century and founded a religious group, notorious for its non-Islamic practices, generally known in the Sudan as al-Zabālᶜah. It seems paradoxical to link a group with such practices to the Shādhiliyya, which is noted for its conformity to the Quran and *sunna*.[82]

The Shādhiliyya was not represented in the Shāyqiyya area as an organization with a body of followers. Rather it was present in the form of teachings and liturgies such as the *Dalāʾil al-khayrāt* of al-Jazūlī.[83]

80 Ibn Ḍayf Allāh (1974), 188-9; see also Yūsuf Badrī, "A Survey of Islamic Learning in the Funj State, 1505-1820 AD.", B.Litt. thesis, Oxford University 1970, 87, and Muḥammad Ibrāhīm Abū Salīm, "*Dawr al-ᶜulamāʾ fī nashr al-Islām fī'l-Sūdān*", Conference paper, Khartoum 1982, 11.

81 Ibn Ḍayf Allāh (1974), 311; see also ᶜAbd al-Majīd (1949), i, 242, and Qarīb Allāh, thesis (1965), 218-20.

82 Shuqayr (1903), i, 57; S. Hillelson, "The people of Abu Jarid", *SNR*, i, (1918). 175-93; Qarīb Allāh, thesis (1965), 217, and Hill (1967), 70.

83 Ibn Ḍayf Allāh (1974), 10. See also, Abū Salīm in NRO, *Majmūᶜat Abī Salīm*, 12; Trimingham (1949), 213; Qarīb Allāh, thesis (1965), 241, and Ḥasan (1975), i, 77.

Conclusion

Although the doctrines of the ancient *ṭarīqas* were widespread and their shaykhs highly venerated throughout the Sudan, they failed to gain ground in the Shāyqiyya area as organized institutions. The reasons for this, and for the gradual change in the nature of Islam in the Shāyqiyya region, need to be seen within the context of the political and economic conditions in the region, as well as through the study of the doctrines of the orders.

The political instability and the continuous wars between the Shāyqiyya and their neighbours and between the various clans themselves hardly encouraged the Sufi shaykhs to visit the region to recruit followers. However, the Shāyqiyya revolt in 1659 (see p.7) was a contributory factor in the infiltration of the Sufi *ṭarīqas* into the region since it caused an economic decline in the area and thus led to the closing of some of the established centres of learning and the emigration of the *ᶜulamāᵓ*, thereby clearing the way for others.[84]

The Qādiriyya, which originated as a *sunnī* or orthodox "way" of Sufism became an eclectic *ṭarīqa* in the Sudan, accommodating a number of non-Islamic practices. Thus Muḥammad al-Hamīm, who was the first of Tāj al-Dīn al-Bahārī's *khalīfas* in the Sudan, had studied only a few chapters of the Quran. It is also said that he married two sisters at one time, while the *qāḍī* who reproached him was miraculously punished. Not surprisingly, al-Hamīm is described as one of the *malāmatiyya* (the blameworthy).[85] This is perhaps why some *ᶜulamāᵓ* in the Shāyqiyya area and elsewhere were unwilling to join the Qādiriyya. These included ᶜAbd Allāh al-ᶜArakī and Ḥamad al-Majdhūb. ᶜAbd al-Qādir b. Idrīs w. al-Arbāb, who studied under al-Aᶜsar w. ᶜAbd al-

84 Badrī, thesis (1970), 67-8, and Awad al-Sid al-Saied Muṣṭafā, "The Majdhubiyya Ṭarīqa: its Doctrine, Organization and Politics", M.Sc. thesis, University of Khartoum 1977, 122.

85 Ibn Ḍayf Allāh (1974), 318-23. On the evolution of the *malāmatiyya* idea within Sufism, see T. P. Hughes, *A Dictionary of Islam*, London 1885, 620; Trimingham (1971), 13 and 264-9, and M. Winter, *Society and Religion in Early Ottoman Egypt. Studies in the Writings of ᶜAbd al-Wahhāb al-Shaᶜrānī*, London 1982, 112-13.

Raḥmān w. Ḥamadtū in Nūrī, tried to persuade his teacher to join the Qādiriyya. But al-Aᶜsar replied,

I have nothing apart from this book [i.e. the *Mukhtaṣar* of Khalīl]. I am doing what is obligatory, recommended and permissible in it, and avoiding what is reprehensible.[86]

A further example is ᶜAbd al-Majīd al-Aghbash (d. 1121/1710-11), of the Bidayrī Ghubush holy clan of Berber. He studied the *Mukhtaṣar* with Shaykh al-Aᶜsar in Nūrī and succeeded his father as a religious teacher in Berber. He carefully prevented his numerous pupils from being initiated into the Sufi orders, reminding them that his only *ṭarīqa* was the Quran and the *ḥizb al-baḥr*, "the litany of the sea", one of Abū'l-Ḥasan al-Shādhilī's litanies.[87]

A final example is Muḥammad w. ᶜAdlān al-Shāyqī al-Hawashābī, who made the pilgrimage and settled in Medina where he studied philosophy, logic and jurisprudence with ᶜAbd Allāh al-Maghribī, a Mālikī jurist. After returning to the Sudan, Muḥammad settled in Tanqāsī, seven miles north of Marawī. He was famous for his learning and was the first to teach philosophy, logic, jurisprudence, Arabic and mysticism using the three works of Muḥammad b. Yūsuf al-Sanūsi al-Tilimsānī known as *al-Sanūsiyya al-Kubrā, al-Wusṭā* and *al-Ṣughrā*. Previously, only the *Ṣughrā* or *Umm al-Barāhīn* was commonly used in the Funj territory. Although Muḥammad w. ᶜAdlān combined *fiqh* with Sufism, he seems to have adopted a personal form of Sufism (*taṣawwuf fardī*) for there is no evidence of his initiation into a specific Sufi *ṭarīqa*.[88]

86 Ibn Ḍayf Allāh (1974), 228 and 308-10.
87 *Ibid.*, 280-1.
88 *Ibid.*, 359-60. On the works of al-Sanūsī, see GAL ii, 250, S ii, 352, and Ḥasan (1975), i, 70.

3

THE CENTRALIZED BROTHERHOODS: THE FIRST PHASE

The Wider Background

The ancient and decentralized *ṭarīqas* had had very little influence on the Shāyqiyya region; by contrast the centralized *ṭarīqas* came to dominate the area during the nineteenth century.

The present chapter discusses the coming of two of these centralized new *ṭarīqas*, the Sammāniyya and the Khatmiyya. Both had their origins in the heart of the Muslim world, the Ḥijāz. They were part of a general revivalist or reformist movement which reached its climax during the second half of the eighteenth and the early nineteenth centuries. This Islamic revival was, in part, a response to the military, political, socio-economic and religious decline within the Muslim world and, in part, to European encroachment. The early reformers, in contrast to later ones who attempted reform through borrowing from the West,[1] sought to reform the Muslim world from within, that is on Islamic terms. Our concern in this study is with the latter.

There were many strands within the reform movement and many common ideas. Three movements are particularly relevant to the present study: the Salafiyya or Wahhābiyya, the *ahl al-ḥadīth* tradition and a number of new Sufi *ṭarīqas*. The first was represented in Arabia by Muḥammad b. ᶜAbd al-Wahhāb (1115/1703 to 1206/1792), whose teachings were largely based on those of Aḥmad Taqī al-Dīn b. Taymiyya (661/1263-4 to 728/1328-9) who called for a "return to the sources", *al-rujūᶜ ilā 'l-uṣūl*, that is the Quran and the *sunna*, as the

1 See, for example, A. Hourani, *Arabic Thought in the Liberal Age, 1798-1939*, London 1967, 103-59 on Jamāl al-Dīn al-Afghānī (1839-97) and Muḥammad ᶜAbduh (1849-1905).

only true basis for Islam.[2] A related strand is represented by such figures as Ṣāliḥ b. Muḥammad al-Fullānī (1166/1752-3 to 1218/1803-4), a West African scholar settled in Medina, and Muḥammad Ḥayyā al-Sindī (d. 1163/1750).[3] Both may be termed anti-Madhhabists or, better, "Traditionists" in that they decisively rejected *taqlīd*, the unquestioning acceptance of the teachings of any one of the law-schools (*madhāhib*), inasmuch as,

> The yardstick against which every action is to be measured is conformity with Quranic injunction or with a saying or a deed of the Prophet.[4]

The new brotherhoods had a number of strands. One included several Naqshbandiyya teachers who were influenced by the Indian reformer, Aḥmad Sirhindī (971/1564 to 1034/1624), known as the *mujaddid al-alf al-thānī*, "the renewer of the second millenium", who worked to purify Sufism in India.[5] Two figures who had links with both the Salafiyya or Wahhābiyya and *ḥadīth* movements were to become of profound significance to the movement for revival and reform throughout Sudanic Africa, from the Red Sea to Senegal. They were Aḥmad al-Tijānī (1150/1737-8 to 1230/1815) and Aḥmad b. Idrīs al-Fāsī (1163/1749-50 to 1253/1837); both were from North Africa.

The Sammāniyya

The first impulse for change came through the Sammāniyya whose origins lay in the tradition of the Khalwatiyya Sufi order, which may be traced back to the fourteenth century. The founder of the Sammāniyya, Muḥammad b. ᶜAbd al-Karīm al-Sammān (1132/1718 to 1189/1775), was a student of a Syrian Khalwati, Muṣṭafā Kamāl al-Dīn al-Bakrī

2 See H. Laoust, "Ibn ᶜAbd al-Wahhāb", in *EI* 2, iii, 677-9; ᶜAbd al-Raḥīm ᶜAbd al-Rahmān ᶜAbd al-Raḥīm, *Min taʾrīkh shibh al-jazīra al-ᶜarabiyya fīʾl-ᶜaṣr al-ḥadīth*. Cairo 1979, i, 31-55.

3 J.O. Voll, "Muḥammad Ḥayyā al-Sindī and Muhammad ibn ᶜAbd al-Wahhāb: an analysis of an intellectual group in eighteenth-century Madīna", *BSOAS*, xxxviii, 1975, 32-9, and J.O. Hunwick, "Ṣāliḥ al-Fullānī (1752/3-1803): the career and teachings of a West African *ᶜālim* in Medina", in *In Quest of an Islamic Humanism*, ed. A.H. Green, Cairo 1984, 147.

4 Hunwick (1984).

5 Sh. ᶜInayatullah, "Shaykh Aḥmad Sirhindi", *EI* 2, i, 297-8.

(1099/1688-9 to 1162/1748-9), who lived for long periods of his life in Damascus, Jerusalem and Cairo. On al-Bakrī's death, his students set up their own independent branches. Among these students was al-Sammān, who established a new Khalwatī branch known as the Sammāniyya.[6] This was brought to the Sudan in about 1764 by Aḥmad al-Ṭayyib w. al-Bashīr (1155/1742-3 to 1239/1824), who had been initiated and appointed *khalīfa* by al-Sammān himself while on the pilgrimage in Medina.

Aḥmad al-Ṭayyib was born at Umm Marriḥ, north of Omdurman. His mother was Ruqayya bt. Raḥma b. Muḥammad Surūr; his father, who was also his mother's cousin, was Bashīr b. Mālik b. Muḥammad Surūr.[7] His pedigree shows that he had a common ancestry with the ᶜArakiyyūn holy clan. After memorizing the Quran at the mosque of his ancestor, Muḥammad w. Surūr, Aḥmad studied under Walad Anas al-ᶜAwaḍābī, a student of Shaykh Khōjalī, on the island of Islānj, north of Omdurman. He then asked the famous Qādirī shaykh, ᶜAbd al-Bāqī al-Nayyal, to initiate him into the Qādiriyya. Al-Nayyal is reported to have communicated with the spirit of Ḥasan w. Ḥassūna, who commanded him not to admit Aḥmad.[8] Aḥmad was also a student of Aḥmad al-Fazārī al-Farḍī of Umm Ṭalḥa in the Gezira. He then decided to return to Umm Marriḥ, where he studied on his own, devoting most of his time to the *Mukhtaṣar* of Khalīl and a major commentary upon it by Bahrām al-Damīrī (d. 805/1402).

When he was sixteen or eighteen, that is in 1758 or 1760, Aḥmad travelled to the Ḥijāz. In Mecca he studied under several leading scholars, among them ᶜAbd Allāh al-Maḥjūb al-Mīrghanī, the founder of the

6 Muḥammad Tawfīq al-Bakrī, *Bayt al-Ṣiddīq*, Cairo (1323/1905-6), 156-65; F. de Jong, "Khalwatiyya", in *EI*[2] iii, 991-3; B. G. Martin, "A Short History of the Khalwati Order of Dervishes", in *Scholars, Saints and Sufis*, ed. N. R. Keddie, Berkeley 1972, 275-305.

7 The two main sources on Aḥmad al-Ṭayyib's life are ᶜAbd al-Maḥmūd Nūr al-Dāʾim, *Azāhīr al-riyāḍ fī manāqib al-ᶜārif bi-llāh al-Shaykh Aḥmad al-Ṭayyib*, Khartoum 1954 and *idem*, *al-ᶜUrf al-fāʾiḥ wa'l-ḍiyāʾ al-lāʾiḥ fī manāqib al-quṭb al-rājiḥ wa-ghawth al-wāḍiḥ sayyidī al-ustādh al-ṣhaykh Aḥmad al-Ṭayyib b. al-Bashīr*, Omdurman 1955; see also Muḥammad Ibrāhīm Abū Salīm, "Ijāza Sammāniyya", *MDS*, 1969, 30. On Muḥammad w. Surūr, see Ibn Ḍayf Allāh (1974), 345.

8 Nūr al-Dāʾim.(1954), 29-39 and 370.

Mīrghaniyya.[9] It was probably because of this relationship and the high esteem in which Aḥmad was held by Muḥammad ᶜUthmān al-Mīrghanī that the Sammāniyya and Khatmiyya developed very intimate relations, especially during the life of Muḥammad al-Ḥasan al-Mīrghanī (see pp. 79-80).

While in Mecca Aḥmad al-Ṭayyib was also initiated by Ibrāhīm b. Muḥammad ᶜAbd al-Salām al-Makkī al-Shāfiᶜī, a student of Muṣṭafā Kamāl al-Dīn al-Bakrī, into the Khalwatiyya and by ᶜAbd al-Raḥmān al-ᶜAydarūs into the Naqshbandiyya.[10] Aḥmad was said to have seen in a vision that his real master was Muḥammad b. ᶜAbd al-Karīm al-Sammān in Medina. He thus moved there and studied under him for seven years, during which he was initiated by his teacher into a number of *ṭarīqas*, among them the Qādiriyya, Khalwatiyya, and Naqshband-iyya.[11] After receiving his diploma (*ijāza*), Aḥmad al-Ṭayyib was ordered by his master to return to the Sudan to initiate followers and "to make manifest the signs of the Religion", *iẓhār maᶜālim al-dīn.*

Aḥmad al-Ṭayyib was to infuse a new spirit into Sudanese Sufism, leading to a renewed emphasis not only on such practical aspects as *dhikr* (recital) and *madīḥ* (songs of praise) but also on the philosophy of Sufism. Aḥmad al-Ṭayyib was said to have found the Qādiriyya and the Shādhiliyya at a very low ebb. He felt the need for reform and began to make contact with the leading shaykhs of his day, seeking to persuade them to unite under his leadership, "to revive its [the land's] people", *li-iḥyā' ahlihā.*[12]

Aḥmad travelled extensively preaching his new order. During a visit to Sinnār he recruited the Hamaj Regent, Nāṣir b. Muḥammad Abī Likaylik, who granted him an estate. He also initiated the scholar Aḥmad w. ᶜĪsā al-Anṣārī, who sent some of his own pupils to be initiated by Aḥmad, among whom was Badawī w. Abū Ṣafiyya (d. *c.* 1848), a religious notable of the Bidayriyya of Kordofan.[13]

9 *Ibid.*, 41, and Aḥmad ᶜAbd Allāh Sāmī, *al-Shāᶜir al-Sūdānī, Muḥammad Saᶜīd al-ᶜAbbāsī*, Khartoum 1968, 24.

10 Nūr al-Dā'im (1954), 41-2, and *idem* (1955), 6-7.

11 Nūr al-Dā'im (1954), 50.

12 *Ibid.*, 66.

13 *Ibid.*, 241. Abū Ṣafiyya led a holy war against the Nūba, converting many to Islam. He transferred from the Sammāniyya to the Khatmiyya, which in turn he later abandoned for the Ismāᶜīliyya. Like al-Kabbāshī, he was hostile to the Turco-Egyptian regime; to an official, he exclaimed, "You call yourself

The Sammāniyya also gained some followers in the Shāyqiyya region, among whom was Ibrāhīm al-Duwayḥī, an uncle of Ibrāhīm al-Rashīd whose coming was allegedly prophesied by Aḥmad al-Ṭayyib, and ᶜAbd al-Jabbār al-Shāyqī who propagated the *ṭarīqa* in Abū Dōm near Marawī.[14]

By the time of Aḥmad's second visit to the Ḥijāz, which took place some years after his first visit in 1758 or 1760, the Sammāniyya had already gained wide popularity, especially in the Gezira. It attracted many of the Qādiriyya, who were impressed with the *ṭarīqa*'s new style as well as with Aḥmad's personality. Thus Aḥmad al-Baṣīr (d. 1829) and Muḥammad Tōm Bānnaqā (d. 1851), Qādirī shaykhs and religious leaders of the Ḥalawiyyīn and the Yaᶜqūbāb clans of the Gezira respectively, joined the Sammāniyya under the influence of Aḥmad.[15]

Aḥmad al-Ṭayyib, however, faced some opposition from the Ṣādqāb Qādiriyya holy clan and, paradoxically, from some of his own relatives, the ᶜArakiyyūn, who probably opposed him because they did not want to be subordinate to the Sammāniyya.[16]

Aḥmad's visit to the Ḥijāz was via Egypt. *En route*, he stayed for some time at al-Dāmar with Ḥamad b. Muḥammad al-Majdhūb, whose grandson Muḥammad al-Majdhūb b. Aḥmad Qamar al-Dīn later became a prominent Sammāniyya leader.[17]

While in Cairo, Aḥmad visited al-Azhar where he attended some lectures given by Muḥammad al-Amīr, a famous Egyptian Mālikī scholar, who was said to have treated Aḥmad with honour. It was probably because of this connexion that Aḥmad al-Salāwī, himself a student of Muḥammad al-Amīr, later after the Turco-Egyptian conquest cultivated

---

Muslim, God alone knows the truth, but to me you are only the oppressors of my country", N. Peney, quoted in Trimingham (1949), 103. See also Hill (1967), 65-66; Mahmūd (1971), 131, and Mahmoud Abdalla Ibrāhīm, "The history of the Ismāᶜīliyya Ṭarīqa in the Sudan: 1792-1914", Ph.D. thesis, University of London 1980, 79-80.

14 Nūr al-Dāʾim (1954), 329 and 338.

15 Trimingham (1949), 221 and 227; see also Hill (1967), 31.

16 Trimingham (1949), 199 and 226-8; Abū Salīm (1969), 30; Badri, thesis (1970), 182, and Holt (1973b), 126. Aḥmad met with some opposition from Yūsuf Abū Shara, an ᶜArakī *khalīfa*, when the latter saw him encroaching upon his followers in the Gezira. Later, the ᶜArakiyyūn went over to the Sammāniyya; see Trimingham (1949), 220.

17 Nūr al-Dāʾim (1954), 68, and *idem* (1955), 14-15.

close relations with Aḥmad, married one of his daughters and named a son after him.[18] Aḥmad continued his journey to the Ḥijāz, where he performed the pilgrimage and stayed for some time with his teacher Muḥammad b. ᶜAbd al-Karīm al-Sammān, who later permitted him (*adhina lahu*) to return to the Sudan to pursue his career.[19]

Aḥmad's death in 1824 marked the beginning of his order's division: "at his death the sun of the *ṭarīqa* set", *gharabat bi-wafātihi shams al-ṭarīqa.*[20] His death without nominating a successor led to long disputes among his sons, and between them and some of his senior adherents. At first Aḥmad's followers split into two groups. The first supported Ibrāhīm al-Disūqī (d. 1269/1852-3), Aḥmad's elder son, because of his age, learning and, more importantly, because he had frequently taken his father's place in leading the prayers. The second group backed Nūr al-Dā'im (d. 29 Shawwāl 1268/7 August 1851), another son of Aḥmad, because his father was said to have remarked of him that *baraka* would be inherent in him and his offspring.[21]

This dispute continued until 1245/1829-30, when Aḥmad al-Baṣīr arrived to build a tomb over his master's grave. Al-Baṣīr, who was greatly respected by the Sammāniyya and believed to be a member of the Prophetic communion (*ḥaḍrat al-rasūl*, see Glossary), was said to have authorized Nūr al-Dā'im to lead the prayers, praying behind him like an ordinary follower. Al-Baṣīr's justification for this was that he had had a vision (*ru'yā*) in which the Prophet declared that Nūr al-Dā'im was Aḥmad's successor.[22]

The Sammāniyya suffered further fragmentation and regionalization. Three new independent branches, which shared the same spiritual genealogy and paid nominal homage to the family of the founder, emerged. The first branch was under the leadership of al-Qurashī w. al-Zayn (d. 1878), a senior follower of Aḥmad.[23] A second branch was

18 Nūr al-Dā'im (1954), 59-60 and 78.

19 *Ibid.*, 66.

20 *Ibid.*, 265-6.

21 *Ibid.*, 354-6.

22 *Ibid.*, 274.

23 Al-Qurashī was from the Ḥalawiyyūn of the Gezira; he established a *khalwa* to teach the Quran and propagate the Sammāniyya at al-Masallamiyya near al-Ḥasaḥayṣa. Muḥammad Aḥmad, the Mahdi, joined him after a dispute with his previous master, Muḥammad Sharīf (see following n. 24). The Mahdi

founded by Aḥmad al-Baṣīr (d. 1830). Finally, a third emerged under Muḥammad Sharīf Nūr al-Dāʾim (d. 1327/1908-9), a grandson of Aḥmad al-Ṭayyib.[24] This branch, which was known as the Ṭayyibiyya Sammāniyya Bakriyya, gained a considerable number of followers not only in the Sudan but also in Egypt.[25]

The Sammāniyya came to the Sudan as a "reformist" *ṭarīqa* but was soon assimilated into the local social order. Like the ancient orders, it split up into a number of autonomous branches, characterized by personal disputes between their heads. The Sammāniyya broke up because of clashes of personality, and ethnic and regional loyalties. Thus during the disputes over the succession, Ibrāhīm al-Disūqī was supported by the Surūrāb and ᶜAwaḍāb clans of the Jummūᶜiyya sub-section of the Jaᶜaliyyūn, whereas his brother Nūr al-Dāʾim was backed by the Jimiᶜāb, another sub-section of the Jaᶜaliyyūn who live north of Omdurman and Khartoum North. A further example of ethnic and regional division is the case of al-Qurashī and Aḥmad al-Baṣīr, who won the support of the Ḥalawiyyīn of the Gezira.[26]

In conclusion, it was because of these rivalries and lack of central leadership that the Sammāniyya failed to become a geographically widespread *ṭarīqa* as the Khatmiyya later became. The Sammāniyya may be considered a "halfway house" between the older orders and the new centralized ones.

---

married a daughter of al-Qurashī by whom he had ᶜAlī al-Mahdī (1881-1944); see Hill (1967), 49, and Holt (1970), 45 and 104.

24 Muḥammad Sharīf was the Mahdi's first Sufi teacher, before the former expelled him from the *ṭarīqa*; see Hill (1967), 247; Abū Salīm (1969), 31, and Holt (1970), 21. Thus, when Muḥammad Aḥmad declared himself the Mahdi in 1881, he was supported by the Sammāniyya branches of al-Qurashī and al-Baṣīr, but opposed by that of Muḥammad Sharīf; see Hill (1967), 274, and al-Ṭāhir Muḥammad ᶜAlī, *al-Ādab al-ṣūfī fī'l-Sūdān*, Khartoum 1970, 89.

25 F. de Jong, *Ṭuruq and Ṭuruq-linked Institutions in Nineteenth Century Egypt*, 179. This branch should not be confused with the Moroccan Ṭayyibiyya which derives its name from Mawlay al-Ṭayyib (d. 1767); see Trimingham (1971), 276.

26 Nūr al-Dāʾim (1954), 274, 356 and 358.

DIAGRAM 2. *Aḥmad al-Ṭayyib w. al-Bashīr.*

Aḥmad al-Ṭayyib w. al Bashīr*
(known as al-Shaykh al-Ṭayyib)
(1155/1742-3 to 1239/1824)

Ibrāhīm al-Disūqī (Aḥmad's eldest son d. 1269/1852-3)	Nūr al-Dāʾim (d. 29 Shawwāl 1268/ 7 August 1851)

* For Aḥmad's numerous sons see, Nūr al-Dāʾim (1954), 351-67.

The School of Aḥmad b. Idrīs

Aḥmad b. Idrīs b. Muḥammad b. cAlī b. Aḥmad was born into a holy family at Maysūr in the district of al-cArāʾish near Fez in Morocco probably in 1163/1749-50.[27] He was a descendant of the *imām* Idrīs b.

27 Muḥammad cUthman al-Mīrghanī, *Manāqib ... al-Sayyid Aḥmad b. Idrīs,* Wad Madanī, 1391/1971, 7, says he was born at Qāra near Fez. The sources disagree on the date of his birth; according to Ṣālih b. *al-ḥājj* Muḥammad b. Ṣāliḥ al-Jacfarī al-Madanī, *al-Muntaqā al-nafīs fī manāqib quṭb dāʾirat al-taqdīs sayyidinā wa-mawlānā al-ṣayyid Aḥmad b. Idrīs,* Cairo 1380/1960, 2; Ibrāhīm al-Rashīd, *Acṭār azhār aghṣān ḥaẓīrat al-taqdīs fī karāmāt... al-sayyid Aḥmad b. Idrīs,* Cairo 1394/1974, 34, and cUmar cAbd al-cAzīz al-Bayyāḍī, *Nasab al-sayyid Aḥmad b. Idrīs,* al-Zayniyya/ al-Uqṣur: published privately by the sons of al-sayyid Muṣṭafā b. cAbd al-cĀl al-Idrīsī, (1979), 1 and 5, he was born in 1163/1749-50. A Sanūsiyya source gives the date as 1173/1760-1; al-Rashīd (1394/1974), 55. Although this latter date is widely given in Western sources (see, for example, Trimingham (1949), 229; *idem* (1971), 114; J.O. Voll, "A History of the Khatmiyya Ṭariqa in the Sudan", Ph. D. thesis 1969, 90 and de Jong (1978), 111), the head of the Idrīsiyya in the Sudan claimed that 1163 was correct; interview 15. See further, R.S. O'Fahey, *Enigmatic Saint. Aḥmad ibn Idrīs and the Idrīsī Tradition,* London 1990, 27-32.

ᶜAbd Allāh of the Idrīsī family of Morocco, tracing his descent back to al-Ḥusayn b. ᶜAlī, the grandson of the Prophet.[28]

Even before reaching manhood, Aḥmad used to seclude himself and devote most of his time to worship, contemplation and lamentation over the deteriorating state of Islam and the Muslims; he soon became known for his piety, asceticism (*taqashshuf*) and the renunciation of the things of the world.[29]

After memorizing the Quran and studying a range of Islamic subjects, he moved, at the age of twenty, to Fez for further study. There he studied under a number of scholars among whom were Muḥammad al-Tāwudī b. Sūda (d. 1209/1794-5), ᶜAbd al-Qādir b. Aḥmad al-ᶜArabī (d. 1216/1801-2) and Muḥammad al-Majīdrī (or al-Mijaydrī) al-Shinqīṭī.[30] He was also taught by a number of Sufi teachers, the first being ᶜAbd al-Wahhāb al-Tāzī, with whom he stayed for four years and by whom he was initiated into the Khaḍiriyya order.[31] On al-Tāzī's death, Aḥmad joined Abū'l-Qāsim al-Wazīr, who initiated him into the Nāṣiriyya Shādhiliyya.[32]

Aḥmad came to Fez at a time when two Moroccan sultans, Muḥammad b. ᶜAbd Allāh (ruled 1757-1790) and his brother's son Sulaymān b. Yazīd (ruled, 1794-1822), were attempting to reform Islamic learning in Morocco. Sultan Muḥammad, for instance, endeavoured to improve the curriculum of the Qarawiyyīn mosque-school in Fez by encouraging the study of the "sources", *uṣūl*, of the Sharia rather than the commentaries written on it.[33]

28 Aḥmad b. Idrīs, *al-ᶜIqd al-nafīs fī naẓm jawāhir al-tadrīs*, Cairo1372/1953, 2, and al-Bayyāḍī (1979), 6-10. On the Idrīsī family, see D. Eustache, "Idris I", in *EI*²,, iii, 1031 and 1053-7.

29 See *Tarjamat al-ustādh Aḥmad b. Idrīs*, NRO, misc., 1/81/1294, f. 5.

30 Al-Madanī (1380/1960), 2, and al-Rashīd (1394/1974), 35.

31 The Khaḍiriyya derives its name from al-Khaḍir, "a servant of Ours", who appears in Quran, XVIII: 59-81; see further A. J. Wensinck, "al-Khaḍir", in *EI* ²,, iv, 902-5. Its *sanad* became the basis of the *sanads* of virtually all the *ṭarīqas* inspired by Ibn Idrīs; see for example, *Sanad al-ṭarīqa al-Khatmiyya*, Bergen, NO 126.6/1. Its founder was ᶜAbd al-ᶜAzīz al-Dabbāgh who was initiated by al-Khaḍir; he was succeeded by Aḥmad b. Mubārak al-Lamaṭī, who was followed by al-Tāzī who had originally been an adherent of the Nāṣiriyya Shādhiliyya. On the Khaḍiriyya, see Trimingham (1971), 114.

32 Al-Mīrghanī (1391/1971), 22-3, where Abū'l-Qāsim is described as one of "the hidden Malāmatī".

33 Al-Rashīd (1394/1974), 9, and Voll, thesis (1969), 92.

Ibn Idrīs began to hold circles (Ar. sing. *ḥalqa*) to which he lectured on Sufism and *ᶜilm*, preaching against such practices as the exaggerated veneration of saints. He based his teachings and ideas on the Quran and the *sunna* and exhorted his audience to follow a purified form of Islam.

When Aḥmad left Fez in the middle of 1212/1797-8 intending to make the pilgrimage, he was already a prominent religious teacher and Sufi shaykh in the Maghrib. On his way to Mecca, he visited Algeria, Tunisia and Libya, where he lectured in the mosque of Benghāzī. Travelling by boat, he arrived at the beginning of 1213/June 1798 at Alexandria in Egypt. Aḥmad's public lectures, especially those which he gave in al-Azhar, were received with admiration and led some of those who heard them to accompany him to Mecca, which he reached at the end of 1213/1798-9.[34]

Ibn Idrīs stayed in Mecca for fourteen years, during which he founded a circle of pupils called by Aḥmad himself, *al-ṭarīqa al-Muḥammadiyya al-Aḥmadiyya* to show its direct link to the Prophet. Some scholars have claimed that Aḥmad established his own *ṭarīqa* known as the Idrīsiyya; this was in fact, as we shall see later, established by his sons after his death in 1837.[35] We may call Aḥmad's group of students *al-madrasa al-Idrīsiyya*, the Idrīsiyya school. It did not, like most of the Sufi orders, confine its activities to the practical aspects of Sufism such as the recital of *wird* and *ḥizb*, but also laid emphasis on Islamic doctrine and on missionary work.

Aḥmad was above all a reformer who sought, as did the Salafiyya movement, to restore the original form of Islam, purified of innovations and superstitions.[36] He rejected *qiyās* (analogy) and *ijmāᶜ* (consensus),

34 al-Rashīd (1394/1974), 37. In the lives appended to Aḥmad b. Idrīs, *Majmūᶜat Awrād aḥzāb wa-rasāʾil,* Cairo 1359/1940, 205 and *idem*, (1372/1953), 3-4, the date of his arrival is given as 1214/1799-1800. C. Padwick, *Muslim Devotions. A Study of Prayer-Manuals in Common Use*, London 1969, xviii, says that Aḥmad had taught in Cairo for twenty years before settling in Mecca in 1234/1818-9, but this latter is the date of his return to Mecca after his prolonged visit to Upper Egypt with his student, al-Mīrghanī. See further, the chronology proposed in O'Fahey (1990), 51-8.

35 See, for example, C.A. Willis, in NRO, Departmental Reports 11/1/4, "The Religious Confraternities", p. 10; *idem*, "Religious confraternities of the Sudan", *SNR*, iv/4, 1921, 184-5; Yūsuf b. Ismāᶜīl al-Nabhānī, *Jāmiᶜ karāmāt al-awliyāʾ*, 2 vols., Cairo (n.d.), i, 314-9, and de Jong (1978), 11.

36 Shams al-Dīn ᶜAbd al-Mutᶜāl, *Kanz al-Saᶜād wa'l-rashād,* Khartoum, 1358/1939, 12-3.

except that of the Prophet's companions, as sources of Islamic law.[37] He was hostile to the schools of law (the *madhhabs*).[38] Among his students in Mecca were Muḥammad Ḥasan Ẓāfir al-Madanī al-Darqāwī;[39] Muḥammad al-Majdhūb al-Ṣaghīr (see Appendix A); ᶜAbd al-Raḥmān b. Sulaymān al-Ahdal, the then *muftī* of Zabīd in the Yemen;[40] Makkī b. ᶜAbd al-ᶜAzīz; Ḥasan Muḥammad Balōl, known as Ḥasan al-Sunnī; and ᶜAbd Allāh al-Mawārzī, known as Abū'l-Maᶜālī. Aḥmad also taught a number of students after he settled at Ṣabyā in the Yemen in 1244/1829-30, among whom were Ibrāhīm al-Rashīd, Muḥammad ᶜUthmān b. Mubashshar, al-Jazūlī b. Idrīs and Shaykh Ṭāhir al-Ḥaymādī (or al-Ḥīmādī).[41]

Aḥmad's success was due, in addition to his own qualities, to the moral and material support which he received from Ghālib of the Zayd clan, *amīr* of Mecca. It was Ghālib who granted him the use of the famous palace (*saray*) of the Jaᶜfariyya in Mecca, which Aḥmad used as a centre for his followers until he left for the Yemen in 1243/1827-8.[42] Aḥmad's stay in Mecca coincided with important political develop-

37 *Ibid.*, 13-4.

38 *Ibid.*, 16; al-Mīrghanī (1391/1971), 46-7; see also Trimingham (1949), 199 and *idem* (1971), 115.

39 Muḥammad Ẓāfir was a son and successor of Muḥammad Ḥasan b. Ḥamza al-Madanī (d. 1846), the founder of the Madaniyya branch of the Darqāwiyya order in Libya. Muḥammad Ẓāfir made the Madaniyya a distinctive order which spread to the Maghrib, Ḥijāz and Turkey where it played a significant role in the pan-Islamic movement; see further, Trimingham (1971), 113 and 126.

40 On al-Ahdal, see *al-Aᶜlām*, iv, 79; ᶜUmar Riḍā Kaḥḥāla, *Muᶜjam al-muʾallifīn, tarājim muṣannifī al-kutub al-ᶜarabiyya*, Damascus 1957-61, v, 140, and al-Rashīd (1394/1974), 38.

41 Al-Ḥaymādī was a Sudanese holy man about whom very little is known. He was originally an adherent of the Khalwatiyya and Shādhiliyya, but joined the Khatmiyya at the instigation of al-Mīrghanī. He accompanied the latter to the Ḥijāz, performed the pilgrimage and joined the school of Ibn Idrīs in the Yemen. He is said to have entered into retreat (*khalwa*) sixty-four times and to have been told by Ibn Idrīs that his initiation would be at the hands of a holy man from the Maghrib whom he would meet in Dār Fūr. He travelled to the western Sudan where he met Muḥammad al-Mukhtār al-Tijānī al-Shinqīṭī; see Muḥammad al-Sayyid al-Tijānī, *Ghāyat al-amānī fī manāqib wa-karāmāt aṣḥāb al-shaykh sayyidī Aḥmad al-Tijānī*, Cairo, n.d., 105-6.

42 Interview 15.

ments, among which was the Wahhābī occupation in 1218/1803. In 1228/1813, on hearing of the approach of the army of Ṭusūn, Muḥammad ᶜAlī Pasha's son, the Wahhābīs retreated to Najd, where they maintained their authority until they were finally defeated by Ibrāhīm b. Muḥammad ᶜAlī's forces in 1816-18.[43]

It was probably no coincidence that in 1813, the year of the Turco-Egyptian occupation of Mecca, Aḥmad went, together with his student al-Mīrghanī, to Upper Egypt. Aḥmad and his student stayed at the village of al-Zayniyya, between Qinā and Isnā. In 1815 Muḥammad al-Mīrghanī went, with his master's consent, as a missionary to the Sudan; Aḥmad himself stayed in Upper Egypt until the end of 1234/1818-9 and then returned to the Ḥijāz. There he performed the pilgrimage and subsequently remained in Mecca up to the middle of 1243/1827-8, when he finally moved to the Yemen.[44]

It is evident that the political instability in Mecca hindered Aḥmad's work. Because of their opposition to his occupation of Mecca, in 1827 Muḥammad ᶜAlī Pasha ordered that the office of the *amīr* of Mecca be transferred from the Zayd clan, which had held it for a number of years, to the ᶜAwn clan.[45] Aḥmad had been on good terms with the Zayd clan. Perhaps this is why he now faced considerable opposition and hostility after the ᶜAwn clan took over the *amīr*ship. The Meccan *ᶜulamāʾ*, who had concealed their hostility toward him over the years, not only found the climate favourable to reveal their resentment of his disapproval of the four *madhhabs*, they openly accused him of heresy.[46] Aḥmad, together with all his principal students, except for al-Sanūsī who remained in Mecca as his representative (*khalīfa*), left in the middle of 1243/1827-8 for the Yemen. He stayed first at Zabīd with his student ᶜAbd al-Raḥmān, but at the end of 1244/1828-9 he moved to a small village in ᶜAsīr called Ṣabyā, which was at that time under the control of the Wahhābīs.[47]

43 Al-Rashīd (1394/1974), 39; see also ᶜAbd al-Raḥīm (1979), i, 329-34.

44 Al-Rashīd (1394/1974), 40.

45 Voll, thesis (1969), 95-6.

46 Al-Mīrghanī (1391/1971), 31, and Trimingham (1971), 115. What they meant by "heresy" is not specified.

47 Al-Rashīd (1394/1974), 41, and NRO, Intel., 6/7/22, "A short history of the Idrisia Tarika and its connection with Senussia", p. 10.

Shortly after his arrival, a famous debate (*munāẓara*), later published as a book known as *al-munāẓara al-Najdiyya*, took place between Aḥmad and a group of Wahhābī scholars led by a certain *faqīh* Nāṣir al-Kubaybī. The debate showed that although Ibn Idrīs had much in common with the Wahhābīs, he also disagreed with them over a number of issues. Aḥmad continued to teach at Ṣabyā, where he died and was buried on 21 Rajab 1253/21 October 1837. He left three sons: Muḥammad (1222/1807-8 to 1307/1889-90), ᶜAbd al-ᶜĀl (1246/1830-1 to 1296/1878-9) and Muṣṭafā, who died a young man some years after his father's death.[48]

The Succession Dispute

Aḥmad's death without nominating a successor was to have far-reaching repercussions on the subsequent development of the Idrīsiyya school. It also confirms the argument that Aḥmad did not establish a *ṭarīqa* as such with a hierarchy and fixed system of succession. The absence of a nominated *khalīfa* led to a series of disputes over the succession among his principal students, al-Sanūsī, al-Mīrghanī, Ibrāhīm al-Rashīd and his own sons.

In these disputes, Ibrāhīm al-Rashīd was supported by Muḥammad, Aḥmad's eldest son, who regarded him as Aḥmad's true successor because his father used to authorize him to lead the prayers in his absence. Moreover, his father had died in Ibrāhīm's arms. Because of Muḥammad's support, Ibrāhīm al-Rashīd succeeded in winning the allegiance of Ibn Idrīs' followers in Ṣabyā. Nonetheless, Ibrāhīm decided to leave for Upper Egypt to be away from the dispute, which was becoming increasingly bitter, especially between al-Sanūsī and al-Mīrghanī. Al-Sanūsī based his claim to the succession on the fact that he had acted as his master's representative in Mecca after he had left for the Yemen.[49] Al-Mīrghanī, on the other hand, considered himself his teacher's sole legitimate successor because he had been the first to join him, had acted as his missionary to Ethiopia and had accompanied him to Upper Egypt, whence he had gone with his consent to the Sudan.

48 Al-Rashīd (1394/1974), 26-7 and 42-5.

49 *Ibid.*, 41. A discussion of the succession dispute is given in O'Fahey (1990), 113-19.

Aḥmad's second son, ᶜAbd al-ᶜĀl, sided with al-Sanūsī against al-Mīrghanī and was later initiated by him into his own order, the Sanūsiyya, which he established after Aḥmad's death. He later went with al-Sanūsī to Libya.[50]

The rivalry among Ibn Idrīs' students culminated in the establishment by each of his own order. Five orders eventually emerged: the Sanūsiyya, the Khatmiyya established by al-Mīrghanī, the Madaniyya of al-Madanī, the Rashīdiyya of Ibrāhīm al-Rashīd and, at a later stage, the Idrīsiyya established by Ibn Idrīs' sons.

The Idrīsiyya School and the Sudan

The students of Ibn Idrīs were to have great influence in the Muslim world. Those who had a direct impact on the Sudan fall into two groups: those who founded their own orders and those who continued to function as independent representatives of the Idrīsiyya school in the Sudan, endeavouring to reform Sudanese Sufism in the light of Aḥmad's teachings and ideas. Among this latter group may be included Ḥasan Muḥammad Balōl, ᶜAbd Allāh al-Mawārzī, Makkī b. ᶜAbd al-ᶜAzīz, Muḥammad ᶜUthmān b. Mubashshar and al-Jazūlī b. Idrīs. The latter two were later to become representatives of the Khatmiyya order in the Shendi area.

Those of Aḥmad's students who influenced the Sudan through their own or later orders may be divided into two groups: those of non-Sudanese origin, al-Mīrghanī and the sons and descendants of Aḥmad himself; and those of Sudanese origin, Muḥammad al-Majdhūb al-Ṣaghīr, Ibrāhīm al-Rashīd and, indirectly, Ismāᶜīl al-Walī.

Muḥammad ᶜUthmān al-Mīrghanī

The first to carry Aḥmad's teachings to the Sudan was al-Mīrghanī (1208/1793-4 to 22 Shawwāl 1268/2 May 1852).[51] He came from a

50 Al-Rashīd (1394/1974), 44-5.

51 Makkī b. ᶜAbd al-ᶜAzīz is said to have returned to the Sudan before al-Mīrghanī's first visit; see Ibn Idrīs al-Ḥasan al-Idrīsī, *"al-Ḥaraka al-Sanūsiyya*

Sharifian family that had lived in Bukhāra before it moved to India and thence to the Ḥijāz and whose descent from the Prophet was widely acknowledged.[52] His father Muḥammad b. Abī Bakr and his grandfather ᶜAbd Allāh b. Ibrāhīm b. Ḥasan, commonly known as al-Maḥjūb (lit. "the secluded"; d. 1207/1792-3) were celebrated Sufi scholars.

Al-Mīrghanī was born at al-Salāma near al-Ṭā'if in 1208/1793-4. When he was about seven, his mother died. Three years later, his father died. It was his childless uncle, Muḥammad Yāsīn b. ᶜAbd Allāh al-Maḥjūb al-Mīrghanī, a noted Meccan Sufi and *ᶜālim*, who took care of him. In his childhood Muḥammad ᶜUthmān, who was said to have been a brilliant pupil, memorized the Quran and was instructed by his uncle in the exoteric sciences (*ᶜulūm al-ẓāhir*) such as grammar, rhetoric, *fiqh* and *tafsīr* (Quranic exegesis). By the age of thirteen or fourteen, he had already acquired a sound knowledge of these Islamic sciences. Having studied the exoteric religious sciences and Mālikī law, Muḥammad ᶜUthmān, then aged about fifteen years, decided to combine them with the esoteric sciences (*ᶜulūm al-ḥaqīqa*, lit. "the sciences of the Reality", i.e. of God), that is Sufism. Al-Mīrghanī was to become a prolific writer enriching Islamic scholarship with a number of works, including a major commentary on the Quran.

Muḥammad ᶜUthmān had affiliated himself to five Sufi orders or traditions before joining the "circle" of Aḥmad b. Idrīs: the Naqshbandiyya,[53] the Qādiriyya, the Shādhiliyya, the Junaydiyya[54] and

---

wa-āthāruhā al-thaqāfī fī shamāl Ifrīqiyya", MA thesis, University of Cairo 1976, 145. There is, however, little evidence to support this claim.

52 The main source for the life of al-Mīrghanī is Aḥmad "b. Idrīs" Muḥammad b. al-Naṣayḥ, ms; the *Kitāb al-ibāna al-nūriyya fī sha'n ṣāḥib al-ṭarīqa al-Khatmiyya* (hereafter cited as, *Kitāb al-Ibāna*); see also Voll (thesis) 1969, 103-15 and *passim*.

53 The Naqshbandiyya is traced back to Muḥammad al-Naqshbandī al-Bukhārī, an eclectic reformer who was influenced by Shīᶜa teachings. According to al-Sanūsī (1968), 89-98, and Nūr al-Dā'im (1954), 78, this *ṭarīqa* was the "Path" of the companions (*ṣaḥāba*) of the Prophet. See further, Montet (1967), 726, and Willis (1921), 188.

Al-Mīrghanī was initiated into the Naqshbandiyya by a number of shaykhs; first by Aḥmad b. Muḥammad Bannā al-Makkī, and then by Saᶜīd al-ᶜAmūdī al-Makkī, who had a religious centre at Jabal Abū Qubays in Mecca. Al-ᶜAmūdī was renowned for his almost continuous recitation of prayers for the Prophet, especially the *Dalā'il al-khayrāt*. His third Naqshbandī teacher was Aḥmad ᶜAbd al-Karīm al-Azbakī, who is said to have guided al-Mīrghanī to Ibn Idrī;, see

the Mīrghaniyya.[55] He then joined Ibn Idrīs, who initiated him for the second time into the same five orders, reflecting the latter's spiritual status.

Aḥmad's school was a missionary one. Thus, Muḥammad ᶜUthmān was sent by his master Ibn Idrīs to Ethiopia and, at a later stage, was allowed by him to travel to the Sudan. In Ethiopia he visited Balghā, where he preached his teacher's doctrines among the Muslim Jabarta. His success is said to have provoked the envy of the King of the Balghā region, who, thinking that Muḥammad ᶜUthmān was threatening his authority, attempted to have him poisoned. Muḥammad ᶜUthmān prudently returned to Mecca to rejoin his master.[56]

Muḥammad ᶜUthmān's second journey, together with his teacher, was to Upper Egypt in 1228/1813. It seems that, apart from avoiding the Turco-Egyptians in the Ḥijāz, the trip was intended as a period of apprenticeship for Muḥammad ᶜUthmān; he was sent by his teacher to preach in Manfalūṭ and Asyūṭ in Upper Egypt.[57]

Tarjamat al-sayyid Muḥammad ᶜUthmān al-Mīrghanī, ms., f. 4, and *Kitāb al-ibāna*, ms., f. 3.

According to Trimingham (1949), 232, al-Mīrghanī was also initiated into the Naqshabandiyya by ᶜAbd al-Raḥmān al-Ahdal, *muftī* of Zabīd.

It was al-ᶜAmūdī who initiated al-Mīrghanī into the Qādiriyya and Shādhiliyya and who taught him the *al-Dawr al-aᶜlā* of Muḥyī'l-Dīn b. al-ᶜArabī; see *Kitāb al-ibāna*, ff. 2-3, and *al-Nafaḥāt al-Makkiyya* in *Majmūᶜat al-nafaḥāt al-rabbāniyya al-mushtamila ᶜalā sabᶜa rasāᵓil Mīrghaniyya*, 1370/1950, 5-6.

54 The Junaydiyya tradition goes back to Abū'l-Qāsim al-Junayd b. Muḥammad al-Junayd al-Baghdādī (d. 260/874-5). According to Ibn al-Athīr, he was "the *imām* of the world of his time", *imām al-dunyā fī zamānihi*, and was described as the shaykh of the Sufi *madhhab* because his teachings were based on the Quran and *sunna*; see al-Sanūsī (1968), 62, and *al-Aᶜlām*, ii, 137-8.

55 The Mīrghaniyya was founded by ᶜAbd Allāh al-Maḥjūb al-Mīrghanī, Muḥammad ᶜUthmān's grandfather. It combined the Naqshbandiyya with the Shādhiliyya; NRO, Intel., 2/32/270, p. 56; Muḥammad b. ᶜAbd al-Majīd al-Sarrāj, *al-Manāḥij al-ᶜaliyya fī tarājim al-sāda al-Mīrghaniyya*, Khartoum 1374/1955, 24, and Voll, thesis (1969), 107.

56 *Kitāb al-ibāna*, ms., f. 6. Balghā is a region in Eritrea; see J.S. Trimingham, *Islam in Ethiopia*, London 1952, 159.

57 *Tarjamat al-sayyid Muḥammad*, ms., f. 5; ᶜAbd al-Malik b. ᶜAbd al-Qādir b. ᶜAlī al-Lībī, *al-Fāwaᵓid al-jaliyya fī taᵓrīkh al-ᶜāᵓila al-Sanūsiyya al-ḥākima fī Lībīya*, Damascus 1966, 13, gives the date of al-Mīrghanī's journey

It is often stated that Muḥammad ᶜUthmān was ordered by his master to travel to the Sudan.[58] But from the letters that were exchanged between Muḥammad ᶜUthmān in Asyūṭ and his teacher in al-Zayniyya, it would seem that it was Muḥammad ᶜUthmān who, in fact, petitioned his master to allow him to go to the Sudan.[59] Aḥmad replied,

> As to what you have mentioned about going to the Sudan, it will be very inconvenient. It will be a very long journey. If you can avoid that, do so. But as for the holy men of the Sudan, they have been bearing excessive burdens, and they want to lay them upon the shoulders of others.[60]

The question of the journey to the Sudan continued to come up, and Aḥmad finally allowed Muḥammad ᶜUthmān to go; Aḥmad wrote that it was only the Prophet who could decide Muḥammad ᶜUthmān's destination, otherwise Aḥmad would have authorized the journey before. It was, therefore, not until Aḥmad had himself received the required Prophetic authority that he allowed his student to travel to the Sudan.[61]

Why did Muḥammad ᶜUthmān suggest the Sudan as his third missionary field, after Ethiopia and Upper Egypt? He may have heard of the weakness of the *ṭarīqas* there. After his apparently limited success in both Ethiopia and Egypt, he may have hoped to win a greater following in the Sudan.[62]

---

as 1230/1814-5, the year after the Turco-Egyptian occupation of the holy cities; Voll, thesis (1969), 111, and O'Fahey (1990), 53.

58 For example, T.W. Arnold, *The Preaching of Islam. A History of the propagation of the Muslim faith*, 2nd edn, London 1913, 327; ᶜĀbdīn (1967), 101, and Trimingham (1949), 232.

59 According to Voll, thesis (1969), 11-2, al-Mīrghanī was in the Sudan between 1817 and 1818. According to *Sayyid* Muḥammad ᶜUthmān b. ᶜAlī al-Mīrghanī, the present (1985) head of the Khatmiyya in the Sudan, his journey began in 1815; see Muḥammad ᶜUthmān b. ᶜAlī al-Mīrghanī, interview in *Majallat al-Fatḥ* (Ramaḍān 1402/June-July 1982), 3. The latter date is partly confirmed by the statement of Ismāᶜīl al-Walī that he was initiated by al-Mīrghanī in al-Ubayyiḍ in Shawwāl 1231/September-October 1816; see Ismāᶜīl b. ᶜAbd Allāh al-Walī, *K. al-ᶜuhūd al-wāfiya*, ms., f. 6.

60 *Tarjamat al-ustādh Aḥmad b. Idrīs*, ms., ff.91-3.

61 *Ibid.*, 121-2.

62 Only two of his Egyptian *khalīfas* are named in *Kitāb al-ibāna*, ms. ff. 37-8. One is Aḥmad Abū Ḥarbiyya, regarded as one of the *ahl al-dīwān*, a Sufi term meaning "the people of the register (of the saints)". He had a large mosque and followers in Upper Egypt. The other was Aḥmad w. Saᶜd (d. c. 1286/1869-70), who was known as *al-dhākir*, "one who remembers (God)". He

The Travels of al-Mīrghanī

Muḥammad ᶜUthmān reached the Sudan in the last years of Funj rule at a time of instability and almost continuous war. He spent some time in Sudanese Nubia, where he visited Kunūz, Sukkūt and the Maḥas regions. Here he achieved great success in recruiting followers and appointed Idrīs b. Muḥammad, a famous Maḥasī holy man, as his *khalīfat al-khulafā*ᵓ, that is a senior representative or deputy (on the question of the foundation of the Khatmiyya, see pp. 64-6).[63]

He then continued south to Dongola where he stayed for a time and recruited many followers. One was Ṣāliḥ Suwār al-Dhahab, a member of the Suwār al-Dhahab holy family, who is said to have accompanied his master to Bāra in Kordofan.[64] From Dongola, Muḥammad ᶜUthmān travelled to al-Dabba where he attracted a number of followers, especially from the Shāyqiyya region, among whom was Ṣāliḥ b. ᶜAbd al-Raḥmān b. Muḥammad b. Ḥājj al-Duwayḥī, father of Ibrāhīm al-Rashīd, who came from his home village to meet al-Mīrghanī.[65] Muḥammad ᶜUthmān is also said to have initiated a number of prominent holy men in the Shāyqiyya region into the order without meeting them personally, but by sending *ijāzas* (certificates) to them in their home areas, relying only on hearsay about their learning, piety and most importantly, willingness to join him. These holy men included Muḥammad Khayr b. Muḥammad Ṣāliḥ al-ᶜIrāqī, Muḥammad Khayr al-Naḍīf and Muḥammad Hammād, known as Shaykh Jiqaydī.

---

spent some time with his master in Muṣṣawaᶜ where he wrote a commentary on the Quran with the same title as that written by al-Mīrghanī, *Tāj al-Tafāsīr.*

63 *Kitāb al-ibāna*, ms., f. 28; on Idrīs see further E.A.W. Budge, *The Egyptian Sudan,* i, London 1907, 458-60.

64 Ṣāliḥ's name is not given in the *Kitāb al-ibāna*, but see Hill (1967), 329; Voll, thesis (1969), 138-9, and Maḥmūd (1971), 129. He is perhaps referred to in a letter dated 1234/1818-9 from al-Mīrghanī in Kordofan to Ibn Idrīs sending greetings from a number of followers, including one Ṣāliḥ, *Tarjamat al-ustādh Aḥmad b. Idrīs,* ms., f. 90.

65 Muḥammad Khalīl al-Hajrasī, *al-Qaṣr al-mushīd fi'l-tawḥīd wa-fī ṭarīqat sayyidī Ibrāhīm al-Rashīd,* Cairo, 1314/1915-6, 89.

Al-Mīrghanī then went from al-Dabba in a large caravan, led by his *khalīfa* Muḥammad Ṣāliḥ Shādūl, to Bāra.[66] He arrived in Kordofan in Shawwāl 1231/September 1816 and stayed for about three years and three months, during which time he also visited Sinnār.[67] In Bāra he married Ruqayya bt. Jallāb, from the Jallāba Hawwāra holy family of Bādī, by whom he later had a son, Muḥammad al-Ḥasan. He is said to have initiated about two hundred persons, including Hammād al-Baytī[68] and ᶜArabī al-Khaṭīb al-Hawwārī. The latter was an *ᶜālim* and a man of letters who was appointed *qāḍī* of Kordofan province by the Turco-Egyptian authorities.[69] Muḥammad ᶜUthmān also recruited Ismāᶜīl al-Walī (1792-1863), who was born in al-ᶜUbayyiḍ into a Bidayrī-Dahmashī holy family which had moved, as part of the Jaᶜaliyyūn diaspora, from Manṣūrkutī near Dongola, to Kordofan. Ismāᶜīl had received a traditional *khalwa* education and before he met Muḥammad ᶜUthmān in Shawwāl 1231/September 1816 he had been living as a *khalwa* teacher. Muḥammad ᶜUthmān, who was impressed by his devotion, appointed him a *murshid*, "guide".

Also among al-Mīrghanī's initiates in Kordofan were Badawī w. Abū Ṣafiyya, Ibrāhīm al-Barqāwī, his brother *al-ḥājj* Mūsā al-Barqāwī and Maḥmud Bādī, a brother of Ruqayya (Muḥammad ᶜUthmān's wife), who was said to have been famous for his knowledge and writings on both Sufism and exoteric sciences (*ᶜulūm al-ẓāhir*).[70] While in Kordofan, Muḥammad ᶜUthmān also recruited three holy men who were said to have played an important role in propagating the Khatmiyya in the Shāyqiyya region, namely Muḥammad w. Mālik, Muḥammad b.

66 Maḥmūd (1971), 129. Muḥammad Ṣāliḥ was a descendant of ᶜAbd al-Mawlā of al-Khandaq who established himself as a *khabīr* (large-scale merchant) in Dār Fūr. On his descendants, see A. Bjørkelo, *Prelude to the Mahdiyya. Peasants and Traders in the Shendi Region, 1821-1885*, Cambridge 1989, 124-5.

67 Al-Walī, *Kitāb al-ᶜuhūd*, ms., f. 6.

68 Al-Baytī is said to have become *imām al-shamāl*, "*imām* of the left hand", a term apparently peculiar to Sudanese Sufism and meaning the one who stands at the left hand of the *quṭb* of the age but who is unable to attain the rank of *ghawthiyya* because of non-Sharifian origin, see *Kitāb al-ibāna*, ms., f. 9.

69 ᶜAbd al-Raḥīm (1952), 93, and Ḥusayn Sīd Aḥmad al-Muftī, *Taṭawwur niẓām al-qaḍāʾ fī'l-Sūdān*, i, 1378/1959, i, 80.

70 *Kitāb al-ibāna*, ms., f. 11.

ᶜAbd al-Ḥalīm, known as *al-naqīb* (a Sufi technical term, see Glossary), and Mālik w. Jinayd.

However, Muḥammad ᶜUthmān's visit to Kordofan was not as successful as his journeys in the northern and eastern Sudan. This was probably because of the hostility of the *maqdūm* Musallam, the Dār Fūr Sultanate's Governor in Kordofan, who imprisoned some of al-Mīrghanī's followers. Al-Mīrghanī is reported to have warned the *maqdūm* of the coming of the Turco-Egyptian invaders and the end of his rule at their hands.[71]

While in Kordofan, two of al-Mīrghanī's sons, Ibrāhīm Tāj al-Khatim and Aḥmad Nūr al-Khatim, died and were buried there.

The next region visited by Muḥammad ᶜUthmān was the Gezira. He stayed for some time at Shādhili village before continuing to Sinnār, where he arrived in 1232/1816-7. Here he suffered from the hostility of some of Sinnār's *ᶜulamāᵓ* and rulers. The *wazīr* al-Arbāb Dafᶜ Allāh w. Aḥmad is said to have been hostile towards Muḥammad ᶜUthmān; it was he who sent to Ibrāhīm w. Baqādī, an eminent *ᶜālim* known as the "Sibawayhī" (the famous Grammarian) of his time, to examine him. This choice itself shows that Muḥammad ᶜUthmān's opponents were familiar with his background and abilities as a Sufi and scholar.[72] Ibrāhīm arrived in Sinnār from his village, Baqādī, but two days later he died of a fever, even before he had met al-Mīrghanī. Ibrāhīm was said to have been warned by the famous holy man Aḥmad w. ᶜĪsā not to put Muḥammad ᶜUthmān to the test.[73]

Despite the hostility of the political establishment in Sinnār, Muḥammad ᶜUthmān won a number of prominent followers. One of these was Aḥmad w. ᶜĪsā, who became an adherent and a close friend of al-Mīrghanī and his family and who exhorted both his students and ordinary people to join Muḥammad ᶜUthmān. Among Aḥmad's students

71 *Ibid*., f. 11; on Musallam, see O'Fahey and Spaulding (1972), 331. Al-Mīrghanī might well have heard of Muḥammad ᶜAlī's plans, since the invasion was being planned in 1818; see G. Douin, *Histoire du Soudan Egyptien*, 1944, i, 77.

72 The Funj Chronicle describes him as a pupil (*tilmīdh*) of Ibn Idrīs; *Makhṭūṭa*, 75-6.

73 Ibrāhīm's death was naturally considered as a *karāma* by al-Mīrghanī's followers.

who supported al-Mīrghanī were Ḥamad w. Muḥammad Nūrayn ᶜAmīr, known as al-Ṣuwayliḥ, and al-Sharīf Ibrāhīm w. Saḥnūn.[74]

Muḥammad ᶜUthmān then returned to al-ᶜUbayyiḍ where he stayed for a time before travelling north again to the commercial centre, al-Matamma, where he established a mosque and stayed for about a year, winning a considerable following. He recruited Shaykh al-Rayyaḥ, one of al-Matamma's leading holy men. Like Aḥmad w. ᶜĪsā, Shaykh al-Rayyaḥ encouraged his students to join Muḥammad ᶜUthmān. Other recruits were Aḥmad al-Ṭirayfī, with whose wide learning al-Mīrghanī was impressed; ᶜAlī al-Ṭirayfī, an *ᶜālim* who was said to be famous for his nearly continuous recitation of the Quran, and Muḥammad al-Majdhūb al-Ṣaghīr.[75]

Muḥammad ᶜUthmān next crossed the river to Shendi, where he stayed for a year and some months. His daughter Umm Kulthūm died and was buried there. He also initiated many followers, including ᶜAlī al-Juzūlī and Muḥammad w. Sāttī ᶜAlī, who was said to have been initiated by Muḥammad ᶜUthmān following a command of the Prophet. Although Muḥammad w. Sāttī was recruited in Shendi, he was appointed *khalīfat al-khulafāʾ* for his home area, al-Khandaq in Dongola. Another adherent was al-Mubashshar,[76] who was appointed *imām* of Muḥammad ᶜUthmān's mosque in Shendi. Among al-Mīrghanī's followers in Shendi was also Muḥammad ᶜUthmān b. Mubashshar, who accompanied him to al-Tāka, Muṣṣawaᶜ and thence to Mecca and the Yemen where he joined his master's teacher, Ibn Idrīs.[77]

Muḥammad ᶜUthmān then moved to al-Dāmar, where he stayed for some time. In al-Dāmar a number of persons were recruited, for instance Muḥammad al-Naṣayḥ, who accompanied his master to al-Jinaydī village, east of the Atbara River, where he was ordered to return to his home village.[78] Al-Mīrghanī had intended to visit Berber and the north,

74 *Makhṭūṭa*, 75-6, and *Kitāb al-ibāna*, ms., f. 12 and 33.

75 On al-Majdhūb, see Appendix A.

76 Whose full name is not known, but who is to be distinguished from Muḥammad ᶜUthmān b. Mubashshar.

77 *Kitāb al-ibāna*, ms., ff. 15-16. See also Nūr al-Dāʾim (1954), 329, and Maḥmūd (1971), 131. Wad Sāttī (not Wad Sātt as appears in the *Kitāb al-ibāna*) is another example of changing *ṭarīqas* on account of a Prophetic command; he had earlier been a Sammānī.

78 Father of the author of the *Kitāb al-ibāna*; he stayed frequently at al-Saniyya with his master, who on one occasion sent him on a mission to Berber;

but hearing that the Turco-Egyptian expedition had reached Abū Ḥamad in 1821, he changed his mind and went east to al-Tāka. He travelled via Qōz Rajab where he spent some time recruiting followers. He then continued to al-Tāka and was received by its leading *ᶜālim*, al-Ḥabīb Yaᶜqūb, who ordered all his pupils to be initiated. It was in al-Tāka in eastern Sudan that Muḥammad ᶜUthmān established his own village, al-Saniyya, "the Sublime", which attracted great numbers of followers from various parts of the Sudan. He told his followers not to be anxious at the coming of the Turco-Egyptian expedition and later gave them a letter of recommendation to Khūrshīd Pasha, the Turkish Governor (1826-38). When Khūrshīd arrived in al-Tāka, al-Mīrghanī's followers showed him their master's letter. Khūrshīd treated them kindly and granted them privileged status (*jāh*) which continued until the end of the Turco-Egyptian regime in 1885. Muḥammad ᶜUthmān stayed for a long time at al-Saniyya which, according to Ibn al-Naṣayḥ, became "as if it was his home area".[79]

Muḥammad ᶜUthmān returned to Mecca via Muṣṣawaᶜ where he re-joined Aḥmad b. Idrīs. There is evidence to suggest that the opinion that Muḥammad ᶜUthmān visited the Sudan only once is incorrect.[80] Muḥammad ᶜUthmān was to return to the Sudan three times. The next visit was, together with his wife Ruqayya and their son Muḥammad al-Ḥasan, via Muṣṣawaᶜ to al-Tāka. The second was to Sawākin, shortly after the death of Muḥammad al-Majdhūb al-Ṣaghīr in 1832, where, despite the hostility of al-Majdhūb's followers, he succeeded in winning a considerable number of followers and establishing several *zāwiyas*.[81] Muḥammad al-Ṣāfī, the eldest and most learned of Muḥammad ᶜUthmān's followers in Sawākin, was invested as *khalīfat al-khulafāʾ* and entrusted with running his master's *zāwiya*. Muḥammad ᶜUthmān left Sawākin for Mecca shortly before a fracas broke out between his follow-

---

the latter once addressed him, "the *khalīfa* of my *khalīfas* from Fazūghlī to Alexandria", *Kitāb al-ibāna*, ms., ff. 25-6.

79 *Ibid.*, f. 19. Khūrshīd campaigned in al-Tāka region in both 1832 and 1834; see Hill (1967), 48-9. Three of al-Mīrghanī's sons, al-Ḥasan, al-Ḥusayn and Muḥammad Ṣāliḥ died and were buried at al-Saniyya.

80 See, for example, Trimingham (1949), 232-3; Voll, thesis (1969), 112-3, and Holt and Daly (1979), 42-3. None of these authors had access to the *Kitāb al-ibāna*.

81 *Kitāb al-ibāna*, ms., ff. 32-4.

ers and the Majdhūbiyya adherents.[82] Al-Mīrghanī's last visit to the Sudan was again from Mecca, travelling together with his son, Muḥammad al-Ḥasan, via Sawākin. It was during this visit that Muḥammad ᶜUthmān formally appointed his son as his representative in the Sudan (see p. 74).

The Establishment of the Khatmiyya

When was the Khatmiyya established as an independent *ṭarīqa*, as the *khātim al-ṭuruq* ("the seal of the orders")? And what was the nature of the spiritual relationship between Ibn Idrīs and al-Mīrghanī? Neither of these questions can be satisfactorily resolved on the evidence presently available. The letters exchanged between master and pupil suggest a difficult relationship, but since virtually none are dated, their language is frequently obscure and because, as we noted earlier, they have yet to be edited or translated, they are difficult to interpret.

Ibn Idrīs had consented to al-Mīrghanī's first journey as the result of a Prophetic order. The Funj Chronicle says that al-Mīrghanī, aged only twenty-six, initiated followers into his "way" (*ṭarīquhu* or *ṭarīqatuhu*), but gives it no name, while making it clear that he was a pupil (*tilmīdh*) of Ibn Idrīs.[83] The first specific reference to the Khatmiyya *ṭarīqa* appears in Ismāᶜīl al-Walī's *Kitāb al-ᶜuhūd al-wāfiya*, written in Ramaḍān 1239/May 1824: "I took the *ṭarīqa* from him, that is his *ṭarīqa* known as the Khatmiyya."[84] There is no reference to the Khatmiyya in the letters and the matter remains obscure.

The letters portray a concerned and loving master and a pupil seeking advice on both personal and spiritual matters. The titles they use to address each other are indicative of both affection and enormous Sufi status; thus Muḥammad ᶜUthmān to his master:

khalifāt al-Raḥmān	"*khalīfa* of the Compassionate"
markaz dāʾirat ahl al-ᶜirfān	"Centre of the circle of the People of knowledge"
sulṭān ḥadrat al-awliyāʾ	"Sultan of the assembly of saints"

82 *Ibid.*, ff. 33 and 36.
83 *Makhṭūṭa*, 75-6.
84 Al-Walī, *K. al-ᶜuhūd*, ms., f. 5.

āyyat Allāh al-kubrā	"The greatest proof of God"
wazīr nuqṭat al-kamāliyyāt al-Muḥammadiyya	"wazīr of the summit of Muḥammadan perfections"
From Ibn Idrīs:	
min al-wālid lī waladihi	"from the father to his son"
qurrat ᶜaynī	"the delight of my eye"
ghāyat al-wilāya al-Muḥammadiyya	"summit of Muḥammadan sanctity"

Ibn Idrīs was always ready to place his knowledge and counsel at his student's disposal. He regularly provided al-Mīrghanī, and others, with collections of prayers, litanies (*ḥizbs* and *wirds*) and formulae for entering retreat:

We have ordered our brother Ibn Mālik to write the formula of retreat [Ar. *khalwa*] for you. But when he wrote he made many mistakes of language in it, may God guide you to unravel them.[85]

Instruct the brothers in this *dhikr* since its consequences are great.[86]

Aḥmad seems not to have expected al-Mīrghanī to remain in the Sudan for so long. In his letters, he repeatedly asks him to join him in the Ḥijāz. Muḥammad ᶜUthmān, in a letter of 1234/1818-9, apologizes for not joining him, justifying his delay by the increase in both his followers and his family. He adds that for financial reasons he would not be able to provide for all of them in the Ḥijāz and concludes by asking his master whether he should bring them or leave them behind. Muḥammad ᶜUthmān seems to have been unwilling to leave the Sudan. Thus Aḥmad in Mecca, acknowledging a letter from Muḥammad ᶜUthmān dated 26 Muḥarram 1235/14 November 1819, replies that they are expecting his arrival in that year (1819) and adds,

Make haste to come to us however you can. It is now time for you to come. You have the good news of fulfilling your intention. Hasten to the holy and sacred precinct ...[87]

85 *Majmūᶜ jawābāt al-sāda al-ᶜiẓām*, in *Tarjamat al-ustādh Aḥmad b. Idrīs*, ms., f. 109. This is probably a reference to a short treatise by Ibn Idrīs, *Ṣīfat dukhūl al-khalwa.*

86 *Ibid.*, f. 116.

87 *Ibid.*, f. 98.

Aḥmad seems to have begun to lose hope of his student's return from the Sudan. Thus he writes,

> Then know, May God make it known to you with every goodness, that we have sent you [a letter] this year urging you to come to us. Thus far the occasion for your journey has not arisen because of your pre-occupation with your [affairs] there. And so we have entrusted you to God, May He be Praised and Exalted, that He may compel you to come by an irresistible divine intervention, which can neither be gainsaid, excused nor escaped.[88]

In the same letter, Aḥmad appears to remind his student of his still-subordinate spiritual relationship:

> But as for your revelation [*fatḥukum*]) in which you will experience the total revealing [by God of Himself, *al-tajallī al-kullī*] and the lifting of the veil from the kingdom of the heavens and the earth, this will only come about after you have come to us.[89]

Muḥammad ᶜUthmān finally rejoined his master in Mecca and moved with him to Ṣabyā in 1243/1827-8. He remained there with his teacher until the latter's death in 1837. After Aḥmad's death, the succession dispute became especially acute between al-Mīrghanī and al-Sanūsī, who both moved, after their teacher's death, to Mecca. There al-Mīrghanī devoted most of his time to establishing his own *ṭarīqa*, the Khatmiyya, as a fully-fledged order with its own doctrine and rules (see Chapters Six and Seven). He also established a number of *zāwiyas* in Mecca, Medina, Jidda and al-Ṭāʾif. Inspired by his master's missionary spirit, Muḥammad ᶜUthmān sent out his sons to preach in different regions. The eldest, Muḥammad Sirr al-Khatim (1230/1814-5 to 1280/1863-4) was sent to the Yemen and Ḥaḍramawt. The second son, Muḥammad al-Ḥasan, was appointed as his father's representative in the Sudan.

Like his master, Muḥammad ᶜUthmān's success drew down upon him the hostility of the Meccan *ᶜulamāʾ*, who forced him to move to his home area in al-Ṭāʾif, where he died on 22 Shawwāl 1268/2 May 1852.[90]

88 *Ibid.*, f. 108.

89 *Ibid.*, ff. 109-10.

90 Trimingham (1949), 233.

Al-Mīrghanī and the Shāyqiyya Region

Muḥammad ᶜUthmān did not personally visit the Shāyqiyya region. His order was propagated there through a network of local representatives who were recruited mainly from established holy clans and religious teachers. The centres of learning of these families and individuals thus became integrated into the order and provided the basis for its propagation in the region.

Al-Mīrghanī's representatives in the Shāyqiyya region may be divided into four groups. First was those who travelled from their home in the Shāyqiyya region to al-Dabba, where they were recruited and appointed as local representatives, *khalīfas*, in their home areas. One example is Ṣāliḥ b. ᶜAbd al-Raḥmān b. Muḥammad b. Ḥājj al-Duwayḥī, a member of the Duwayḥiyya clan. The second group comprises those who received their *ijāzas* without even meeting al-Mīrghanī; an example is Muḥammad Khayr b. Muḥammad Ṣāliḥ al-ᶜIrāqī, of the ᶜIrāqāb of Nūrī. Muḥammad ᶜUthmān appointed him *khalīfat al-khulafāᶜ*, that is a senior representative, on the basis of his learning, righteousness and piety. He is said to have travelled, at a later stage, to Muṣṣawaᶜ in order to ask his master's permission to perform the Pilgrimage. Being so permitted, Muḥammad Khayr pursued his journey to the Ḥijāz, where he died and was buried. Other examples are Muḥammad Khayr al-Naḍīf and Muḥammad Ḥammād, known as al-Shaykh Jiqaydī, two prominent religious teachers of the Naḍifāb clan of Abū Rannāt Island (see pp. 144-50). Finally, mention should be made of Muḥammad w. Ibrāhīm Khuḍr Mattī al-Bidayrī al-Dahmashī, who propagated the Khatmiyya in his home area of al-Arāk, just north of Karīma.[91]

The third group of al-Mīrghanī's local representatives include those who met him in Kordofan, accompanied him on his journeys and stayed with him at his centre, al-Saniyya, before returning home. Among these were Muḥammad b. Mālik, commonly known as Wad Mālik, and Muḥammad b. ᶜAbd al-Ḥalīm, known as *al-naqīb*, a nickname given him by his teacher. Al-Naqīb and Wad Mālik were both ordered by their master to return to their home areas, Kūrtī and Qanatī respectively, to spread the *ṭarīqa*. Al-Naqīb's death is regarded as a

91 *Kitāb al-ibāna*, ms., f. 28; interviews 9, 12 and 19.

karāma in that he is alleged to have gone to Egypt with the intention of preaching the order there, but did not obtain his master's permission; so he died upon his arrival in Egypt.[92] After al-Naqīb's death, another holy man from the Shāyqiyya region was appointed as *khalīfat al-khulafā'*, namely Mālik w. Jinayd who was directed by al-Mīrghanī to take over. Mālik remained in the office until his death in 1307/1889-90.[93]

The final group comprises those who travelled from the Shāyqiyya region as far as al-Saniyya and Muṣṣawaᶜ to meet al-Mīrghanī and to be initiated by him. One of these was Muḥammad ᶜAlī, known as al-Darwīsh, who travelled from his village, al-Zūma, north of Karīma, to Muṣṣawaᶜ where he was initiated, appointed *khalīfa* and then ordered to return to his village.[94]

The Causes of al-Mīrghanī's Success

In his travels, Muḥammad ᶜUthmān came into contact with people from many different groups and social classes. He was opposed by some and supported by others. Our concern here is to establish who supported and who opposed him and to attempt to investigate the motives determining their attitudes.

Which groups were attracted to al-Mīrghanī? His missionary activities were especially successful in the northern and eastern Sudan. These two regions were at that time under only the nominal control of the Funj Government. This was probably why the "ancient" orders, which were closely associated with the ruling class, had failed to gain ground there. Most importantly he won the support of the merchant class, figures such as Muḥammad Ṣāliḥ Shādūl of the Khandaq area and members of the Bidayriyya, Hawwāra and Ṭirayfiyya *jallāba* of Kūrtī and Kordofan. The support of this class for the Khatmiyya in the Shāyqiyya region reached its climax in the time of Muḥammad al-Ḥasan al-Mīrghanī. Muḥammad ᶜUthmān was also supported by a number of local *khalwa* teachers, some of the major holy families and some tribal leaders. Thus, al-Mīrghanī was backed by the family of Suwār al-Dhahab, who transferred its spiritual loyalty from the Qādiriyya to the

92 *Kitāb al-ibāna*, ms., ff. 27-8.
93 *Ibid.*, f. 28.
94 *Ibid.*, ff. 27-8; *Makhṭūṭa*, and interview 11.

Khatmiyya. The changing of allegiance from one order to the other was common, not only in the Sudan but throughout the Muslim world.[95] Another example is Aḥmad w. ᶜĪsā, who was originally a Sammānī but abandoned the order for the Khatmiyya.

Al-Mīrghanī's appeal to these scholars and religious families lay perhaps in his personality, abilities as a Sufi and scholar and the doctrine which he propagated. Al-Mīrghanī's background also contributed to his success. He was a member of a family of scholars; his appeal to Aḥmad w. ᶜĪsā, for instance, may have been because al-Mīrghanī's grandfather, ᶜAbd Allāh al-Maḥjūb al-Mīrghanī, was a teacher of Wad ᶜĪsā's master, Aḥmad al-Ṭayyib w. al-Bashīr. Furthermore, al-Mīrghanī was a leading student of the renowned scholar Ibn Idrīs, who was said, together with his student al-Mīrghanī, to have spoken of Aḥmad al-Ṭayyib with great respect.[96] Because al-Mīrghanī and Aḥmad al-Ṭayyib had developed very intimate relations, the latter did not oppose the former when he initiated some Sammāniyya into his own order. The relationship between the two orders grew very close in the time of Muḥammad al-Ḥasan al-Mīrghanī, who became a Sammānī himself.

Another factor which contributed to al-Mīrghanī's success was the belief that he had strong blood ties with the Prophet; hence the common phrase, *al-Sayyid* Muḥammad ᶜUthmān, *al* [= *alladhī*] *jadduhu al-nabī*, "his ancestor was the Prophet". The claim to Sharifian descent was, of course, common throughout the Islamic world, but al-Mīrghanī's claim seems to have been widely acknowledged as being more elevated than the general pretension to such descent.

Muḥammad ᶜUthmān's success may also be attributed to the way he treated his own followers and other holy men. His *ṭarīqa*'s discipline and the rules which he set for its members also attracted followers. Al-Mīrghanī disliked the exaggerated dress and asceticism (*taqashshuf*) of the dervishes. He exhorted his followers always to maintain a decent appearance. According to the *Kitāb al-ibāna* he established the tradition of granting each of his senior representatives a long robe with long sleeves, usually made of silk or cotton, called *quftān*, and an ordinary outer robe called *jibba*. He used also to give each of them a woollen cloak called *ᶜibāya* and a robe called *farajiyya* to be worn in winter time.[97]

95 For West Africa, see Jenkins in Willis, ed. (1979), 51.
96 Nūr al-Dāʾim (1954), 71-2.
97 *Kitab al-ibāna*, ms., f. 106.

Affiliation with al-Mīrghanī was undoubtedly considered by some of the more ambitious as a step towards advanced education in the school of Ibn Idrīs in the Ḥijāz. Two of Muḥammad ᶜUthmān's representatives in the Shendi area went with him to Arabia and joined his master's school in the Yemen.

Al-Mīrghanī attracted a number of holy families in the Shāyqiyya region. According to one informant, most of these families were not affiliated with specific Sufi orders before al-Mīrghanī came to al-Dabba. Most of these holy families were not themselves Shāyqiyya, but mainly Duwayḥiyya, ᶜIrāqāb, Bidayriyya and Ṣawārda. The appeal of al-Mīrghanī to these families and, at a later stage, to a number of other families and persons, of both Shāyqī and non-Shāyqī origin, should be seen within the context of the political instability and the continuous wars between the Shāyqiyya and their neighbours, and between the various Shāyqiyya clans themselves. More important was the external threat which was represented by the Mamlūk attacks against the Shāyqiyya in 1813, shortly before the coming of al-Mīrghanī, and the Turco-Egyptian invasion in 1820, shortly after his arrival. Al-Mīrghanī, who was a stranger to the Sudan, was politically neutral and was not involved in its society, may have been seen as a "Wise Stranger" who could bring stability to a social order in upheaval and give its ethnic minorities a sense of identity.[98]

Ibn al-Naṣayḥ gives the impression that the time was ripe for al-Mīrghanī's success. A number of prominent Sudanese holy men had allegedly prophesied the coming of Muḥammad ᶜUthmān. Among these was a famous holy man of the Shāyqiyya region, Wad al-Karsanī; he is reported to have said,

> There will come to this land a new order in accordance with the Book and the Sunna. Whoever accepts it shall be victorious and triumphant. Whoever holds back from it and does not accept it; who greets its followers, but neither joins them nor leaves them shall be saved but excluded [*maḥrūm*, *sc.* from the elect]. And whosoever joins and then leaves, shall perish. Our refuge is in God.[99]

Al-Mīrghanī's appeal seems to have been greater to what may be considered, in Sudanese terms, a middle class (traders and urban holy

98 On the concept of "Wise Stranger", see Holt (1973b), 76-8.

99 *Kitāb al-ibāna*, ms., ff.71-2. There is a tradition among the descendants of Wad al-Karsanī that it was Shaykh Aḥmad al-Karsanī of al-Barkal in the Shāyqiyya region who prophesied the coming of al-Mīrghanī. Interview 14.

men), hence his success in trading towns such as al-Matamma, Shendi, al-Dabba and al-Ubayyiḍ. This middle class, seeking for greater Islamic orthodoxy to buttress their position *vis-à-vis* the political elite, would have found al-Mīrghanī's teachings attractive.[100] This suggestion gains support from looking at those who were hostile to him: the *wazīr* al-Arbāb Dafᶜ Allāh in Sinnār, Musallam in Kordofan and *makk* Nimr in Shendi - in other words the political establishment.[101]

Muḥammad ᶜUthmān's willingness to co-operate with the Turco-Egyptians may have been the reason for the defection of two of his principal adherents in the Sudan, Ismāᶜīl al-Walī and Muḥammad al-Majdhūb al-Ṣaghīr. The former had been initiated by al-Mīrghanī in Kordofan but in 1241/1825-6 broke away from his teacher and established his own order, the Ismāᶜīliyya. Ismāᶜīl justified his defection by a divine order (*al-amr al-ilāhī*) and permission from the Prophet (*al-idhn al-nabawī*).[102] Al-Majdhūb's defection was also based on a Prophetic order; while in Medina, the Prophet appeared to him, ordering him to abandon the Khatmiyya and return to the order of his grandfathers, that is the Shādhiliyya.[103] There may well have been political motives in both cases. Both may have disliked their master's willingness to deal with the Turco-Egyptian regime, which may have been viewed by them, as by most of the Sudanese, as alien and oppressive. Al-Walī was imprisoned for three days by the Turco-Egyptian Government; the reasons for this are not given in Ismāᶜīliyya's sources, but according to the *Kitāb al-ibāna* al-Walī entered into a series of spiritual states (*aḥwāl*) to the point where he claimed the sun would not rise or set without his command and it was because of these ideas that he was imprisoned.[104] Mahmoud Abdalla Ibrahim notes that by 1239/1823-4, the writings of al-Walī:

100 On socio-economic developments in this period, see J. L. Spaulding, "Slavery, land tenure and social class in the northern Turkish Sudan", *IJAHS*, xv/ 1, 1982, 1-20.

101 Whose downfall was attributed by Ibn Idrīs to their hostility to al-Mīrghanī; *Makhṭūṭa*, 74.

102 Al-Walī, *K. al-ᶜuhūd*, ms., ff.6-7.

103 *Makhṭūṭa*, 111.

104 *Kitāb al-ibāna*, ms., f. 10.

Betrayed a feeling of frustration and dissatisfaction with the religious and political situation around him. His *Intiẓhām al-ri'āsa* was an expression of his desire for change.[105]

Despite the hostility of the ruling class and political instability, especially at the time of his first visit, al-Mīrghanī had laid the foundations of the Khatmiyya. He had created a network of qualified and reliable local representatives; and he had founded the village of al-Saniyya (later renamed al-Khatmiyya) as a seat for the order. Al-Mīrghanī thus paved the way for his son and representative in the Sudan, Muḥammad al-Ḥasan, who was to consolidate the position of the Khatmiyya in the Sudan, especially in the Shāyqiyya region.

105 Ibrāhīm, thesis (1980), 58.

4

THE CONSOLIDATION OF THE KHATMIYYA

Muḥammad al-Ḥasan al-Mīrghanī

After Muḥammad ᶜUthmān al-Mīrghanī's death on 22 Shawwāl/2 May 1852, the headship of the Khatmiyya passed to his eldest son, Muḥammad, known as *Sirr al-khatim*.[1] Upon the latter's death, the *ṭarīqa* split into four regional branches each with its own shaykh. Despite this regionalization the Khatmiyya maintained a considerable degree of unity through shared doctrines and intermarriage within the Mīrghanī family.

The Sudan branch was established by Muḥammad al-Ḥasan b. Muḥammad ᶜUthmān al-Mīrghanī, commonly known in the Sudan as *al-sayyid* al-Ḥasan and sometimes as Abū Jallābiyya.[2] He was born at Bāra in Kordofan on 12 Jumādā II 1235/28 March 1819, shortly before the Turco-Egyptian invasion.[3] The news of al-Ḥasan's birth reached his father while the latter was in the Shendi area.[4]

1 *Kitāb al-ibāna*, ms., f. 44; see also NRO, Intel. 2/32/270, p. 27, and Trimingham (1949), 233. Hill (1967), 274, confuses Muḥammad Sirr al-Khatim with his son and namesake who died in 1917. The latter was generally known as Muḥammad al-Mīrghanī to distinguish him from his father.

2 *Kitāb al-ibāna*, ms., f. 53; Muṣṭafā Ibrāhīm Ṭāhā, "*al-Adab al-shaᶜbī ᶜinda'l-Shāyqiyya*", MA thesis, University of Khartoum 1967, 85, and Qurashī Muḥammad Ḥasan, *Maᶜa shuᶜarāʾ al-madāʾiḥ*, 2nd edn, Khartoum 1972, 241. The nickname Abū Jallābiyya alludes to the fact that he wore a *jallābiyya*, which was not common in the Sudan at that time; see H.B. Barclay, *Buuri al Lamaab*, Ithaca 1964, 8.

3 Aḥmad b. Idrīs b. al-Naṣayḥ, *Manāqib al-sayyid al-Ḥasan al-Mīrghanī*, ms., f. 4, and *idem*, *Kitāb al-ibāna*, ms., f. 49. Later sources give different dates; Zaghlūl Muḥammad al-Waṭanī, *Abṭāl al-Khatmiyya*, i, Cairo 1953, 15, gives *c.* 1235/1819-20, and Muḥammad ᶜUthmān al-Amawī, "Dhikrā

DIAGRAM 3. *The Mīrghanī Family: The Sudan Branch*

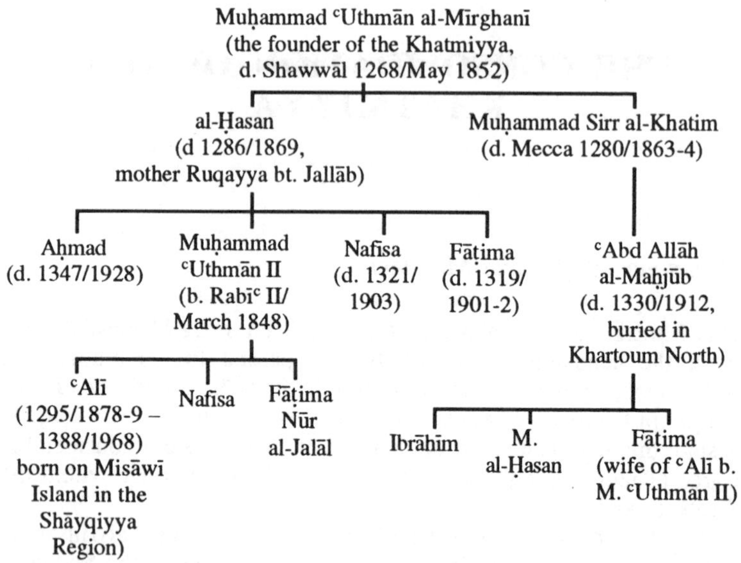

In about 1822-3, *al-ḥājj* Idrīs w. Jallāb, a maternal uncle of al-Ḥasan, took him and his mother to Dongola and thence to the Ḥijāz via Upper Egypt. Upon reaching Mecca they found that his father had left for Muṣṣawaᶜ. They stayed for some time with Aḥmad b. Idrīs; al-Ḥasan's mother asked Aḥmad to pray to God to bless her son. Aḥmad is reported to have replied,

---

al-Sayyid al-Ḥasan al-Mīrghanī", *Ṣawt al-Sūdān,* 8 February 1963, proposes 1234/1818-9.

4 There is a popular tradition that a holy man in Bāra, Shaykh Muṣṭafā, prophesied that Ruqayya would marry a Sharīf from Mecca and would be the mother of a saint. Another tradition has it that Usuman dan Fodio (1754-1817), having heard of the prophecy, went to Bāra to marry Ruqayya, but found her already married to al-Mīrghanī; interview 23.

Rejoice, for your son is the leader who holds the reins of the most holy caravan [*al-qāfila al-qudsiyya*].[5]

Al-ḥājj Idrīs then took al-Ḥasan and his mother to Muṣṣawaᶜ to join Muḥammad ᶜUthmān. After some time in Muṣṣawaᶜ, the latter travelled with them to al-Tāka, where he directed *al-ḥājj* Idrīs to escort al-Ḥasan and his mother back to Bāra. In about 1249/1833, when al-Ḥasan was fourteen years of age, he travelled, together with his mother and some of his maternal uncles, via Berber and Sawākin to join his father in Mecca.

In the Ḥijāz, al-Ḥasan memorized the Quran under a religious teacher from Medina, Muḥammad Shaykh al-Dalāᵓil. He was also thoroughly educated by his father in a wide range of Islamic subjects. He was taught by a woman, a former student of his great-grandfather ᶜAbd Allāh al-Maḥjūb al-Mīrghanī, a litany known as *wird al-basmala*. Al-Ḥasan recited the *wird* continuously for nineteen days before being ordered in a vision by al-Khaḍir to recite instead another *wird* called *Yā ḥayy, Yā qayyūm*.[6] Al-Ḥasan spent eight months wandering in the mountains between Mecca and al-Ṭāᵓif preoccupied with the recitation of his new litany. In a further vision of al-Khaḍir, he was ordered to enter into a spiritual retreat (*khalwa*) in Mecca. Al-Ḥasan then travelled to Medina, where he performed the visitation to the grave of the Prophet. Al-Ḥasan's long stay in Medina worried his father, who wrote to him several times asking him to return to Mecca. Al-Ḥasan finally did so and afterwards left with his father for Sawākin, where they stayed for two or three months. His father ordered him to travel throughout the Sudan to propagate the order and act as his representative there.

As has been noted by Voll, it was al-Ḥasan who successfully consolidated the Khatmiyya, especially in the northern and eastern Sudan.[7] The success of this consolidation can be seen in the ability of the Khatmiyya to face challenges to its influence, even in al-Ḥasan's lifetime. Other Sufi orders which, like the Khatmiyya, originated within the Idrīsī tradition, also found their way into the northern Sudan (see below, Chapter Five). None succeeded in attracting as large a number of followers as the Khatmiyya. The fact that the Khatmiyya came into the region before the others may have helped. Nevertheless, the reasons for

5 *Kitāb al-ibāna*, ms., ff. 50-1.
6 *Ibid*., ff. 51-2, and *Manāqib al-sayyid al-Ḥasan*, ms., ff. 4-5.
7 Voll, thesis (1969), 153.

its success need to be studied within the context of the conditions prevailing at the time of the Khatmiyya's advent. Muḥammad ᶜUthmān al-Mīrghanī had propagated his *ṭarīqa* during the last years of the Funj Sultanate, which were dominated by war and political disorder. Conditions had changed by the time al-Ḥasan arrived as his father's representative. The Turco-Egyptian invaders were in the process of destroying the traditional order in the Sudan, groups such as the Shāyqiyya being brought under the control of the central Government. To these Shāyqiyya, and indeed to most of the riverain communities which suffered from the invaders, al-Ḥasan al-Mīrghanī came as a holy man with charismatic appeal. They may have found in his *ṭarīqa* a substitute for their traditional institutions.

Muḥammad ᶜUthmān, who, like his master Ibn Idrīs, kept aloof from the rulers of the day, exhorted his son al-Ḥasan not to follow in his footsteps in this respect and urged him to associate with the Turco-Egyptian Government and to behave politely towards it.[8]

Following his father's orders, al-Ḥasan apparently moved to al-Saniyya, the order's headquarters, at the foot of Kasala Mountain, probably in 1840, the same year as a Turco-Egyptian expedition to the area. Although this campaign, which was led by Aḥmad Pasha Abū Widān, the then Governor-general, failed to achieve its main goal (the complete subjugation of the Hadanduwa) it succeeded in establishing the town of Kasala as the main administrative centre in the eastern Sudan.[9]

A contemporary European source records that during his war against the Hadanduwa, Abū Widān requested a holy man at Kasala to use his

8 *Kitāb al-ibāna*, ms., f. 52. Ibn al-Naṣayḥ's wording may have been influenced by the audience for whom the *K. al-Ibāna* was written (see p. 195). Muḥammad ᶜUthmān's attitude towards the Turks is alluded to in an undated letter (early nineteenth century) from a Khatmiyya *khalīfa*, *al-ḥajj* Muḥammad, to another Khatmiyya *khalīfa* in the Dongola region, Muḥammad b. al-Ṣādiq. The former reported that Muḥammad ᶜUthmān had told his son, "The Turks are coming here [i.e. Sawākin]. He [Muḥammad ᶜUthmān] said to us [al-Ḥasan], 'If they [the Turks] come here, I shall leave and travel to Muṣṣawaᶜ'". Al-Ḥasan continued that his father would move on to Sinkāt if the Turks reached Muṣṣawaᶜ; see NRO, Misc., 1/27/376, Letter from *al-ḥājj* Muḥammad ... to *al-khalīfa* Muḥammad b. al-Ṣādiq.

9 On Abū Widān's campaign, see Holt and Daly (1979), 64-8. Our primary sources, the *Kitāb al-ibāna* and *Manāqib al-sayyid al-Ḥasan al-Mīrghanī*, do not give a date for al-Ḥasan's arrival at al-Saniyya; later sources suggest 1840, see G.J. Fleming, "Kasala", *SNR*, v, 1922, 69.

influence to persuade their chief, Shaykh Muḥammad Dīn, to submit to the Government. According to Hill, the translator and editor of this source, this holy man may have been Muḥammad ᶜUthmān al-Mīrghanī.[10] However, Muḥammad ᶜUthmān was not in the Kasala area at the time, having returned from Sawākin to the Ḥijāz; the holy man was more probably al-Ḥasan al-Mīrghanī. Although Abū Widān had assured the holy man that no harm would befall Muḥammad Dīn, the latter was arrested, shackled and sent to Khartoum where he died of smallpox in the following year.[11] It was perhaps because of Abū Widān's deceitful behaviour that his relations with al-Ḥasan are said to have been hostile.

Al-Ḥasan then began an intensive missionary tour which covered all the regions where his father had followers. Al-Ḥasan's first visit was to Berber, where he was warmly welcomed by his father's followers and representatives. His reception was so enthusiastic that it aroused the suspicions of the Governor of Berber, who relayed them to Abū Widān. The latter, who was on tour in the Nuba mountains in Kordofan, promised the Governor that he would bring al-Ḥasan under control. Al-Ḥasan, who had arrived in Khartoum, was informed by some of his followers of Abū Widān's intention, but the latter died in Ramaḍān 1259/September/October 1843, immediately after his return from Kordofan.[12]

While in Berber district, al-Ḥasan appointed a number of local representatives. Among these was Aḥmad b. Muḥammad al-Naṣayḥ, known as Aḥmad b. Idrīs al-Rubāṭābī, who was appointed a *khalīfat al-khulafāʾ* like his father, who had been invested with the same office by Muḥammad ᶜUthmān. Aḥmad is said to have become a close confidant of his master. This association was cemented by al-Ḥasan's marriage into Aḥmad's family. It was by this Rubāṭābī wife, who moved to live with al-Ḥasan in Shendi and later al-Saniyya, that al-Ḥasan became the father of a son and three daughters.[13] Al-Naṣayḥ was a poet and the au-

10 Hill (1970), 94.

11 *Kitāb al-Ibāna*, ms., f. 52.

12 *Ibid.*, f. 53; see also *Taʾrīkh mulūk al-Sūdān* (1947), 33.

13 While in the village of al-Jiwayr in the Shendi area, al-Ḥasan married a second wife who was later to become the mother of his daughter Fāṭima (d. 1319/1901-2). Nafīsa and her sister Fāṭima were later to marry their cousins ᶜAbd Allāh al-Maḥjūb b. Muḥammad Sirr al-Khatim I and Bakrī b. Jaᶜfar b. Muḥammad ᶜUthmān al-Mīrghanī I, respectively. See interviews 17 and 23 and

thor of some devotional works. Specifically, he is known for his works the *Kitāb al-ibāna al-nūriyya fī shā'n ṣāḥib al-ṭarīqa al-Khatmiyya* and *Manāqib al-sayyid al-Ḥasan al-Mīrghanī.* Al-Naṣayḥ's loyalty to the Khatmiyya continued after his master's death on 18 Shaᶜbān 1286/23 November 1869, especially after the outbreak of the Mahdiyya.

Al-Ḥasan al-Mīrghanī maintained close relations with a number of contemporary holy men and families. He made a prolonged stay at Qubbat Khōjalī, in the present-day Khartoum North. While al-Ḥasan was at Qubbat Khōjalī, a number of Shaykh Khōjalī's descendants abandoned their original *ṭarīqa,* the Shādhiliyya, for the Khatmiyya. This Khōjalī branch of the Shādhiliyya had begun to lose momentum after Shaykh Khōjalī's death. After the defeat of the Shāyqiyya by the Turco-Egyptians, 400 Shāyqiyya had joined the invaders as irregular soldiers. After the punitive campaign of the *daftardār,* which ravaged most of the riverain communities, the ᶜAbdallāb lands at Qarrī and Ḥalfāyat al-Mulūk were granted to the Shāyqiyya in return for their support.[14] Undoubtedly, these losses had affected the Maḥas and their holy men, whose influence had been largely bound to the ᶜAbdallāb and Funj regimes. Furthermore, in 1240/1824-5 the *daftardār* had destroyed the mosque of a famous Maḥasī holy man, Shaykh Arbāb w. Kāmil w. *al-fakī* ᶜAlī, a great-grandson of Shaykh Arbāb al-ᶜAqā'id, and then brutally executed Arbāb himself with a cannon.[15]

Within the context of these grim events, the Khōjalāb, according to a descendant, changed their spiritual allegiance from the Shādhiliyya to the Khatmiyya because they had been impressed by al-Ḥasan al-Mīrghanī.[16] According to Voll, this change was motivated by the desire of Shaykh Khōjalī's descendants to benefit from al-Mīrghanī's association with the Turco-Egyptian Government, whose centre of administration was just across the river from their village.[17]

The ties of the Khōjalāb with the Khatmiyya were consolidated by al-Ḥasan's marriage to Fāṭima bt. Muḥammad al-Amīn (known as al-ᶜAjab) b. Ṭāhā, the future mother of al-Ḥasan's sons Aḥmad and Muḥammad ᶜUthmān II. Shaykh al-Amīn, a brother of Fāṭima, granted

---

letter, dated 20.7.1984, to the present writer from ᶜAlī al-Shaykh Jiqaydī. See also *Kitāb al-ibāna,* ms., ff. 55-6.

14 Interview 4; see also Lobban, thesis (1973), 48-9.

15 *Makhṭūṭa,* 97.

16 Interview 4.

17 Voll, thesis (1969), 230.

him an estate on which he built a *khalwa* and a grotto (*ghār*) for his private worship and other spiritual purposes.[18]

Al-Ḥasan also initiated a number of other Maḥas holy men living at the Khōjalāb village. Among these was Abū Bakr Muḥammad al-Mutᶜāriḍ b. Abī'l-Maᶜālī b. Ḥamad w. Umm Maryūm. Abū Bakr, commonly known as Wad al-Mutᶜāriḍ, was also related through his mother, Rābiᶜa bt. al-Badrī, to another famous holy man, Shaykh Khōjalī b. ᶜAbd al-Raḥmān. Abū Bakr, who was a Quranic teacher and was appointed a *khalīfa* by al-Ḥasan, accompanied his master on his journeys through the northern and eastern Sudan. He later settled on Misāwī Island in the Shāyqiyya region and married locally. He fathered several sons, including Muḥammad, ᶜUthmān, ᶜAbd Allāh and Muḥammad al-Ḥasan. Misāwī Island, which was (and still is) one of the main Khatmiyya centres in the Shāyqiyya area, was to be the birthplace of Sayyid ᶜAlī, a grandson of al-Ḥasan al-Mīrghanī, who became one of the principal Sudanese religious figures after the defeat of the Mahdist state in 1898 and until the time of his death in 1968.

Abū Bakr was a man of letters and a talented poet, composing a number of Sufi poems or songs (*qaṣāʾid*) and songs of praise (*madāʾiḥ*), which are still popular among the followers of the order. Learning of al-Ḥasan's death on 23 November 1869, Abū Bakr and several followers, travelled from the Shāyqiyya region to al-Saniyya to offer his condolences to the Mīrghanī family and the senior representatives of the order. He lamented his master's death in a number of elegies.[19]

Abū Bakr's allegiance to the Khatmiyya continued until his death in 1884. Like most of the Khatmiyya, he refused to support the Mahdist cause. According to oral sources, Aḥmad al-Ḥuday, a member of the Sawarāb branch of the Shāyqiyya and a Maḥdist *amīr*, forced Abū Bakr, together with a number of Khatmiyya local representatives, to join him in 1884 in an attack on Muṣṭafā Pasha Yāwar, the Governor of Dongola. The first battle took place at al-Karad, just north of al-Dabba; Abū Bakr, together with several Khatmiyya *khalīfas* and followers, were killed in the battle.[20]

18 Interview 4; see also al-Sarrāj (1374/1955), 49.

19 Interviews 10, 19 and 23. For examples of Abū Bakr's poetry, see *Kitāb al-ibāna*, ms., ff. 59-63, and *Majmūᶜat al-nafaḥāt al-rabbāniyya* (1370/1950), 245-6.

20 Interviews 6, 16 and 23; see also Hill (1967), 196.

Al-Ḥasan and his Contemporaries

According to *Inshiqāq al-qamar*, al-Ḥasan al-Mīrghanī frequently visited the village of al-Kabbāshī with a large group of his followers. Al-Ḥasan was respected by al-Kabbāshī and his adherents and they used to exchange correspondence on various religious matters. This relationship continued even after the death of both al-Ḥasan and al-Kabbāshī himself. Shaykh Ibrāhīm w. Aḥmad, commonly known as Abū Nafīsa (1871-1951), a Sufi poet and leading follower of the Kabbāshī branch of the Qādiriyya, composed a poem in praise of al-Ḥasan, referring to him as *al-wasīla*, the intermediary with God.[21]

Al-Ḥasan also had close ties with al-Shaykh al-ᶜUbayd w. Badr. Muḥammad ᶜUthmān al-Mīrghanī, who had met al-ᶜUbayd in Mecca, is said to have prophesied that upon the latter's return to the Sudan he should find a tree filled with flies where he would establish his religious centre. Thus, the establishment of al-ᶜUbayd's *khalwa* and Sufi centre at Umm Ḍubbān (lit. "the mother of flies"), near the present-day Khartoum North, was considered as one of al-Mīrghanī's numerous miracles.[22]

Al-Ḥasan's time also saw the abandonment of the Qādiriyya for the Khatmiyya by the successors of the famous Qādirī Shaykh, Idrīs w. al-Arbāb. This family, like the descendants of Shaykh Khōjalī, were at a low ebb during the first years of Turco-Egyptian rule. Their religious centre at al-ᶜAylafūn had been sacked during the *daftardār*'s reprisal campaign. They also faced the rivalry of al-Shaykh al-ᶜUbayd, whose centre at Umm Ḍubbān was very close to that of Shaykh Idrīs. As Voll has suggested, the descendants of Shaykh Idrīs might have felt the need for Khatmiyya support in their competition with Shaykh w. Badr.[23]

Relations between the Khatmiyya and the Sammāniyya were consolidated under al-Ḥasan. Al-Ḥasan was a frequent visitor to the Sammāniyya centre at Umm Marriḥ, north of Omdurmān, where he used to spend hours inside the tomb of Aḥmad al-Ṭayyib. According to

21 Al-Kabbāshī (1971), 16-9, and al-Bashīr (1976), 274.

22 J. Reid, *Tribes and Prominent Families in the Blue Nile Province*, Khartoum 1935, 70. This centre is now known as Umm Ḍawnbān.

23 Voll, thesis (1969), 230.

Azāhīr al-riyāḍ, al-Ḥasan was initiated into the Sammāniyya by Shaykh Ḥasīb b. Imām al-Maghribī, a student of Aḥmad al-Ṭayyib. Al-Ḥasan began to initiate people into the Sammāniyya as well as into his own *ṭarīqa*. Moreover, he ordered his own followers to copy the *Rātib al-saᶜāda*, which is a collection of prayers composed by Aḥmad al-Ṭayyib, to be used together with the Khatmiyya devotions.[24] Al-Mīrghanī was also friendly with the Sammāniyya branch of Shaykh al-Qurashī w. al-Zayn (d. 1878) of the Ḥalāwiyyīn in the Gezira. While in the Gezira, al-Ḥasan paid a visit to Shaykh al-Qurashī during which he copied more of the Sammāniyya teachings.[25]

Al-Ḥasan visited Bāra in Kordofan and met his maternal relatives and his father's local representatives and followers. He also visited al-Ubayyiḍ, where he faced a certain amount of hostility from his father's former student, Ismāᶜīl al-Walī. The *Kitāb al-ibāna* gives few details but claims that despite his attitude towards his master's son, al-Walī remained loyal to the Khatmiyya.[26] Even after he had broken away from the Khatmiyya and founded his own order, al-Walī continued to initiate followers into the two *ṭarīqas*. This practice is said to have been kept up by al-Walī's son and successor, Muḥammad al-Makkī (1237/1821-2 to 1324/1906).[27]

Al-Ḥasan al-Mīrghanī was on friendly terms with the followers of Aḥmad b. Idrīs, especially Ibrāhīm al-Rashīd. He also maintained close relations with his brothers and other members of the Mīrghanī family, who, because of the deeply-rooted belief in their hereditary *baraka*, enjoyed equal veneration in all areas where the order had followers. This relationship was cemented by marriage connections (see p. 77, n. 13). Al-Ḥasan exchanged letters with these relatives, discussing with them religious as well as personal matters.

Although al-Ḥasan al-Mīrghanī never left the Sudan after his appointment as his father's representative there, he was regularly visited by his brothers and relatives who lived outside the Sudan. His brother Jaᶜfar stayed with him from 1275/1858-9 to 1277/1860-1. Jaᶜfar was warmly welcomed and enjoyed the hospitality of the followers of the order; his letter to the followers of the Khatmiyya in the Abū Rannāt

24 Nūr al-Dā'im (1954), 73 and 285-6.
25 *Ibid.*, 286.
26 *Kitāb al-ibāna*, ms., f. 11.
27 Al-Sarrāj (1374/1955), 28-9.

area in the Shāyqiyya region confirms that he had received gifts from them.[28]

Al-Ḥasan enjoyed great social status and political influence. He was frequently asked by the Government to intervene to settle disputes. He played a significant role as an intermediary during the serious mutiny of the *jihādiyya* at Kasala in 1864-5.[29] In return for his support for the Government, al-Ḥasan was granted privileges and his centre of learning at al-Saniyya was subsidized. Al-Ḥasan al-Mīrghanī used to receive a monthly subsidy of 250 Egyptian piasters and four *ardabbs* (750 litres) of sorghum. Following al-Ḥasan's death, Jaᶜfar Pasha Maẓhar, the Governor-general, suggested to the Khedive that the Government should continue this subsidy to al-Ḥasan's two sons, Aḥmad and Muḥammad ᶜUthmān II, their two sisters and mothers.[30]

Although the Khatmiyya supported the Government and enjoyed the latter's patronage, the relationship between them was not always cordial. Al-Ḥasan did not involve himself directly in politics; he thus laid the foundation of the strategy of not openly involving themselves in politics that was to be maintained by his sons and their descendants to the present day.

Al-Ḥasan al-Mīrghanī and the Shāyqiyya Region

Al-Ḥasan's travels included the Shāyqiyya region, which had not been visited by his father. The Khatmiyya had been propagated there by local representatives, drawn from religious families in the region.

The Khatmiyya had not consolidated themselves among the Shāyqiyya before the arrival of al-Ḥasan. The destruction of the traditional system by the Turco-Egyptian invaders had indirectly contributed to the spread of the Khatmiyya. This may be illustrated by the case of the Ḥamadtūiyāb holy family of Nūrī. This family had enjoyed consid-

28 *Kitāb al-ibāna*, ms., ff. 46-7, the letter of Sayyid Jaᶜfar al-Mīrghanī is in the possession of *khalīfa* ᶜAlī Muḥammad al-Shaykh Jiqaydī, Kobar, Khartoum North.

29 G. Douin, *Histoire du Regne du khedive Ismail*, Cairo 1936, iii/1, 175-200; see also *Kitāb al-ibāna*, ms., f. 55.

30 A letter from Jaᶜfar Pasha Maẓhar to the Khedive Ismāᶜīl, ENA, Cairo, *maᶜiyya Turkī*, case *ḥāʾ*/2, 46, document no. 361. The letter is published in ᶜAbd al-Majīd (1949), iii, 178.

erable influence during the Funj period and had been granted estates and privileges by both the Funj sultans and the Shāyqiyya *māliks*. This is perhaps why this family was at the time of Muḥammad ᶜUthmān's visit reluctant to abandon the Qādiriyya. The Ḥamadtūiyāb may also have felt that affiliation to a *ṭarīqa* led by a Sufi and scholar such as Muḥammad ᶜUthmān would place them in a subordinate position.

By the time of al-Ḥasan's visit and prolonged stay in the Shāyqiyya region in the early 1840s, the Turco-Egyptian administration had already been established. It was evident that al-Ḥasan was a very influential holy man, who enjoyed political as well as religious prestige. The Ḥamadtūiyāb might have felt, as several other religious families did, that in the changed political circumstances it would be advantageous to join the Khatmiyya. This decision may have been prompted by the fact that the Ḥamadtūiyāb's neighbours, the ᶜIrāqāb of Nūrī, who had joined the Khatmiyya at the time of Muḥammad ᶜUthmān al-Mīrghanī's visit to al-Dabba in about 1815 and had been invested with the office of *khalīfat al-khulafā'*, began to enjoy great religious influence. This office gave the ᶜIrāqāb considerable religious authority over a number of holy families in the Shāyqiyya region.[31]

Thus, according to an oral tradition among the Ḥamadtūiyāb, their ancestors abandoned the Qādiriyya for the Khatmiyya as a result of a Prophetic order. Muḥammad Karrār b. ᶜAbd al-Raḥmān Muḥammad Madanī (known as al-Nāṭiq) saw a vision in which he was ordered by the Prophet to accept initiation into the Khatmiyya by al-Ḥasan al-Mīrghanī, a justification which was not, of course, unique to the Ḥamadtūiyāb.

Muḥammad Karrār, who was appointed a *khalīfa* by al-Ḥasan, had been educated in the family's centre at Nūrī. Upon his death he was succeeded as *khalīfa* by his son, ᶜAbd al-Raḥmān, whose period of office continued until his death in the last years of the nineteenth century.

While in Nūrī, al-Ḥasan also initiated other members of the Ḥamadtūiyāb, among whom were Shaykh w. Ibrāhīm, al-ᶜAbbās Madanī and ᶜAbd al-Raḥmān al-Nāṭiq. However, from al-Ḥasan's letter of 10 Rabīᶜ I 1283/23 July 1866 to the Ḥamadtūiyāb it would seem that the Khatmiyya order was not yet well established among them and its rituals not yet systematically practised. Al-Ḥasan thus also ap-

31 Interview 19.

pointed Ḥamadtū b. Muḥammad Madanī al-Nāṭiq as *khalīfa* and entrusted him with the duty of the proper establishment of the *ṭarīqa* among his family. In the same letter al-Ḥasan exhorted the rest of the Ḥamadtūiyāb to give their support to his new representative.[32]

Al-Ḥasan made a prolonged visit to al-Zūma, north of Karīma. He was welcomed by Muḥammad Aḥmad and Idrīs, sons and successors of Muḥammad ᶜAlī, known as al-Darwīsh, who had joined the Khatmiyya at the time of Muḥammad ᶜUthmān and who died while on the pilgrimage to Mecca. The family of these two *khalīfas*, commonly known as Awlād al-Darwīsh, played a significant role in consolidating the Khatmiyya in the Shāyqiyya region. Their efforts were enhanced by al-Ḥasan's prolonged stay and marriage into the influential family of Wad al-Zūma. A number of al-Zūma's other holy families and individuals joined the Khatmiyya. Among these was ᶜAlī Muḥammad w. al-Tīkal, who became one of the main Khatmiyya supporters in the Shāyqiyya area. His descendants are still today (1982) influential in the order.

During his stay in al-Zūma, al-Ḥasan was given plots of land and a number of palm trees by his followers. His stone house there, commonly known as *qalᶜat* al-Sayyid al-Ḥasan, and its open space where he used to lead the prayers, are still places of visitation (*ziyāra*) for the followers.[33]

Another Khatmiyya centre which was also visited by al-Ḥasan was that of the Naḍīfāb of Abū Rannāt Island. This community is discussed in greater detail below (pp. 144-50).

Al-Ḥasan also initiated members of the Rikābiyya holy clan who lived at al-Karāfāb near al-Qurayr. Their earlier association with the Khatmiyya received renewed impetus through al-Ḥasan's visit. Among those initiated was Shaykh Nāfiᶜ b. al-Amīn, a descendant of Ibrāhīm al-Būlād. While al-Ḥasan al-Mīrghanī was in the Shāyqiyya region, Ibrāhīm al-Rashīd arrived from the Ḥijāz to propagate the teachings of Ibn Idrīs on the grounds that he was the latter's legitimate successor. The followers of the Khatmiyya claimed throughout the region that he was a heretic. Al-Rashīd had in fact been accused in 1273/1856-7 of heresy by the board of *ᶜulamāʾ* in Mecca but had successfully rebutted the claim. Having heard of his followers' hostility to al-Rashīd, al-Ḥasan ordered Nāfiᶜ to visit al-Rashīd in his home village, al-Kurū,

32 Interviews 20 and 25; see also Bergen NO 163. 8/6, letter from Muḥammad al-Ḥasan al-Mīrghanī to the Ḥamadtūiyāb of Nūrī.

33 Interviews 11, 23 and personal observation (1982).

north of Karīma, and investigate the matter. Nāfiᶜ was cordially received by al-Rashīd and his followers, and eventually accepted instruction from him into the teachings of Ibn Idrīs. Upon his return to al-Karāfāb, Nāfiᶜ reported what had happened to al-Ḥasan. The latter expressed his admiration for al-Rashīd and ordered his followers not to insult him.[34]

Another Khatmiyya centre which was frequently visited by al-Ḥasan was al-Ghurayba, just south of Kūrtī. Al-Ghurayba's ties with the Khatmiyya had already been established when Muḥammad ᶜUthmān went there. At the time of al-Ḥasan's visit, the affairs of the Khatmiyya were administered by *khalīfat al-khulafā*ᵓ Mālik b. ᶜAbd al-Raḥmān b. Jinayd (d. 1307/1889-90), who had been invested with the office by the founder himself. Mālik was assisted by a number of *khalīfas*, who included were Muḥammad ᶜUthmān, Sīd Aḥmad al-Naqīb, Aḥmad and Muḥammad Maᶜrūf and the sons of Ḥāmid al-Muftī, Muḥammad, ᶜUmar and Maḥmūd. This latter son was also responsible for the teaching of the Quran and Quranic sciences in the *khalwa* of al-Ghurayba; he was moreover the *muftī* and the *maᵓdhūn* of the area.[35]

During his stay at al-Ghurayba, al-Ḥasan al-Mīrghanī appointed a number of new *khalīfas*; among them were the two brothers of Muḥammad ᶜUthmān and Muḥammad Sirr al-Khatim, who, having received their education in al-Ghurayba, established their own Quranic schools at Ḥuzayma in the Shāyqiyya region and Kasala, respectively. Muḥammad ᶜUthmān al-Ṣāfī was a frequent visitor to the headquarters of the order in the eastern Sudan, especially after his brother, Muḥammad Sirr al-Khatim, had established his religious school in Kasala.[36]

Al-Ḥasan also visited Kūrtī, which was at that time a substantial trading centre with about seventy-five large-scale merchants. There, he initiated members of the trading community of Bidayriyya and Ṭirayfiyya origin. One of these was Kanbāl Ḥamad, who was the head merchant of Kūrtī, trading in gum arabic and ostrich feathers. Kanbāl, like

34 NRO, Misc., 1/18/208, *K. fī dhikrat al-sayyid Ghulām Allāh*, ms., ff. 43-4.

35 Interview 6. See also Bergen NO 167. 9/1, letter, Dhū'l-ḥijja 1272/August-September 1856, from al-Ḥasan al-Mīrghanī to the people of al-Ghurayba.

36 Interview 6. See also *Taᵓrīkh al-khulafā*ᵓ (in the Ghurayba area), ms. Bergen NO 169.9/3. Presents from al-Ghurayba brought by Muḥammad ᶜUthmān al-Ṣāfī are acknowledged in a letter from al-Ḥasan; see n. 35 above.

several other local Khatmiyya representatives, was killed in the sack of Kūrtī by the forces of Muṣṭafā Yāwar in 1884.[37]

There is a popular tradition among the Khatmiyya concerning the relationship of the Kawārta with al-Ḥasan al-Mīrghanī; al-Ḥasan returned the hospitality of the Kawārta by praying to God to bless their trade. The subsequent flourishing of the Kawārta's commercial activities, especially in the time of Kanbāl's sons and successor, Ḥasan (*c.* 1845-1933), was attributed by many to al-Mīrghanī's supplications.

Eventually, al-Ḥasan al-Mīrghanī returned to the eastern Sudan where he continued his efforts to consolidate the Khatmiyya. While on a visit to Jabal Taqorba in the Banī ᶜĀmir area, he died of a fever on 18 Shaᶜbān 1286/23 November 1869. His body was carried by his followers to Kasala where it was buried at the village of al-Saniyya. He left two sons, Aḥmad and Muḥammad ᶜUthmān, and two daughters, Nafīsa and Fāṭima. A tomb was constructed over his grave and a large mosque was built in his memory by his son, Muḥammad ᶜUthmān.[38]

The Causes of al-Ḥasan's Success

Al-Ḥasan al-Mīrghanī consolidated the position of the Khatmiyya among the Shāyqiyya. Was his success primarily because he was seen as favoured by the authorities of the day? Or was it because he was a charismatic figure in the Sudanese holy man tradition (he was, of course, half-Sudanese) that he was able to reconcile Khatmiyya discipline to the needs of Sudanese spirituality?

Some scholars attribute the spread and consolidation of the Khatmiyya *ṭarīqa* in the Sudan to its association with the Shāyqiyya as well as to the favour that both of them enjoyed under the Turco-Egyptian rule.[39] This hypothesis, however, should not be accepted uncritically. In fact, most of the key followers of the Khatmiyya, inasmuch as they came from the old holy families in the Shāyqiyya region, were of non-Shāyqī origin. Nor was the favour of the Turco-

37 Interviews 1, 6, 17 and 23; on Kanbāl, see Hill (1967), 196.

38 *Kitāb al-ibāna*, ms., f. 56, and al-Sarrāj (1374/1955), 41.

39 For example, Shuqayr (1903), iii, 112; Voll, thesis (1969), 213 and 236; Ibrahim, thesis (1980), 83, and Ahmed al-Shahi, "A Noah's Ark: the Continuity of the Khatmiyya Order in Northern Sudan", *Bulletin, British Society for Middle Eastern Studies,* viii/1, 1981, 16.

Egyptian Government confined to the Khatmiyya; it also extended to other Sufi orders and to a number of *khalwa* teachers. The Government gave the family of Aḥmad al-Ṭayyib a monthly subvention of money and millet.[40] Ismāᶜīl al-Walī was hostile to the Turco-Egyptian rule in its opening years, especially after he had been imprisoned for three days. Al-Walī, however, changed his attitude towards the Government at the time of Muḥammad ᶜAlī Pasha's visit to the Sudan in 1838-9. During the visit, Muḥammad ᶜAlī received a letter from al-Walī expressing his gratitude for the privileges that he enjoyed as a religious leader under the regime. A document dated 13 Shawwāl 1273/8 June 1856 confirms that all the land and properties of Shaykh al-Walī, like those of several other holy men in the Sudan, were exempted from taxes.[41]

Nor were relations between the Khatmiyya and the Shāyqiyya on the one hand and the Turco-Egyptian regime on the other always cordial. The hostility of the Government attained serious proportions after al-Ḥasan al-Mīrghanī's death; a large number of the Khatmiyya local representatives were arrested and their privileges were abolished.

Muḥammad ᶜUthmān was a Meccan *ᶜālim*; his writings include works on *tafsīr*, *tawḥīd*, *ḥadīth* and treaties on Sufism.[42] By contrast, his son has left only short works of a devotional nature. This may be a clue as to how he was perceived by his contemporaries and later described in the *manāqib* literature written a generation after his death, as a miracle-working holy man whose life and works were a manifestation in themselves of this *baraka*. Here al-Ḥasan stands in contrast not only to his father, but also to his father's master, Ibn Idrīs; al-Ḥasan was assimilated into Sudanese Islam.

The *Kitāb al-ibāna* brings this out vividly:

40 ENA, Cairo: *daftar*, no. 1282 *ṣādir ᶜarḍuḥālat Turkī*, an Arabic translation of a Turkish document (no. 3, p. 20), dated 16 Rajab 1286/22 October 1869, and *sijill*, no. 583, p. 16, document no. 12, 21 Shaᶜbān 1286/26 November 1869. See also ᶜAbd al-Majīd (1949), iii, 172 and 176, and Antūnī Sūrīyāl ᶜAbd al-Sīd, "Juhūd Miṣr al-thaqāfiyya fī'l-Sūdān, 1820-1879", MA thesis, University of Cairo 1972, 62 and 105.

41 For al-Walī's letter, see ENA, Cairo, case no. 265, a copy of an Arabic dispatch, *ḥamrā*ᵓ, no. 154, 4 Dhū'l-ḥijja 1254/18 February 1838. See also ᶜAbd al-Majīd (1949), ii, 19.

42 GAL S II, 809-10.

In this respect he (al-Ḥasan) told us something very strange, may God help us to believe, namely that he was the saint of divine guidance and prosperity. He said to us time and time again in the presence of a group of his followers: "I remember the time of my birth. I even remember which women were present and I know what they were saying to each other". We were astonished at what he said, although we did not doubt its veracity for such things often happen to holy men and women [*ahl Allāh*] and are recorded in their writings and works about miracles. What has been said by our Lord Jesus son of Mary, peace upon him, should suffice as an example.[43]

Muḥammad ᶜUthmān II

According to Voll, after al-Ḥasan al-Mīrghanī's death several members of the family, living outside the Sudan, played an active part in the affairs of the Khatmiyya in the Sudan.[44] One was Muḥammad Sirr al-Khatim II (d. 1917), head of the Egyptian branch of the Khatmiyya and a son of Muḥammad Sirr al-Khatim b. Muḥammad ᶜUthmān al-Mīrghanī. Muḥammad Sirr al-Khatim II, who was commonly known as Muḥammad al-Mīrghanī to distinguish him from his father, appointed a number of *khalīfas* in the Sukkūt, Maḥas and the Shāyqiyya regions, especially after the death of Muḥammad ᶜUthmān II, in 1886.[45] Muḥammad Sirr al-Khatim II visited the Sudan at the end of 1883 in response to a Government request to use his religious influence to counter the Mahdist cause (see pp. 101-2).

Another who came was Bakrī b. Jaᶜfar b. Muḥammad ᶜUthmān al-Mīrghanī, who arrived after al-Ḥasan's death to assist his cousin, Muḥammad ᶜUthmān II, in the administration of the order. Bakrī, who was married to his cousin Fāṭima bt. al-Ḥasan al-Mīrghanī, was also active in the military and religious struggle against the Mahdist movement. Finally, ᶜAbd Allāh al-Maḥjūb, a brother of Muḥammad Sirr al-Khatim II and the husband of Nafīsa bt. al-Ḥasan al-Mīrghanī, also

43 *Kitāb al-ibāna*, ms., f. 50.

44 Voll, thesis (1969), 255-6.

45 *Sanad wa-ijāza kubrā al-ṭarīqa al-Khatmiyya*, ms., NRO, Misc. 1/22/248, and Voll, thesis (1969), 257.

moved from the Ḥijāz to the Sudan and remained there until he died and was buried in a large tomb in Khartoum North in 1912.[46]

The participation of these members of the family in the administration of the Khatmiyya does not mean that the order lacked central leadership. Upon al-Ḥasan's death, his son Muḥammad ᶜUthmān (born 1848) was recognized by the family and followers as his successor despite the presence of his elder brother, Aḥmad (born 1846).[47] However, Muḥammad ᶜUthmān II began, immediately after his father's death, to face a number of problems. This may explain why other members of the family came to help in preserving the influence of the order.

Muḥammad ᶜUthmān b. Muḥammad al-Ḥasan al-Mīrghanī was sometimes called *al-ṣughayr*, "the younger", and more commonly *al-aqrab*, "the second" (lit. "the nearer [in terms of time]") to distinguish him from his grandfather; for convenience, the present study refers to him as Muḥammad ᶜUthmān II. He was born at Qubbat Khōjalī on 10 Rabīᶜ II 1265/4 March 1848 amid much rejoicing.[48]

Muḥammad ᶜUthmān II memorized the Quran under his father. In 1860, when he was twelve years of age, he was, together with his brother Aḥmad, circumcised. In about 1863, when Muḥammad ᶜUthmān II was fifteen, he completed the memorization of the Quran and mastered the rules of its recitation. He was then encouraged by his father to combine that with the study of the other Islamic sciences. Muḥammad ᶜUthmān II pursued his studies on his own and taught himself a wide range of Islamic subjects, including *fiqh* and *tawḥīd*. He, and his brother Aḥmad, were taught the basis of Sufism by their father, who also allowed them to attend his meetings and lessons with the senior followers of the order. His father used to speak highly of his younger son and repeatedly asserted that he was following in the footsteps of the founder of the order. The father, shortly before he died, issued him an *ijāza*, nominating him as his successor.[49]

Muḥammad ᶜUthmān II's period of office saw a number of challenges to the Khatmiyya. The first came from the Government, which changed its policy towards the religious families and institutions and cancelled their privileges. The change in policy should be seen within

46 Al-Sarrāj (1374/1955), 47.

47 *Kitāb al-ibāna*, ms., f. 56; al-Sarrāj (1374/1955), 52, and Trimingham (1949), 233.

48 Al-Sarrāj (1374/1955), 49-50.

49 *Ibid.*, 51-2.

the context of a general economic decline in the Sudan at that time. The decline was particularly acute in Dongola and Berber provinces, strongholds of the Khatmiyya in the northern Sudan. At the time of al-Ḥasan al-Mīrghanī's death in November 1869 these provinces were already suffering from shortages of vegetables and cereals.[50]

The Government appointed Ḥusayn Bey Khalīfa, a Sudanese of ᶜAbbādī origin, governor of Berber province in 1869 in the hope that he would reverse the economic decay. In 1871 he became the governor of the amalgamated provinces of Dongola and Berber. He attempted to improve conditions by reducing Government expenditure and bringing more land under cultivation. These policies led to hostility between Ḥusayn Khalīfa and the Khatmiyya; consequently, a large number of them were arrested.[51]

Ḥusayn Khalīfa's attitude towards the Khatmiyya is evident in his letter of 19 Rajab 1289/23 September 1872 to the Khedive. He portrayed the Khatmiyya as propagators of false beliefs among the common people and especially women. He described their *khalīfas* as idlers who supported their activities by illegally going from door to door begging for contributions in cash or kind. Ḥusayn's letter, based on a survey of the province, continues that there were 141 Khatmiyya *khalīfas*, out of whom fifty-one were in the sub-district (*khuṭṭ*) of Marawī. The authorities in the different sections of the province were told to stop these *khalīfas* from begging and to oblige them to build new waterwheels (Ar. sing. *sāqiya*) on the estates that the Government had granted to them to earn their living. The letter adds that this policy would enable the Government to benefit from these *khalīfas*. It also mentions that each of the *khalīfas* who were living in the sub-district of Marawī was obliged to build a *sāqiya*, whereas every four or five *khalīfas* in the rest of the province were ordered to build one. Their tax-exempt status was abolished and an official was appointed to collect the taxes due from these *khalīfas*.[52]

Although Ḥusayn Khalīfa achieved some success, he was removed from office in 1873, accused of maladministration and nepotism; several of his relatives were charged with the illegal possession of a num-

50 See further Bjørkelo (1989), 75-6.

51 Voll, thesis (1969), 264. On Ḥusayn Khalīfa's policies, see further Bjørkelo (1989), 94-6.

52 ENA, Cairo, a Turkish document in *daftar*, no. 1864, *maᶜiyya*, p. 23; translated in ᶜAbd al-Majīd (1949), iii, 184.

ber of *sāqiyas*.[53] In a recent study Bjørkelo attributes Ḥusayn's removal to pressure on the Government by some Turks, notables and merchants who felt that Ḥusayn's reforms had endangered their interests.[54] It seems reasonable to assume, although we have no direct evidence, that the Khatmiyya, who managed through the efforts of Muḥammad ᶜUthmān II to resume their cordial relations with the Government, also played a role in the removal of Ḥusayn Khalīfa.

A further challenge to the Khatmiyya came from Ibrāhīm al-Rashīd, who already in al-Ḥasan Mīrghanī's lifetime began to propagate the teachings of Ibn Idrīs in the Shāyqiyya region. After al-Rashīd's death in 1874, his activities were carried on by his students, ᶜAbdullāhi al-Dufārī and Muḥammad al-Dandarāwī. The same teachings of Ibn Idrīs were also taught in the name of the Aḥmadiyya Idrīsiyya order by his son, ᶜAbd al-ᶜĀl, who arrived in Dongola from Upper Egypt in July 1878 (see pp. 118-19). Finally, the most serious threat to the Khatmiyya was the outbreak of the Sudanese Mahdiyya in 1881, which coincided with the infiltration of the Tijāniyya order into areas where the Khatmiyya had followers. However, Muḥammad ᶜUthmān II followed his father's example and preserved the missionary spirit of the order. He also kept up the tradition of visiting the followers in their home areas. Muḥammad ᶜUthmān's efforts to administer the Khatmiyya coincided with those of the Khedive Ismāᶜīl (1863-79) to establish the Turco-Egyptian administration in the Sudan on a sounder basis. Ismāᶜīl improved the routes and introduced telegraph communication and steamers into the Sudan. These innovations facilitated the administration of the Khatmiyya order, which had followers in various areas of the Sudan.

Muḥammad ᶜUthmān II married a woman of Ethiopian origin, who lived with him in the Mīrghanī house at Qubbat Khōjalī and became the mother of his eldest son Aḥmad (1293/1877-8 to 1347/1928) and his daughter Fāṭima Nūr al-Jalāl, who was commonly known as Sitt Nūr.[55]

Muḥammad ᶜUthmān II travelled extensively in the eastern and northern Sudan. He visited Shendi, where he maintained his father's house, which, later became a centre of opposition to the Mahdist

53 Bjørkelo (1989), 97.

54 *Ibid.*

55 NRO, Kassala, 2/124/523, *Religion-Tarikas*, and al-Sarrāj (1374/1955), 79.

movement in the region. While in Berber, he visited Artolī Island, the home of the Inqirriyāb, who were related to the ᶜAbdallāb. He enjoyed the people's hospitality and married Āmina, a daughter of a local holy man, Shaykh al-Nūr.[56] Muḥammad ᶜUthmān II, accompanied by his wife Āmina, a large group of followers and *khalīfas* (who included his father's senior representative and relative by marriage, Aḥmad b. Idrīs Muḥammad al-Naṣayḥ) continued to the Shāyqiyya region, where he made an extended stay. He visited many villages in the region, initiating followers and appointing *khalīfas*. He also established a number of mosques and *zāwiyas*.

Like other members of his family, Muḥammad ᶜUthmān II was credited with the power of performing *karāma*. While in the village of Juwārī, just north of Kūrtī, he is said to have restored the eyesight of a woman who was supporting a number of orphan children. Ibn Idrīs al-Naṣayḥ, who witnessed the incident, reported that his master's comment was that it was He, Almighty God, who had rescued the poor woman and to Him should be offered thanks.[57]

Muḥammad ᶜUthmān II eventually reached the village of Nūrī, where he remained for some years. At first he lived with the *khalīfat al-khulafāʾ* Muḥammad ᶜUthmān Muḥammad Khayr, a member of the ᶜIrāqāb holy family of Nūrī and the senior representative of the Khatmiyya in the Shāyqiyya region. Shortly afterwards Muḥammad ᶜUthmān II, who was given considerable land by his followers, built a splendid house whose remains can still be seen (in 1982).

Early in 1295/1878-9, Muḥammad ᶜUthmān II, together with his pregnant wife Āmina, left Nūrī for Misāwī Island, just opposite Kūrtī. On his way he made short stops at the religious centres of his local representatives. For instance, he visited the mosque of the sons of Ḥājj Nūr at the village of al-Jirayf, north of Nūrī. Muḥammad ᶜUthmān II and his suite were warmly received at Misāwī, which had established its ties with Khatmiyya during the life of al-Ḥasan al-Mīrghanī. There, Muḥammad ᶜUthmān II left his wife behind and travelled to Kasala, where he shortly afterwards received news of his son's birth. Muḥammad ᶜUthmān II sent a telegram to *khalīfat al-khulafāʾ* Muḥammad ᶜUthmān Muḥammad Khayr al-ᶜIrāqī, with instructions that his

56 Al-Sarrāj (1374/1955), 80, and *Manāqib al-sayyid ᶜAlī al-Mīrghanī*, Khartoum 1390/1970, 11.

57 Al-Sarrāj (1374/1955), 56-7.

newly born son was to be named ᶜAlī. It was this child who later became one of the key religious figures in the modern Sudan.[58]

The followers of the Khatmiyya, and those of other orders, were accustomed to show their loyalty to their spiritual masters by granting them shares (Ar. sing. *shaqīqa*) in their agricultural land or by offering them one or more of their palm trees. Some of the Khatmiyya, however, went much further in demonstrating their loyalty and gave away some of their sons and daughters to serve as attendants to members of the Mīrghanī family. These sons and daughters, who were known as *awlād al-bayt* or *banāt al-bayt*, that is attendants of the male and female members of the Mīrghanī household respectively, spent their lives in the service of their masters or mistresses. A number of female adherents in the Shāyqiyya region as well as in other areas voluntarily offered their service as *ḥuwārāt* (Ar. sing. *ḥuwāra*), namely acting as links between the female members of the Mīrghanī family, known collectively as *al-sharīfāt*, and the female followers of the *ṭarīqa*.[59]

The Khatmiyya and the Mahdiyya

The most serious challenge that the Khatmiyya faced was the Mahdist revolution. From the beginning the Khatmiyya, like the Turco-Egyptian administration, underestimated the Mahdist movement. It was only when the Mahdist cause began to gain momentum and attracted supporters in areas which were considered Khatmiyya strongholds that the members of the Mīrghanī family and their adherents began to take measures against it.

It was Kordofan that saw the early and decisive stages of the Mahdist movement, from where it gradually spread to the other parts of the Sudan. Members of the riverain groups, especially the Bidayriyya, who lived in the western Sudan in contrast to their kinsmen who remained on the Nile, supported the Mahdist cause from the outset.[60] Before his public manifestation as the Mahdi, Muḥammad Aḥmad vis-

58 The above is based on interviews 16, 19 and 20. Khalīfa Muḥammad ᶜAbd al-Ḥamīd al-ᶜIrāqī (interview 19) allowed the present author to read the telegram which is preserved among his private papers.

59 Interview 9, and al-Sarrāj (1374/1955), 54. These voluntary servants provided Muḥammad ᶜUthmān II with a large retinue.

60 Holt (1970), 109, and Ibrahim, thesis (1980), 73-80.

ited al-Ubayyiḍ twice and stayed with several holy families and individuals from the Bidayriyya, including Muḥammad al-Makkī b. Ismāᶜīl al-Walī, the head of the Ismāᶜīliyya, and the family of Ṣalīḥ Suwār al-Dhahab (d. 1875).[61] On his second visit Muḥammad Aḥmad secretly informed these families that the Mahdiship had been bestowed upon him by the Prophet.

The Mahdiyya was to divide these families deeply. Muḥammad al-Makkī and Ismāᶜīl b. ᶜAbd al-Qādir al-Kurdufānī (d. 1897), a grandson of Ismāᶜīl al-Walī, who was a poet, a *muftī* and later became the Mahdist chronicler, were among the earliest and most faithful supporters of the Mahdi. In contrast, Aḥmad al-Azharī, a brother of Muḥammad al-Makkī, supported the Turco-Egyptian Government against the Mahdi and wrote a pamphlet refuting his claims to the Mahdiship. He was killed in October 1882 in a battle fought near Bāra against the Mahdists.

Another example is Muḥammad b. Ṣāliḥ Suwār al-Dhahab who, again in contrast to his brother Ibrāhīm who became a Mahdist *amīr*, remained loyal to the Turco-Egyptian regime and died in al-Ubayyiḍ after its occupation by the Mahdist forces in January 1883.[62] A final example is the Bādī family of Bāra. This family was among the earliest supporters of Muḥammad ᶜUthmān al-Mīrghanī I, who cemented his ties with it by marrying a daughter, Ruqayya, the mother of al-Ḥasan al-Mīrghanī. After the outbreak of the Mahdiyya, however, several members of this family abandoned the Khatmiyya and joined the Mahdi. These included Fawzī Maḥmūd Bādī and his brothers, Aḥmadī and Mukhtār, who became close confidants of the Mahdi and were appointed as his secretaries. Fawzī was moreover invested with the office of the keeper of the Mahdi's seal, *amīn khatm al-Mahdī*, and after the fall of Khartoum in January 1885, he was appointed as one of the seven commissioners who constituted the Mahdi's administrative council, *majlis ᶜumanāʾ al-Mahdī*. Mukhtār was also appointed a director of the lithograph press, *amīr maṭbaᶜat al-ḥajar*, which was seized by the Mahdist forces.[63]

61 Holt (1970), 53.

62 Hill (1967), 62.

63 Shuqayr (1903), iii, 357; Muḥammad Ibrāhīm Abū Salīm, "Makhṭūṭ fī taʾrīkh muʾassis al-Khatmiyya", *MDS*,. 1968, 38, and *idem*, *al-Ḥaraka al-fikriyya fī'l-Mahdiyya*, Khartoum 1970, 86.

How are we to explain this phenomenon of the split of these important families over the question of the Mahdiyya? One may suggest that these divided loyalties were a kind of insurance policy, whether or not the people involved were doing this consciously, against the loss of their family's position. This can be illustrated by the family of Suwār al-Dhahab, which resumed its position as the Khatmiyya local representatives in al-Ubayyiḍ when the members of the Mīrghanī family managed to re-establish the Khatmiyya after the fall of the Mahdist state in 1898.[64]

The Mīrghanī family began to react to the new threat, especially when the Mahdist revolution spread to the eastern Sudan, led by ᶜUthmān Diqna (*c.* 1840-1926). ᶜUthmān, who was partly of Beja origin and a follower of a Sufi order, the Majdhūbiyya, rivals of the Khatmiyya since the time of Muḥammad ᶜUthmān al-Mīrghanī I, joined the Mahdi after the fall of al-Ubayyiḍ in 1883. He swore allegiance and the Mahdi subsequently appointed him *amīr* over the eastern Sudan. When Diqna returned to the Red Sea Hills, he began to distribute the Mahdi's proclamations and administer the oath of allegiance on his master's behalf. He eventually reached Qubāb, the centre of his Sufi teacher Shaykh al-Ṭāhir al-Majdhūb, the local head of the Majdhūbiyya. The swearing of allegiance to the Mahdi by Shaykh al-Ṭāhir al-Majdhūb and his followers greatly strengthened the Mahdist cause.[65]

Victory followed victory, and the Mahdist revolution spread rapidly into other Khatmiyya areas, the Berber and Dongola regions. The arrival of Gordon in February 1884 with orders to evacuate the Turco-Egyptian troops from the Sudan, encouraged all those who were halfhearted to give their support to the Mahdist cause. One example is Muḥammad al-Khayr ᶜAbd Allāh Khōjalī of Berber, a former teacher of Muḥammad Aḥmad, the Mahdi. Muḥammad al-Khayr, who was subsidized by the Government, received several letters from Muḥammad Aḥmad in which he informed him about his Mahdiship and urged him to join his movement. In a letter dated 1299/1881-2, the Mahdi reproved his former teacher for his delay in joining his cause and urged him to support it either by declaring a *jihād* in the Berber region or by emigrating

64 Ibrahim, thesis (1980), 38.

65 Abū Salīm, (1970), 27 and 55; *idem*, ed. *Mudhakkirāt ᶜUthmān Diqna*, Khartoum 1974, 40-1, and Holt (1970), 81-4.

(*yuhājir*) to join him.[66] It was not until Gordon's arrival that Muḥammad al-Khayr emigrated to the Mahdi in Kordofan and swore allegiance to him. On 3 Jumādā II 1301/31 March 1884, the Mahdi appointed him as *amīr* of Berber and instructed him to begin a *jihād* in the province, where he arrived on 27 April 1884.[67]

Ahmad al-Shahi argues that the Mahdist followers used only to make incursions into the Shāyqiyya homeland, and that they never settled there.[68] This statement, however, may be disputed since the Sawarāb sub-section of the Shāyqiyya supported the Mahdiyya; the Mahdi appointed some of its members *ᶜāmils* (commissioners) and *amīrs*. The earliest of these followers were Aḥmad al-Huday and Shaykh al-Ṭayyib al-Sawarābī, who propagated the teachings of the Mahdi, together with (despite the Mahdi's prohibition of the Sufi orders) those of the Tijāniyya order. Before Aḥmad al-Huday joined the Mahdist cause, Muṣṭafā Yāwar, the then Governor of Dongola, replied to a letter which he had received from the Mahdi expressing his desire to join the Mahdiyya. The Mahdi, who was delighted by Yāwar's positive response, appointed him *ᶜāmil* (administrative agent) for Dongola province. Some of the Mahdist supporters reported to the Mahdi that Yāwar's conversion was only a pretence.[69] This is presumably why the Mahdi conferred the same office of *ᶜāmil* of Dongola upon Aḥmad al-Huday after the latter had sworn allegiance to Muḥammad al-Khayr, the Mahdi's agent in Berber province.

Al-Huday and his agent in the Sāyqiyya region, *amīr* al-Ṭayyib al-Sawarābī, fought a number of unsuccessful battles against Muṣṭafā Yāwar, in which two local senior Khatmiyya representatives, Abū Bakr Wad al-Mutᶜāriḍ and Kanbāl Ḥamad al-Kawārtī, who had been forced to join in the fighting, were killed. Other Khatmiyya leaders who died in the fighting include Idrīs b. Muḥammad ᶜAlī al-Darwīsh, a member of the Awlād al-Darwīsh of al-Zūma; Shaykh Ḥamad, nicknamed *al-ḍibaylān*, "the feeble", of the Ḥawājnīr clan of al-Jirayf, north of Nūrī; and Muḥammad b. ᶜAbd al-Raḥman b. Madanī al-Nāṭiq, of the Ḥamadtūiyāb of Nūrī.[70]

66 Muḥammad Ibrāhīm Abū Salīm, "*al-Murshid ilā wathāʾiq al-Mahdī*", mimeograph, Khartoum 1969, 34-5, no. 64.

67 Shuqayr (1903), iii, 234, and Holt (1970), 98.

68 Al-Shahi, thesis (1971), 309.

69 Abū Salīm, mimeograph (1969), 318-9, no. 649.

70 Interviews 11, 16 and 20.

The loyalty of some Shāyqiyya to the Turco-Egyptian regime should not be interpreted to mean that the entire community was anti-Mahdist. Members of the Sawarāb, Ḥinikāb and ᶜAwniyya sub-sections of the Shāyqiyya, who lived in Berber province, were on good terms with the Mahdi; in a letter dated 7 Ṣafar 1302/26 November 1884 the latter ordered that no one should interfere with their property.[71] Furthermore, and in contrast to Wingate's claim that "even eight days after the fall of Khartoum, if a Shaigi [Shāyqī] was seen, he was instantly killed", the Mahdi appointed al-Shafīᶜ Raḥma al-Shāyqī as *amīn* (commissioner) in the administrative board, *majlis al-umanāʾ*, which he set up shortly after the fall of Khartoum.[72]

The Mahdist threat to the Khatmiyya became even more serious when Muḥammad al-Dandarāwī and ᶜAbdullāhi ᶜAbd al-Ḥafīẓ al-Dufārī, students of Ibrāhīm al-Rashīd and who had won some support in the Shāyqiyya region, swore allegiance to the Mahdi. Indeed, Muḥammad Aḥmad, before declaring himself the Mahdi, had been taught the doctrines of Ibn Idrīs and issued an *ijāza* by ᶜAbdullāhi al-Dufārī.

The Khatmiyya opposed the Sudanese Mahdiyya by both peaceful and military means. But did the Khatmiyya believe in the Mahdist idea as such? The answer is that they, like most Muslims, did. Muḥammad ᶜUthmān al-Mīrghanī I who called himself *al-khatim*, "the seal of [*sc.* all the saints]", believed that his rank in the divine hierarchy would be the sixth, immediately after that of the Mahdi. He noted that the first four places in the hierarchy would be occupied by the Prophet, his daughter Fāṭima and her two sons al-Ḥasan and al-Ḥusayn, respectively. Muḥammad ᶜUthmān affirmed the inferiority of his position to that of the Mahdi by stating that he would have a seat near to *al-ᶜarsh*, "the throne [*sc.* of God]", immediately behind that of the Mahdi.[73] Al-Mīrghanī also noted that he had composed a book of devotions called *al-Rātib*, and its contents were beyond the comprehension of all, save the Prophet and the expected Mahdi.[74] Muḥammad ᶜUthmān I, unlike

71 Abū Salīm, mimeograph (1969), 226, no. 446. A number of informants in both the Shāyqiyya region and Khartoum confirmed that many of the Shāyqiyya who had emigrated to the Shendi area during the nineteenth century voluntarily joined the Mahdist cause.

72 F.R. Wingate, *Mahdiism and the Egyptian Sudan*, 2nd edn, London 1968, 143, and Shuqayr (1903), iii, 557.

73 *Kitāb al-ibāna*, ms., f. 74.

74 *Ibid.*, ff. 74-5.

most of the Muslims, did not associate the Mahdi's manifestation with the end of time. He also considered that the expected Mahdi would manifest himself in the east.[75]

But the Mīrghaniyya did not recognize Muḥammad Aḥmad as the Mahdi. In the beginning, they underestimated the strength of the Mahdist movement, which they repeatedly referred to as "the sedition", *al-fitna*; they circulated Government anti-Mahdist proclamations and wrote to their own followers and other influential figures refuting the Mahdi's claims and exhorting them to remain loyal to the regime.

The Mahdi, who knew of the belief of the Mīrghanī family in the Mahdist idea, repeatedly reproached its members for their delay in supporting his movement. In his letter of 14 Ṣafar 1302/15 December 1883 to Muḥammad ᶜUthmān al-Mīrghanī II the Mahdi stated that he had sent him many messages and letters of warning (*indhārāt*) that had evoked no response. He concluded by urging al-Mīrghanī to support the Mahdist cause either by making the *hijra*, "emigration", and joining him or by waging the *jihād* under the command of Shaykh al-Ṭāhir al-Majdhūb and ᶜUthmān Diqna in the eastern Sudan.[76]

Soᶜād al-Fātiḥ argues that Muḥammad ᶜUthmān al-Mīrghanī II, and indeed all the members of the Mīrghanī family, would have been most unwilling to subordinate themselves to ᶜUthmān Diqna, and I would add his Sufi master Shaykh al-Ṭāhir, who belonged to their rivals, the Majādhīb.[77]

Some of the Mīrghaniyya may have wavered or prevaricated. On 13 Muḥarram 1301/14 November 1883, the Mahdi writes to Muḥammad Abū Bakr (commonly known as Bakrī) b. Jaᶜfar al-Mīrghanī I, acknowledging the receipt of Bakrī's letter in which he had declared his loyalty to the Mahdiyya but also expressing his unwillingness to obey Diqna. The Mahdi continues that he had already given Bakrī the chance of choosing between joining Diqna or making of the *hijra* to the Mahdi himself. The Mahdi concluded by saying that despite his awareness of Bakrī's anti-Mahdist feelings, revealed in some of his correspondence captured by the *Anṣār*, he would pardon the latter if he hastened to join him.

75 *Ibid*., f. 74, and NRO Majmūᶜat Abī Salīm, 7/1/10, ms., p. 9.

76 Abū Salīm, mimeograph (1969), 96, no. 189.

77 Soᶜād al-Fātiḥ, "The Teachings of Muḥammad Aḥmad, the Sudanese Mahdi", MA thesis, University of London 1961, 97.

The activities of Muḥammad ᶜUthmān al-Mīrghanī II against the Mahdiyya have been described by a number of scholars; he used his headquarters, al-Khatmiyya, in Kasala as a base to oppose Mahdism in the eastern Sudan. He travelled widely in the region preaching against the Mahdiyya and exhorting the people to remain loyal to the Government. He left his wife and his daughter in his father's house at Shendi to keep the Mahdists from encroaching upon his followers in the area. And when Khartoum was besieged by the Mahdist forces, Gordon instructed that his correspondence with Egypt should be sent through Muḥammad ᶜUthmān al-Mīrghanī II, whom he trusted.[78]

The people of Kasala appealed to the Government for reinforcements. Their request evoked no response and this is presumably why they wrote to the Mahdi expressing their readiness to surrender.[79] The Mahdi sent al-Ḥusayn w. al-Zahrā, an influential *ᶜālim*, as head of a delegation to supervise the evacuation of the Government troops from Kasala.[80] But Muḥammad ᶜUthmān II advised the forces not to surrender. Despite his knowledge of this, the Mahdi wrote to Muḥammad ᶜUthmān II on 11 Shaᶜbān 1302/27 May 1885, when Kasala was still under siege, stating that he greatly cared for al-Mīrghanī and adding that the latter's delay in supporting the Mahdiyya was not appropriate to his great status. The Mahdi also noted that he had sent him an *amān*, "pardon" or "safe-conduct", with Ḥasan Badawī Ḥāshī and had instructed al-Ḥusayn w. al-Zahrā to treat him with kindness.[81] Illness forced Muḥammad ᶜUthmān to withdraw from Kasala to Sawākin, where he stayed until the end of August 1886, when, leaving his family behind, he moved to Cairo, where he died and was buried. His son Aḥmad and daughter Fāṭima remained as prisoners until the fall of the Mahdist state in 1898.[82] His other son, ᶜAlī, stayed in Sawākin with Muḥammad Sirr al-Khatim II, and later travelled with him to Cairo, where he studied at al-Azhar. ᶜAlī returned to Kasala after the re-occupa-

78 The above is based on Wingate (1968), 162; Shuqayr (1903), iii, 332-6; Hill (1967), 279, and Voll, thesis (1969), 273-84.

79 Abū Salīm, mimeograph (1969), 341, no. 701; see also Voll, thesis (1969), 282.

80 Abū Salīm, mimeograph (1969), 336, no. 687; *idem* (1970), 195-6, and Holt (1970), 210-11.

81 Abū Salīm, mimeograph (1969), 346, no. 712.

82 *Kitāb al-ibāna*, ms., ff. 55-6; Shuqayr (1903), iii, 336 and 401, and Hill (1967), 279.

tion of the Sudan by the Anglo-Egyptian forces in 1898, and succeeded, with his brother Aḥmad, in restoring the influence of the Khatmiyya.[83]

After the departure of Muḥammad ᶜUthmān II from the Sudan, Bakrī al-Mīrghanī became the leader of the Khatmiyya in Kasala. He was circumspect in his dealings with the Mahdi and his followers; he swore allegiance to the Mahdiyya and apparently urged the people of Kasala to submit to the Mahdists. Thus, in a letter of 3 Shaᶜbān 1302/19 May 1885 to Bakrī, the Mahdi acknowledges the latter's role in arranging for the surrender of Kasala. In the same letter, the Mahdi informed Bakrī about the delegation which would come to undertake the evacuation of Kasala, and concluded by offering him a pardon, urging him to migrate to join him.[84] However, Bakrī himself continued to circulate anti-Mahdist letters and played an active part in the military operations against the *Anṣār*. He was severely wounded in a battle and was taken by his followers to Sawākin, and later to the Ḥijāz, where he died in 1304/1886-7.[85] Kasala finally surrendered in May 1885 and was immediately plundered by the Mahdist forces, who also destroyed al-Ḥasan al-Mīrghanī's tomb and mosque.[86]

The Mahdist forces in the eastern Sudan fought on a number of fronts simultaneously. In February 1884, Tōkar surrendered; Sharīfa Maryam bt. Hāshim al-Mīrghanī and some of her followers were imprisoned by the *Anṣār* and were not released until an Anglo-Egyptian expedition from Sawākin defeated the Mahdists and occupied the area in 1891.[87] Shortly before the fall of Tōkar, the British had intervened to protect Sawākin, a strategic Red Sea port, from the Mahdists. The British, using Sawākin as a base, fought several successful battles against the Mahdist forces. They were actively supported by ᶜUthmān Tāj al-Sirr b. Muḥammad Sirr al-Khatim, who managed to win over a considerable number of people from the Mahdist cause. Sawākin, which never fell into the hands of the *Anṣār*, became a refuge for many anti-

83 *Manāqib al-sayyid ᶜAlī al-Mīrghanī* (1970), 13-4, and Khartoum, NRO, Intel. 2/32/270, p. 12.

84 Abū Salīm, mimeograph (1969), 339, no. 697.

85 *Ibid.*, 89-90, no. 179, and Shuqayr (1903), iii, 340.

86 *Kitāb al-ibāna*, ms., f. 56, Shuqayr (1903), iii, 402, and Holt (1970), 106.

87 *Kitāb al-ibāna*, ms., ff. 47-8, and Holt and Daly (1979), 109-10.

Mahdists, especially after the fall of Kasala in 1885. ᶜUthmān Tāj al-Sirr himself remained there until he died in 1903.[88]

Sawākin also served as a base for Muḥammad Sirr al-Khatim II, who at the request of the Khedive arrived from Cairo on 1 Rabīᶜ al-Awwal 1301/31 December 1883 and put his religious authority at the disposal of the Government.[89]

ᶜUthmān Diqna described Muḥammad Sirr al-Khatim as the greatest opponent of the Mahdiyya on the face of the Earth. He added that Sirr al-Khatim claimed that he was authorized by the Prophet himself to combat the Mahdist sedition. Sirr al-Khatim required those who wished to see him to spend three days washing themselves in order to be purified from the contamination of Mahdism. He also advised all those who felt the slightest temptation to join the Mahdiyya to ask for God's forgiveness. Sirr al-Khatim is said to have ordered the followers of the Khatmiyya to swear daily by the Quran that the Mahdiship of the Sudanese Mahdi was false.[90]

Muḥammad Sirr al-Khatim II wrote a number of anti-Mahdist letters that were sent to people in various parts of the Sudan. One surviving letter is that sent to Tamām Agha and his brothers, to ᶜAbd Allāh Ḥamza and his brothers, and to all the merchants and the people of al-Khandaq. ᶜAbd Allāh Ḥamza (*c.* 1824-1937) was a substantial merchant who was a descendant of Muḥammad Ṣāliḥ Shādūl, a caravan guide and a *khalīfa* of Muḥammad ᶜUthmān al-Mīrghanī I. He had strong commercial ties with the Turco-Egyptian officials. In September 1884 he supported Muṣṭafā Yāwar, the Governor of Dongola, against the Mahdist forces. The latter, however, joined the Mahdiyya, presumably realizing that the Turco-Egyptian regime was finished.

ᶜAbd Allāh Ḥamza and the people of al-Khandaq received a letter from the Mahdi, dated 22 Shaᶜbān 1302/7 June 1885, acknowledging their letter in which they had attributed their support for Muṣṭafā Yāwar to the fact that he had been appointed as *ᶜāmil* over Dongola by the Mahdi himself. They had, in the same letter, expressed their regret about what had happened and affirmed their loyalty to the Mahdi.[91]

88 *Kitāb al-ibāna*, ms., f. 45; Abū Salīm (1974), 74, and Hill (1967), 141-2.

89 Abū Salīm (1974), 74-5, and NRO, Intel. 2/32/270.

90 Abū Salīm (1974), 74-5.

91 Abū Salīm, mimeograph (1969), 363, no. 752.

In his letter to ᶜAbd Allāh Ḥamza and the people of al-Khandaq, Muḥammad Sirr al-Khatim II refers to the Mahdist movement as "a blind and deaf sedition whose advocates were at the gates of hell". He adds that it is better to die than to follow its cause. He then reproaches ᶜAbd Allāh and the people of al-Khandaq for supporting it:

What you have done during these years is contrary to the pure Muḥammadan Sharia, to the Islamic community, and to both compassion and humanity.

Muḥammad Sirr al-Khatim II devotes a considerable part of his letter to reminding the people of al-Khandaq of the security and prosperity that they had enjoyed under Turco-Egyptian rule:

I can not remain silent because of the obligation of our past friendship and the brotherhood of faith and the *ṭarīqa* [the Khatmiyya] and because I fear I should be questioned about it before God, May He be Exalted and Praised. Therefore, I have written this to you in the hope that you will be given understanding and regain your reason.[92]

92 Bergen, NI 298. 15/26 a and b, lithographed appeal from Muḥammad Sirr al-Khatim al-Mīrghanī to ᶜAbd Allāh Ḥamza and his brothers, 8 Dhū'l-Qaᶜda 1302/19 August 1885.

5

THE CENTRALIZED BROTHERHOODS: THE NEXT GENERATION

Among the students of Ibn Idrīs, a distinction can be made between those who themselves founded orders and those whose missionary activities were only formalized after their death. The former included al-Mīrghanī, al-Sanūsī and, indirectly, Ismāᶜīl al-Walī; the latter included Ibn Idrīs' own descendants (known as the Adārisa) and Ibrāhīm al-Rashīd and Muḥammad al-Dandarāwī.

Ibrāhīm al-Rashīd

DIAGRAM 4. *The Family of Ibrāhīm al-Rashīd*

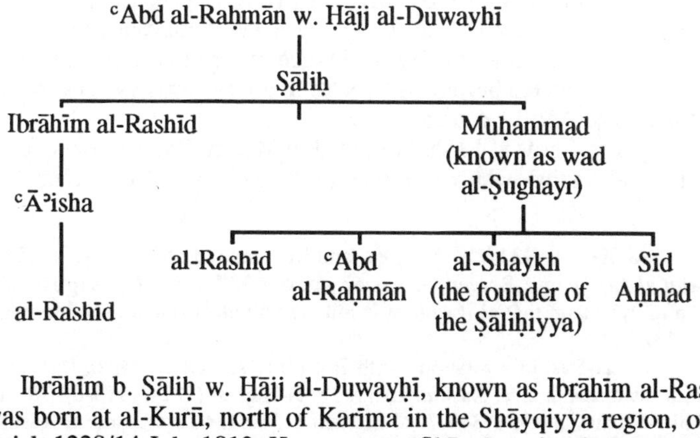

Ibrāhīm b. Ṣāliḥ w. Ḥājj al-Duwayḥī, known as Ibrāhīm al-Rashīd, was born at al-Kurū, north of Karīma in the Shāyqiyya region, on 15 Rajab 1228/14 July 1813. He was not a Shāyqī, as is often stated,[1] but belonged to the Duwayḥiyya, a section of Juhayna. His family, which

1 See, for example, Hill (1967), 177; ᶜĀbdīn (1967), 102, and F. de Jong, "al-Duwayḥī, Ibrāhīm", *EI*^{2}, supplement, 278.

claimed ᶜĀlid descent, had a long religious tradition, being descended from a noted religious teacher, ᶜAbd al-Raḥmān w. Ḥājj al-Duwayḥī, after whom the village of Duwaym Wad Ḥājj, near Marawī, is named, and where his great *qubba* still stands. His mother was Khāliṣa bt. al-Makk al-Nāfaᶜābī, from al-Zawara in the Manāṣīr area. This is presumably why al-Rashīd later won a considerable number of followers in that region.

When Ibrāhīm was about two or three years old, his father, Ṣāliḥ, took him to meet Muḥammad ᶜUthmān al-Mīrghanī I at al-Dabba. After the father "took the Path" from the Mīrghanī, he asked him to initiate his son as well. Al-Mīrghanī allegedly refused, saying that his real master would be Aḥmad b. Idrīs.[2]

After memorizing the Quran and studying various Islamic subjects with his father, Ibrāhīm left for the Ḥijāz in 1247/1832-3. There he performed the pilgrimage and then continued on to the Yemen, where he joined the circle (*ḥalqa*) of Ibn Idrīs, staying until the latter's death in 1837.[3]

During the succession dispute following Aḥmad's death, the latter's eldest son, Muḥammad, seems to have regarded al-Rashīd as his father's true successor. Al-Rashīd, who won the support of most of his master's followers at Ṣabyā, decided to leave for Upper Egypt so as to avoid the dispute. There he visited the house and the mosque which Ibn Idrīs had established at al-Zayniyya. He then moved to Luxor and established a *zāwiya*, which became the centre of a local Idrīsiyya school under Muḥammad Abū'l-Qāsim al-Ḥijāzī.[4]

Shortly afterwards al-Rashīd returned to Mecca. But, following a request from al-Sanūsī, who was forced by the hostility of the *ᶜulamāʾ* of

2 Al-Hajrasī (1314/1915-6), 89, and Muḥammad al-Ḥasan al-Tuhāmī, *R. al-dīn al-naṣīḥa*, ms. Bergen, accession number 237, f. 58. Not suprisingly, the Khatmiyya claim that al-Rashīd was initiated by al-Mīrghanī; see Maḥmūd (1971), 132.

3 On al-Rashīd's relations with Ibn Idrīs, see NRO, Misc.,1/15/179, *Manāqib wa-karāmāt ... al-Rashīd*, ms., f. 15; al-Hajrasī (1314/1915-6), 78 and 90-1; al-Nabhānī (n.d.), i, 344-7; al-Madanī (1380/1960), 44, and al-Rashīd (1394/1974), 20. De Jong in *EI*², supplement, 278, gives the date of al-Rashīd's arrival in Ṣabyā as 1246/1830.

4 Al-Hajrasī (1314/1915-6), 98-9; Trimingham (1949), 231, and ᶜAlī Ṣāliḥ Karrār, "*Athar al-taᶜālīm al-Idrīsiyya fī'l-ṭuruq al-ṣufiyya fī'l-Sūdān*", MA thesis, University of Khartoum 1977, 73.

Mecca to leave for Upper Egypt in 1841, al-Rashīd went with him to Jerusalem, from where they returned to Egypt. After a short stay, the two of them, accompanied by ᶜAbd al-ᶜĀl, went to Libya.[5] Ibrāhīm al-Rashīd returned to Upper Egypt and moved from there to the Sudan via Sawākin. On his way to the Shāyqiyya region, he visited Qubbat Khōjalī and then entered into spiritual retreat on Tūtī Island. Eventually, he arrived at his home village, al-Kurū, where he made a prolonged stay. There he used the famous mosque of his ancestors as a centre for teaching the ideas of his master, Ibn Idrīs. He then undertook a series of missionary tours covering a considerable part of the northern Sudan. During these tours he initiated many followers and established a number of *zāwiyas*, especially in the Shāyqiyya and Danāqla regions.[6]

Among al-Rashīd's numerous students were Ḥusayn Bey Khalīfa, Muḥammad al-Amīn al-Hindī, (the father of al-Sharīf Yūsuf al-Hindī, founder of the Hindiyya *ṭarīqa*), Muḥammad al-Taqalāwī at Omdurman, Muḥammad Mūsā Ghānim of Shendi and, finally, Muḥammad al-Amīn w. al-Tuwaym of Salawa, south of Shendi.[7]

In the Shāyqiyya and Bidayriyya regions, al-Rashīd's followers included members of the Bīlī religious family (commonly known as the Bīliyāb) of Manṣūrkutī. These were the descendants of a famous holy man of the sixteenth or seventeenth century, Aḥmad al-Bīlī, who lived, died and was buried in Tanqāsī in the Shāyqiyya region.

5 NRO, misc., 1/27/376; al-Rashīd (1394/1974), 45; al-Tuhāmī, *R. al-dīn al-naṣīḥa*, ms., f. 60, and E.E. Evans-Pritchard, *The Sanusi of Cyrenaica*, Oxford 1949, 13.

6 On al-Rashīd in the Sudan, interviews 2 and 22; *K. fī dhikrat al-sayyid Ghulām Allāh*, ms., f. 43; al-Tuhāmī, *R. al-dīn al-naṣīḥa*, ms., f. 60, and Karrār, thesis (1977), 74.

7 NRO, Intel., 2/32/262, H.A. MacMichael, "Notes on the Tijania Tarika", and Karrār, thesis (1977), 74-5. On the Hindī family, see Abū Salīm (1970), 18, and R. S. O'Fahey, "A history of the Awlād Hindī", *Bulletin of Information, Fontes Historiae Africanae*, 7/8, Evanston 1982/3, 43-50.

DIAGRAM 5. *The Bīliyāb Family*

Aḥmad al-Bīlī

ʿAwwūḍa | ʿAlī | ʿAbd al-Raḥīm | Ibrāhīm

ʿAbd al-Raḥīm → Muḥammad Abū al-Qāsim → Ismāʿīl (known as Wad Maḥārī)

The Bīliyāb do not belong to the ʿAwniyya branch of the Shāyqiyya as Shuqayr asserts, but to the Bidayriyya.[8] This confusion probably arose because a branch of the Bīliyāb married into the ʿAwniyya. The Bīliyāb, however, like most holy families, claimed Sharifian descent. The branch of Shaykh ʿAlī al-Bīlī, who played a role in the religious life of Kordofan, was related to the family of Ismāʿīl al-Wālī through marriage.

The most prominent of al-Rashīd's followers among the Bīliyāb was, however, Ismāʿīl al-Bīliyābī, known as Wad Maḥārī, a descendant of ʿAbd al-Raḥīm b. Aḥmad al-Bīlī.[9]

It is clear from an undated letter from al-Rashīd to his student, al-Bīliyābī, that the latter was highly respected by his teacher. In the same letter al-Rashīd advised his student on some religious matters and urged him to initiate people into the order.[10]

Al-Rashīd's followers in Manṣūrkutī included members of the families of Āb Aḥmayda and Salmān. Al-Rashīd also initiated members of the Rikābiyya, among whom were ʿUthmān Ḥamad al-Rikābī of Ḥusaynārtī, north of Kūrtī, and Nāfiʿ al-Amīn of al-Karāfāb village in the Shāyqiyya region, who was also a student of al-Ḥasan al-Mīrghanī. Among al-Rashīd's other Shāyqiyya students was al-Ḥājj al-Māḥī (1794-1869) of al-Kāsinger, near Karīma, who was a leading composer

8 Shuqayr (1903), i, 85, and *Nasab al-Bīliyāb*, ms. in the possession of Muḥammad al-Ḥasan Sīd Aḥmad al-Bīlī, Khartoum.

9 *Ibid.*, and interview 22.

10 Al-Rashīd (1394/1974), 70-1.

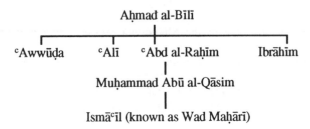

and chanter of religious praise songs (*madḥ*), and Muḥammad Bashīr Agha, a Shāyqī notable of al-Qurayr, near Marawī.[11]

Al-Rashīd enjoyed cordial relations with the Sammāniyya. In 1269/1852-3, he visited Aḥmad al-Ṭayyib's tomb at Umm Marriḥ and is reported by a Sammāniyya source as saying:

> All the Sudanese holy men are mere students in comparison with *ustādh* Aḥmad al-Ṭayyib.[12]

Towards the end of 1269/1852-3, al-Rashīd returned to Upper Egypt, where he visited Qinā, al-Zayniyya and Qūṣ. In the latter, he initiated a famous religious man called Shaykh ᶜAbd Allāh Mūsā Agha Rāsim.[13] Al-Rashīd finally arrived in Mecca in 1271/1854-5 and established a religious centre near Jabal Abū Qubays. It was here that he composed his famous devotional work: *Risālat tawthīq al-ᶜurā li-man arāda hudā khayr al-warā fī taᶜālīm al-ṭarīq al-Aḥmadī al-Idrīsī*.[14]

While in Mecca, al-Rashīd declared himself the heir to the spiritual status (*maqām*) of his teacher. He considered himself to be identical to his master:

> O God, don't make for me any name or exemplar other than those of my master Aḥmad b. Idrīs.[15]

This was presumably the basis of the accusation of heresy brought against him twice by followers and members of the Mīrghanī family in 1273/1856-7. The charges, although their nature is not specified, were brought before the board of Meccan *ᶜulamāʾ*. Al-Rashīd, however, successfully rebutted them and, consequently, attracted many followers, especially from among the Syrian and Indian pilgrims. An Indian

11 Interview 8; Qurashī Muḥammad Ḥasan, Maᶜa shuᶜarāʾ al-madāʾiḥ, 2nd edn, Khartoum 1972, 263, and Karrār, thesis (1977), 73-4. One of *al-ḥājj* al-Māḥī's teachers, Ibrāhīm ᶜAlī w. Halīb of al-Zuma, was also taught by al-Rashīd; Ḥasan (1972), 24.

12 Nūr al-Dāʾim (1954), 74. The same source says that al-Rashīd described the Sammānī Shaykh, al-Qurashī w. al-Zayn, with the Sufi title, *quṭb al-shamāl* (see Glossary).

13 Al-Hajrasī (1314/1915-6), 98-100.

14 Al-Tuhāmī, *R. al-dīn al-naṣīḥa*, ms., f. 60.

15 *Ibid.*, f. 59.

Begum was so impressed that she sent him a gift of 1,000 gold rupees, which he used to build a splendid *zāwiya.*[16]

Ibn Idrīs' family gave its support to al-Rashīd. This is evident from Muṣṭafā b. Aḥmad b. Idrīs' letter of Shawwāl 1273/May-June 1857 to al-Rashīd, in which he acknowledges the receipt of two letters from the latter, informing him of his trial. The letter demonstrates that al-Rashīd was held in high esteem by his master's family:

> Our brother and beloved and sincere friend ... the Shaykh of the *ṭarīqa* and the *imām* of the "Truth" ..., the perfect saint (*al-walī al-kāmil*), who is following in the footsteps of the Prophet ...

Muṣṭafā continues by expressing his sorrow over the unjust accusations levelled against al-Rashīd and his delight at the news of the latter's triumph before the board of *ᶜulamāʾ*:

> It is not, of course, concealed from you that God never puts a person to the test without loving him. The example of the Prophets should suffice; though they are the noblest of the created beings to God and are loved by Him, yet He has put them to the test.[17]

Nor did al-Rashīd's cordial relations with his master's family wane over the years. A letter from Ibn Idrīs' eldest son, Muḥammad, dated 1288/1871-2, praises al-Rashīd. He ends the letter by expressing his gratitude for gifts of tea, coffee and a copy of al-Ghazālī's *Iḥyāʾ ᶜulūm al-dīn.*[18] In return, al-Rashīd constantly acknowledged the spiritual authority of his late teacher. Thus:

> This is the spiritual descent [*sanad*] of the Aḥmadiyya Muḥammadiyya *ṭarīqa*. Whoever enters it, is secure from every peril and affliction, and possesses some attributes pleasing to God, and takes on the characteristics of the merciful.[19]

Shortly before his death in Mecca in 1874, al-Rashīd was joined by two students, namely ᶜAbdullāhi ᶜAbd al-Ḥafīz al-Dufārī and Muḥammad Aḥmad al-Dandarāwī, of Sudanese and Egyptian origin respectively. These two students were later to play a major part in

16 A. Le Châtelier, *Les Confréries musulmanes du Hedjaz*, Paris 1887, 96, and Trimingham (1949), 231. The reason for al-Rashid's popularity among Indians is not explained.

17 Al-Rashīd (1974), 65-6.

18 *Ibid.*, 64-5.

19 *Manāqib wa-karāmāt ... al-Rashīd*, ms., f. 38; al-Tuhāmī, *R. al-dīn al-naṣīḥa*, ms., f. 60, and Trimingham (1949), 231.

preaching the doctrine of Ibn Idrīs in the Sudan, especially in the Shāyqiyya region. Ibrāhīm al-Rashīd died on 7 Shaᶜbān 1291/20 August 1874 and was buried in Mecca. He left only one daughter, ᶜĀ'isha, and the succession went to his nephew al-Shaykh b. Muḥammad b. Ṣāliḥ (*c.* 1854-1919).[20]

The Rashīdiyya and Ṣāliḥiyya

Al-Shaykh was born at al-Kurū in the Shāyqiyya area in about 1854. He studied Mālikī law with his father Muḥammad, known as Wad al-Ṣughayr, who was a noted religious teacher in the region. After al-Rashīd's death, al-Shaykh left for Mecca to continue the work of his late uncle. There he married a woman of Moroccan origin, who was to become the mother of several sons, including al-Rashīd, Aḥmad and Ibrāhīm.[21]

During al-Shaykh's first years in Mecca he sought to organize his uncle's followers into an order that came to be known as al-Rashīdiyya.[22] However, in about 1887, for reasons that are unclear, al-Shaykh established an offshoot of the Rashīdiyya which he called the Ṣāliḥiyya.[23] This latter *ṭarīqa* would be viewed as being part of the Idrīsī tradition, simply because its teachings were based almost entirely on those of Ibn Idrīs.

The Ṣāliḥiyya rapidly gained popularity and found its way into parts of Asia and East Africa. It was especially successful along the coast of Somalia, where Somali religious figures, who had been initiated by al-Shaykh while on pilgrimage in Mecca, propagated the order. One of these Somali local representatives was Muḥammad Qūlid al-Rashīdī, who recruited many followers and established several agricultural settlements, an economic role which echoes that of the Grand Sanūsī in

20 Karrār, thesis (1977), 76. Some Western sources give Muḥammad Ṣāliḥ as al-Rashīd's successor; see, for example, Trimingham (1949), 231, and B.G. Martin, *Muslim Brotherhoods in Nineteenth Century Africa*, Cambridge 1976, 179. This is an error based on reading "al-Shaykh" as a title and not as a name; see Karrār, thesis (1977), 76 and the oral sources cited there.

21 Le Châtelier (1887), 96, and de Jong, *EI*^{2},, supplement, 279.

22 Trimingham (1952), 243-4; I.M. Lewis, "Sufism in Somaliland", *BSOAS*, xvii, 1955, 580-602, and Martin (1976), 179.

23 *Ibid.*

Libya and, more recently, Aḥmad Bamba in Senegal.[24] Another local representative of the Ṣāliḥiyya in the Somalia was Muḥammad ᶜAbd Allāh Ḥasan, the so-called "Mad Mullah" (1864-1920), who led his country's resistance to the British and Italians between 1899 and 1920.[25]

The popularity of Ibrāhīm al-Rashīd, especially among wealthy Indian pilgrims, had enabled him to accumulate considerable wealth and thus to send regular aid, both in kind and in cash, to his relations in the Shāyqiyya region. The surviving correspondence of al-Rashid's successor, al-Shaykh, who combined religion with trade and drew considerable wealth from the agricultural lands of his own *ṭarīqa*, the Ṣāliḥiyya, in Somalia, shows that he kept up the tradition of aiding his relatives in the Shāyqiyya area.[26]

ᶜAbdullāhī al-Dufārī and the Mahdist Cause

ᶜAbdullāhī b. ᶜAbd al-Ḥafīz b. ᶜAbdullāhī b. ᶜAlī was commonly known as ᶜAbdullāhī al-Dufārī because his great-grandfather, *al-faqīh* Idrīs, once lived at the village of al-Nūq in the Dufār area. Al-Dufārī was born on Ḥusaynārtī Island in 1244/1828-9. His family, which had branches in Kūrtī, Tūtī Island, and al-Kawa and al-Qitayna in the White Nile area, was well known for its religious status.[27]

ᶜAbdullāhī al-Dufārī was a Bidayrī, but his pedigree also gives him, on his father's side, a Bakrī origin, that is descent from Abū Bakr al-Ṣiddīq, the Prophet's successor. His family shared a common ancestry with another famous holy family in the Shāyqiyya region, namely the

24 *Ibid*, and O'Fahey (1990), 163-5. On the Sanūsiyya, see Evans-Pritchard (1949), and on Bamba, O'Brien (1971).

25 The hostile colonial view of Muḥammad ᶜAbd Allāh Ḥasan has been modified by modern scholarship; see, for example, Martin (1976), 177-201, and Said Samatar, *Oral Poetry and Somali Nationalism*, Cambridge 1982.

26 Letter from the Duwayḥiyya of Duwaym Wad Ḥājj to al-Shaykh b. Muḥammad Ṣāliḥ al-Rashīd in Mecca; dated 21 Ṣafar 1329/21 February 1911, Bergen NO 155. 7/11, and interview 2.

27 The following is based on two sources from within the Dufārī tradition, namely *Manāqib al-ḥājj ᶜAbdullāhi al-Dufārī*, ms. in the possession of his descendants, and ᶜAydarūs ᶜAbd al-Karīm, *Manāqib al-quṭb al-ḥājj ᶜAbdullāhi al-Dufārī*, n.p., n.d.

Ḥamadtūiyāb of Nūrī. Through his mother, Zaynab bt. ᶜAbd al-Karīm, al-Dufārī was also a close relative of al-Ḥasan al-Mīrghanī through the latter's mother, Ruqayya.

After memorizing the Quran and receiving the normal education at the local Quranic school of ᶜUthmān Ḥammād, al-Dufārī travelled with his parents to meet al-Ḥasan al-Mīrghanī at al-Jiwayr in the Shendi area. There he studied under al-Mīrghanī and stayed with him for eight years. But his master told him that his real teacher would be Ibrāhīm al-Rashīd.[28]

Al-Dufārī, together with his family, returned to his home village Ḥusaynārtī, where he lived for some years. He then travelled to the Ḥijāz, where he made the pilgrimage and met Ibrāhīm al-Rashīd. Al-Dufārī eventually returned to his village in the Sudan and began to initiate followers into the Aḥmadiyya Muḥammadiyya *ṭarīqa.* Among his students was Ṣāliḥ b. Faḍl of Mōrā in the Shāyqiyya region.

Shaykh Ṣāliḥ was of Rikābī origin. His grandfather Ḥasan w. Bilayl, had been a follower of al-Ḥasan al-Mīrghanī. Although a young man when initiated by al-Dufārī, he was appointed a *khalīfa.* Shaykh Ṣāliḥ, who was famed for his mastery of the rules of Quranic recitation (*tajwīd*), used his religious school at Mōrā as a centre for the Aḥmadiyya. He initiated a considerable number of followers in Mōrā, Manṣūrkutī, al-Kuray, Qanatī and Maqāshī. Like his teacher al-Dufārī, Shaykh Ṣāliḥ also supported the Mahdist cause. His followers, together with those of his master, were, and still are, known as the Aḥmadiyya-Anṣār. After his death in 1932, Shaykh Ṣāliḥ was succeeded by his son Aḥmad, who is currently (1982) the head of the religious school and the Aḥmadiyya *khalīfa* at Mōrā.[29]

After some years at Ḥusaynārtī al-Dufārī moved, in response to a Prophetic order, to the Gezira. He visited Umm Marriḥ, the centre of Aḥmad al-Ṭayyib; in this sense al-Dufārī kept up the tradition of close ties with the Sammāniyya followed by all those influenced by Ibn Idrīs. This was further confirmed by his visit to the centre of al-Qurashī at al-Ḥalāwiyyīn. A Sammāniyya source reports that when al-Dufārī was in

28 *Manāqib ... al-Dufārī*, ms., f. 15, and ᶜAbd al-Karīm, *Manāqib*, n.d.,7. While at al-Jiwayr, al-Dufārī's parents had two other sons, ᶜAbd al-Karīm and Munawwar, who were both to become followers of the "way" of Ibn Idrīs and supporters of the Mahdi.

29 The above is based on ᶜAbd al-Karīm, *Manāqib*, 12-3; *K. fī dhikrat al-sayyid Ghulām Allāh*, ms., 95-6, and interviews 8 and 22.

Mecca he asked al-Rashīd about the place (*maqām*) of al-Qurashī in the Sufi hierarchy. Al-Rashīd is reported to have said:

He [al-Qurashī] is the *quṭb* of the north. I frequently listened to his sayings, which prove that he is the *sultan* of the people of his age.[30]

Al-Dufārī also visited Qarrī, where he stayed with *al-ḥājj* Ḥasan al-Sunnī, a student of Aḥmad b. Idrīs.[31] Although our sources make it difficult to establish a chronology for al-Dufārī's travels, it seems that he toured most of the Gezira before finally settling at al-Kawa in the White Nile area. There he established a religious centre and initiated many followers into the Way of Ibn Idrīs, the Aḥmadiyya Muḥammadiyya *ṭarīqa*. Among his students were Muḥammad Aḥmad, the future Mahdi, and the famous scholar al-Ḥusayn w. al-Zahrā.[32]

Thus it was al-Dufārī, the student of al-Rashīd, who provided the link between the Sudanese Mahdi and Aḥmad b. Idrīs. This may explain why the Mahdi showed great respect to all those who were associated with the Idrīsiyya school. We saw earlier how he tried to win over the members of the Mīrghanī family, offering them safe-conduct despite their hostility. Moreover, the Mahdi quoted in one of his earliest proclamations, dated Shaᶜbān 1298/June-July 1881, the following sayings of Ibn Idrīs about the Mahdist idea:

Shaykh Aḥmad b. Idrīs said: "fourteen generations of the people of God (*ahl Allah*) have denied the coming of the Mahdi".

He then said: "He [the Mahdi] will appear from a place unknown to them and in a condition that they will deny".[33]

Al-Dufārī and many of his students, including those of the Shāyqiyya region, were among the earliest supporters of the Mahdiyya. After the Mahdi had migrated to Jabal Qadīr on 7 Dhū'l-ḥijja 1298/1 November 1881, he wrote to al-Dufārī thanking him for his belief in his Mahdiship and urging him to come to him. Al-Dufārī went without delay and made a prolonged stay with his former student at Jabal Qadīr.[34]

30 Nūr al-Dā'im (1954), 307; see also ᶜAbd al-Karīm, *Manāqib*, 9-10.

31 ᶜAbd al-Karīm, *Manāqib*, 13-4.

32 *Ibid.*, 17; *Manāqib ... al-Dufārī*, ms., f. 19; Karrār, thesis (1977), 78.

33 Muḥammad Ibrāhīm Abū Salīm, ed., *Manshūrāt al-Mahdiyya*, Beirut 1969a, 19-22.

34 Abū Salīm, mimeograph (1969), 400, no. 839. See also ᶜAbd al-Karīm, *Manāqib*, 16.

Another example of the followers of the Aḥmadiyya Muḥammadiyya who supported the Mahdiyya from the beginning was Muḥammad al-Amīn al-Hindī, who was, at that time, a religious teacher in the Jaylī area, just north of the present-day Khartoum North. The Mahdi wrote to him in Shaᶜbān 1299/June-July 1882, authorizing him to administer the oath of allegiance (*bayᶜa*) on his behalf. In the same letter the Mahdi exhorted him to reject the *madhhabs* and to rely on the sources of Islam, the Quran and the *sunna*. He concluded by urging al-Hindī and his students to make the migration, *hijra*, and join him. This al-Hindī did, and remained with the Mahdi until his death at al-Rahad on 23 Rajab 1300/30 May 1883.[35]

Another such follower was Muḥammad al-Amīn w. al-Tuwaym of Salawa, near Shendi. He was one of the descendants of Shaykh al-Tuwaym, known as al-Tuwaymāb, of the village of al-Kuray in the Shāyqiyya region. Muḥammad al-Tuwaym was a famous poet (*mādiḥ*). At the outset of the Mahdiyya, he and several of his relatives in the Shendi and the Shāyqiyya areas became supporters. Muḥammad al-Tuwaym became a close friend of the Mahdi and his family. The latter repeatedly addressed him as *Ṣafiyunā wa-ḥabībunā*, "our beloved and best friend", and conferred upon him the title of *khalīfa* Ḥassān, that is the successor of Ḥassān b. Thābit, the Prophet's poet.

The Mahdi apparently held his former teacher al-Dufārī in respect. According to a *Manāqib* on al-Dufārī, the Mahdi once told some of his followers:

> By God he [al-Dufārī] is a *quṭb*, and whoever rejects him will cut off his inheritance in Paradise.[36]

The Mahdi received the support of al-Dufārī's younger brothers, Munawwar and ᶜAbd al-Karīm, and appointed the latter as *amīr* for the Kawa area.[37] Al-Dufārī survived the Mahdiyya and continued his teaching activities until his death on 14 Dhū'l-ḥijja 1325/29 January 1908 at al-Kawa, where he was buried.[38]

The Mahdi's positive attitude toward the followers of the school of Ibn Idrīs may explain the clemency he offered to one of its adherents,

35 Abū Salīm, mimeograph (1969), 24, no. 44. See also O'Fahey (1982/3), 43-50.

36 ᶜAbd al-Karīm, *Manāqib*, 11 and 15-16.

37 *Ibid.*, 16-17.

38 *Ibid.*, 31-2; see also Karrār, thesis (1977), 79.

Ḥusayn Khalīfa, the Turco-Egyptian Governor of Berber. After the fall of Berber to the Mahdist forces, Ḥusayn swore allegiance to the Mahdi, who pardoned him and his sons and instructed Aḥmad Sulaymān, the commissioner of the Mahdist treasury, *amīn bayt al-māl*, to grant them an appropriate sum of money. The Mahdi wrote, on 24 Rajab 1302/10 May 1885, to Muḥammad al-Khayr, his agent in the Berber area, telling him that Ḥusayn Khalīfa had been appointed *ᶜāmil ᶜumūm al-jihāt al-Miṣriyya*, that is agent for the Mahdist cause among his own people, the ᶜAbābda.[39]

Muḥammad Aḥmad al-Dandarāwī

Like his master, Ibrāhīm al-Rashīd, Muḥammad Aḥmad al-Dandarāwī is erroneously stated to have founded an independent *ṭarīqa*; it was, in fact, established by his son.[40] Muḥammad al-Dandarāwī was born in 1255/1839-40 at Dandara, in Upper Egypt, into a religious family that claimed Sharifian descent. He was educated at his family's Quranic school, and became a teacher in his turn. He then travelled to the Ḥijāz, where he performed the pilgrimage and met Ibrāhīm al-Rashīd, who taught him the doctrines of Ibn Idrīs.[41]

After the death of al-Rashīd in 1874, al-Dandarāwī left Mecca for the Sudan. There he made an extended stay in the Shāyqiyya region, where he was warmly welcomed. Some of the local people offered him plots of land and some palm trees.[42]

Muḥammad al-Dandarāwī lived for some time with his teacher's family at al-Kurū and Duwaym Wad Ḥājj in the Shāyqiyya area; it was he who built a tomb over the grave of his master's ancestor, ᶜAbd al-Raḥmān w. Ḥājj, at Duwaym Wad Ḥājj.[43]

39 Abū Salīm, mimeograph (1969), 149-50, no. 290; 266, no. 535, and 328, no. 668.

40 Martin (1976), 178, and *al-Muṣṣawar*, no. 2988, 20 Rabīᶜ I 1402/15 January 1982, 38.

41 Interview 3; see also Karrār, thesis (1977), 79, and O'Fahey (1990), 165-6.

42 Interviews 3 and 22, and letter to the author from Professor Mohammed Omer Beshir, 10 October 1983.

43 Karrār, thesis (1977), 79.

In the missionary spirit of the school of Ibn Idrīs, al-Dandarāwī undertook an extensive preaching tour in the northern Sudan. His travels in the Shāyqiyya region took him to Manṣūrkutī, Karīma, al-Dahasīra and al-Kāsinger, where he initiated a number of followers. While at the last-named place, he built a tomb over the grave of al-Ḥājj al-Māḥī, a student of al-Rashīd.[44]

Like al-Dufārī and other followers of the Aḥmadiyya Muḥammadiyya, al-Dandarāwī, although he was an Egyptian, also supported the Sudanese Mahdi. He travelled with a group of his followers from the Shāyqiyya region to meet the Mahdi in Omdurman. When they arrived at Shendi, they were met with hostility by some of the Anṣār and their personal effects were confiscated by the *amīr* Wad Ḥamza, the Mahdi's representative in the area. The latter sent a dispatch with *amīr* ᶜAbd al-Karīm, a brother of al-Dufārī, to Wad Ḥamza reproving him and ordering him to return the confiscated items. Wad Ḥamza expressed his regret for what had happened.[45] Al-Dandarāwī was prevented by illness from going to the Mahdi, but he authorized al-Dufārī, who was in Omdurman at the time, to swear allegiance to the Mahdi on his behalf.

Muḥammad al-Dandarāwī then returned to the Shāyqiyya region where he declared himself the spiritual heir of Ibrāhīm al-Rashīd. This caused resentment among many, especially those who had been initiated by al-Rashīd himself. Thus Muḥammad al-Tuwaym, a student of al-Rashīd, wrote from his home village, Salawa, to al-Dandarāwī reproaching him for his claim.[46]

Our sources on al-Dandarāwī are too few to show the sequence of his travels. It seems that his visit to the Sudan was followed by one to Somalia.[47] It is also not clear when al-Dandarāwī returned to his home in Dandara, Upper Egypt, where he died in 1328/1910-11.[48] He was succeeded by his son, Abū'l-ᶜAbbās (d. 1953), who broke away from

44 Interview 3.

45 ᶜAbd al-Karīm, *Manāqib*, 19-20. Wad Ḥamza's loss of sight in a family dispute was later regarded as a *karāma* of al-Dandarāwī.

46 The letter, which is undated, is in the possession of *khalīfa* Muḥammad al-Tuhāmī al-Ḥasan, Khartoum.

47 Martin (1976), 178 and 233 n. 9.

48 Karrār, thesis (1977), 80.

the Rashīdiyya and established an independent branch to be known as al-Dandarāwiyya after his father.[49]

The Idrīsiyya

Ibn Idrīs' sons, Muḥammad and ᶜAbd al-ᶜĀl, institutionalized their father's teachings into an order called the Idrīsiyya, or more formally *ṭarīqa Muḥammadiyya Aḥmadiyya Idrīsiyya*.[50]

Although the seat of this new *ṭarīqa* was situated in the Dongola area, and at a later stage Omdurman, it also influenced the Shāyqiyya region through the students of al-Rashīd and the family's own pupils, whatever their *ṭarīqa*. This is because all of them recognized the spiritual authority of the sons and descendants of Ibn Idrīs, who were venerated as possessors of *baraka*.[51] Although it is not clear when the Idrīsiyya was established, one may suggest that it was not until the death of Ibrāhīm al-Rashīd in 1874 that the Idrīsiyya *ṭarīqa* came into being. Al-Rashīd, who was regarded by the sons of Ibn Idrīs as their father's successor, died without leaving a son to follow him, and thus the succession passed to his nephew, whose first years in the office saw a decline in the adherents of the school of Ibn Idrīs.[52]

It was Muḥammad b. Aḥmad b. Idrīs and his descendants who was responsible for the spread of the Idrīsiyya in the Yemen and in parts of Muslim Asia, whereas his brother ᶜAbd al-ᶜĀl, and the latter's son Muḥammad, were responsible for its propagation in Upper Egypt, the

49 *Al-Muṣṣawar* (1982), 38. For the teachings of the Dandarāwiyya, see ᶜAlī ᶜĪsā al-Aḥmadī, *K. al-Iḍāḥ li-ahl al-falāḥ*, ms., written by the former *khalīfa* (d. 1980) of the Dandarāwiyya in the Karīma district, now in the possession of his son, Abū'l-ᶜAbbās ᶜAlī, Karīma.

50 Interview 15; see also NRO, Intel., 2/32/270, p. 12, and Voll, thesis (1969), 101.

51 Interview 22.

52 De Jong, *EI*², supplement, 278-9.

DIAGRAM 6. *The Adārisa: the Sudan branch.*

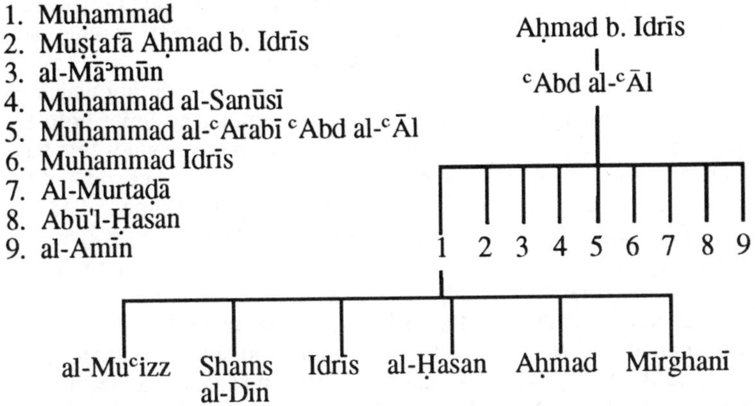

Sudan and other parts of Muslim Africa.[53] Although the former also had close contacts and influence, especially in the Dongola area in the Sudan, our concern here is mainly with the latter.[54]

ᶜAbd al-ᶜĀl was born at Ṣabyā in the Yemen in 1246/1830-1; he was only seven years old when his father died. He memorized the Quran and studied other Islamic subjects with some of his father's students. His principal teacher, however, was al-Sanūsī, with whom he travelled to Upper Egypt and from there to Libya, where he remained until al-Sanūsī's death at Jaghbūb on 9 Ṣafar 1276/7 September 1859.[55]

After al-Sanūsī's death, ᶜAbd al-ᶜĀl left for Egypt on his way to the Ḥijāz. In Cairo he met ᶜAlī ᶜAbd al-Ḥaqq al-Qūṣī, one of the students of Ibn Idrīs in al-Zayniyya, who asked him to come with him to Upper Egypt to meet the followers there. When ᶜAbd al-ᶜĀl arrived at al-

53 Karrār, thesis (1977).

54 NRO, Intel., 2/32/270, p. 13.

55 Al-Rashīd (1394/1974), 45; NRO, Northern Province, 1/25/263, and Intel., 6/7/22.

Zayniyya he found that the followers had transformed his father's house into a place of pilgrimage.[56]

ᶜAbd al-ᶜĀl was warmly received by the followers, who asked him to honour and bless them by marrying some of their daughters. Thus he married a daughter of *al-ḥājj* ᶜAbd al-Raḥīm, one of al-Zayniyya's notables. Shortly afterwards, ᶜAbd al-ᶜĀl married three other women and became the father of nine sons (see Diagram 6).[57]

ᶜAbd al-ᶜĀl stayed at al-Zayniyya for twelve years, during which he firmly established the Idrīsiyya. He also attempted to unite both the Sanūsiyya and the Khatmiyya under his *ṭarīqa* on the grounds that their founders were his father's students. To achieve this, he sent some of his sons to study and "receive the Path" from both Muḥammad al-Mahdī al-Sanūsī and Muḥammad Sirr al-Khatim II, the head of the Khatmiyya in Egypt. Thus he sent his son Muḥammad to the latter, who initiated him into the Khatmiyya. Later Sirr al-Khatim also educated and initiated another member of the Adārisa, Muḥammad Idrīs b. ᶜAlī b. Muḥammad.[58] However, ᶜAbd al-ᶜĀl failed to unite the brotherhoods.

In 1294/1877 ᶜAbd al-ᶜĀl and his eldest son Muḥammad left for the Yemen via the Sudan. They reached Dongola in Rajab 1294/July-August 1877, where they were requested by Muṣṭafā Yāwar, the Governor of Dongola, and the people of the area to spend some time with them. They stayed for over a year; then on 28 Dhū'l-Qaᶜda 1296/24 November 1878 ᶜAbd al-ᶜĀl died and was buried in the main mosque of Dongola.[59] A large tomb was built and the anniversary of his death (*ḥawliyya*) was, and still is, celebrated by the followers. Representatives of the adherents of Ibrāhīm al-Rashīd and his students in the Shāyqiyya region also used to attend this and other occasions associated with the Idrīsiyya tradition.[60]

ᶜAbd al-ᶜĀl was succeeded by his son Muḥammad, who married into the people and lived at the village of Bayūḍ, near Arqū, which became an important centre for the Idrīsiyya. Muḥammad also maintained the missionary spirit of the Idrīsiyya and visited several villages and

56 NRO, Intel., 2/32/261, English title, "A general note on Tarikas in the Sudan"; contains Ar. ms. *Makhṭūṭ taʾrīkh dukhūl al-ṭarāʾiq li'l-Sūdān.*

57 Al-Rashīd (1394/1974), 45.

58 NRO, Intel., 2/32/261, and Abū Salīm in 7/1/10, p. 10. See also Karrār, thesis (1977), 85.

59 NRO, Intel., 6/7/22.

60 Interview 22.

towns in the northern Sudan, establishing mosques and Quranic schools at al-Qaᶜb in Dongola, al-Duyyūm al-Qadīma in Khartoum (now Khartoum Two) and Omdurman. He also established a *takiyya* in the Ḥalfa region.[61]

The sons and descendants of Ibn Idrīs propagated the Idrīsiyya in Sudanese Nubia, which was under the influence of the Khatmiyya, especially the branch of Muḥammad Sirr al-Khatim II of Egypt, and won many followers. This led to a dispute between the leaders of the two orders. The Khatmiyya considered the Idrīsiyya *ṭarīqa* as subordinate to the Aḥmadiyya Muḥammadiyya (which is how they described the Rashīdiyya) on the grounds that Muḥammad b. Aḥmad b. Idrīs had sworn allegiance to al-Rashīd as Ibn Idrīs' successor.[62] Dr. Abū Salīm argues that the Idrīsiyya gained ground in Sudanese Nubia mainly because the Khatmiyya were led by local *khalīfas*, loyal to the Egyptian branch of the Khatmiyya.[63] The absence of the Mīrghanī family in the area enhanced the position of the Idrīsī family. By contrast, the Idrīsī family did not win as many followers in the Shāyqiyya region because their efforts there coincided with those of Muḥammad ᶜUthmān al-Mīrghanī II himself.

Like the Mīrghanī family, the Adārisa also enjoyed great influence and received gifts of lands and palm trees from the followers. A levy of 8 to 10 *midd* on each agricultural unit (*sāqiya*, lit. "waterwheel") used to be collected by a local representative from the adherents after the harvest. This was sold and the proceeds sent to the head of the order as contributions from the followers to cover the expenses of the *ṭarīqa*. When the head of the order visited an area, the *khalīfas* would collect from each house a sum of 4 or 5 piasters or its equivalent in kind - for example, wheat, barley, or dates.[64]

The ties of the Idrīsī family to the Shāyqiyya region were indirect, being mainly through the followers of al-Rashīd. They also, however, sent voluntary gifts, both in cash and kind, to the descendants of Ibn

61 Kāmil Muḥammad Ḥasan al-Aḥmadī (n.d.), *Dumūᶜ al-wafāʾ ᶜalā imām al-aṣfiyāʾ [al-sayyid Muḥammad al-Sharīf b. ᶜAbd al-Mutaᶜāl]*, Khartoum, and Karrār, thesis (1977), 87.

62 NRO, Intel., 2/32/261.

63 NRO, Abū Salīm in 7/1/10, p. 5.

64 NRO, Northern Province, 1/19/127 "Abu el-Hasan Abdel Mutaal", and Karrār, thesis (1977), 88.

Idrīs.[65] The members of the Idrīsī family, for their part, also showed respect for and maintained friendly relations with the students and followers of Ibrāhīm al-Rashīd.

Following the evacuation of Dongola by the Government troops in 1887 because of the Mahdist revolt, Muḥammad b. ᶜAbd al-ᶜĀl took his family to al-Zayniyya, where he remained until 1897 when he returned to Dongola after its occupation by the British forces. He resumed his activities until his death in July 1936. He was succeeded by Mīrghanī, who had settled on Tanqasī Island in about 1905-6; after his father's death he moved to Dongola.[66]

The Tijāniyya

Aḥmad al-Tijānī was one of the key figures of Islam in nineteenth century Africa.

Concerning al-Tijānī's early life and travels, our knowledge is limited, being based effectively on only one source, which as Professor Abun-Nasr notes:

> Left out many details which might have put his life and career in a different perspective.[67]

Within this context, it is worthwhile to note that there are traditions in the Sudan that al-Tijānī had lived as a merchant for five years in al-Ubayyiḍ in Kordofan.[68] He then returned to Morocco from where, in 1186/1772-3, he moved to the Ḥijāz. On his way he stopped at Algeria, where he was initiated by a local *muqaddam* into the Khalwatiyya.[69]

While in Medina, al-Tijānī's ties to the Khalwatiyya were confirmed when he was initiated by Muḥammad ᶜAbd al-Karīm al-Sammān into the Sammāniyya Khalwatiyya. On his way back home from the Ḥijāz

65 Interview 22.

66 NRO, Northern Province, 1/25/263, and Karrār, thesis (1977), 89.

67 J.M. Abun Nasr, *The Tijaniyya. A Sufi Order in the Modern World*, London 1965, 15.

68 Maḥmūd (1971), 58, and al-Idrīsī, thesis (1976), 43.

69 Abun-Nasr (1965), 18.

he visited Cairo, where he was again initiated into the Khalwatiyya, this time by Maḥmūd al-Kurdī al-Khalwatī (d. 1195/1780).[70]

There is a tradition among the followers of Ibn Idrīs that their master, presumably before he left Fez for Mecca in the middle of 1212/1797-8, had appointed Aḥmad al-Tijānī as a representative.[71] Aḥmad al-Tijānī established his own *ṭarīqa*, the Tijāniyya in 1196/1781-2, declaring that he had received Prophetic permission to initiate others.[72] His order spread in North Africa and across the Sahara to West Africa.

The Tijāniyya was introduced into the western Sudan by a religious man of Hausa origin, ᶜUmar Janbo, a pupil of Muḥammad al-Ṣaghīr b. ᶜAlī, a student of the founder. He propagated the order in Dār Fūr and Kordofan, travelled widely in the region and also visited Egypt and the Ḥijāz. After the fall of the Mahdist state in 1898-9, he lived at al-Fāshir under the auspices of Sultan ᶜAlī Dinār (reigned 1898-1916), the Fūr sultan. But the Sultan suspected ᶜUmar Janbo of making him ill by magic and he fled in 1908 to al-Ubayyiḍ, and later to Omdurman. He continued onto the Ḥijāz, where he died and was buried in Mecca.[73]

The propagation of the Tijāniyya in the northern parts of the Sudan was, however, the work of another Tijānī missionary, Muḥammad b. al-Mukhtār b. ᶜAbd al-Raḥmān al-Shinqīṭī, known as Abū'l-ᶜĀliya. He was born at Tashīt in Mauritania in about 1820. He received his education from members of his family; his mother, Fāṭima bt. al-ᶜĀliya, was also well versed in the Islamic sciences.[74]

Abū'l-ᶜĀliya combined religion with trade and travelled extensively. He visited Egypt, where he studied; he then left for the Ḥijāz, where he performed the pilgrimage. While in Medina in 1847, he received an *ijāzā* for the rank of *muqaddam* from Ṣāliḥ b. Aḥmad Balqāsim. He then returned to his home area and from there travelled to Timbuktu,

70 al-Ḥasan b. *al-ḥājj* Muhammad al-Shādhili, *K. Ṭabaqāt al-Shādhiliyya al-kubrā*, Cairo (1347/1928-29), 164-5.

71 *Tarjamat al-ᶜalāma al-sayyid Aḥmad b. Idrīs* (1315/1897-8), 5. Al-Nabhānī (n.d.), i, 349, places his biography of al-Tijānī immediately after his long notice of Ibn Idrīs (i, 341-9) and opens his account of al-Tijānī with the words, "*ajall khulafā' sayyidī Aḥmad b. Idrīs*": "The most prominent of the *khalīfas* of Ibn Idrīs".

72 Abun-Nasr (1965), 19.

73 NRO, Intel., 2/32/270, p. 26.

74 Al-Tijānī, *Ghāyat al-amānī*, 104.

Borno, Wadai and, finally, the Sudan. In Dār Fūr he initiated Sultan Muḥammad al-Ḥusayn (ruled 1838-73) and acted as his ambassador to Egypt. While in Cairo, he initiated Muḥammad Saᶜīd Pasha (ruled 1854-63), the Viceroy of Egypt, and returned in 1858 with presents from him to Sultan Muḥammad al-Ḥusayn.[75]

Abū'l-ᶜĀliya travelled to Sawākin, where he lived for some years. He then moved to Berber with a certain Zayn al-ᶜĀbdīn al-Maghribī. In Berber, Abū'l-ᶜĀliya initiated many followers, including Muḥammad al-Khayr, a teacher of the Mahdi and later his representative in Berber; Abū'l-Qāsim Aḥmad Hāshim (d. 1939), a scholar and legal notable, and some of his sons and brothers; and finally Muddathir Ibrāhīm al-Ḥajjāz (1855-1937), a religious notable who served the Mahdi and the Khalīfa as secretary and was the keeper of the latter's private seal. After Zayn al-ᶜĀbdīn's death, a dispute over his property took place between his relatives and Abū'l-ᶜĀliya, who eventually moved and settled on Umm Ḥarāḥir Island, south of Shendi. There he married into the local people and acquired large landed properties.[76] Before his death in 1882, he had initiated many followers; among them was Aḥmad al-Huday al-Sawarābī, who introduced the Tijāniyya into the Shāyqiyya region.

Aḥmad al-Huday was born about the mid-nineteenth century at the village of Uslī, west of Misāwī Island in the Shāyqiyya region. His family belonged to the Kufunja branch of the Sawarāb sub-section of the Shāyqiyya. They moved after the Turco-Egyptian invasion of 1821 and settled at Wādī Bishāra, at the northern end of al-Sabalūqa gorge. Al-Huday visited Abū'l-ᶜĀliya at Umm Ḥarāḥir and was initiated by him into the Tijāniyya.[77]

It is not clear when al-Huday began to preach the Tijāniyya in the Shāyqiyya region. According to an oral source, he had visited the Shāyqiyya area already during the colonial period and initiated followers into his order; one may suggest that it was not until the beginning of the Mahdiyya in 1881 that the Tijāniyya began openly to gain followers. This may be supported by the fact that "the Tijāniyya were persecuted under the Egyptian occupation", and that they used to conceal

75 *Ibid.*, 105; Trimingham (1949), 237, and Hill (1967), 267.

76 NRO, Intel., 3/32/261, p. 10 and Intel, 2/32/262. See also Hill (1967), 23 and 243.

77 NRO, Intel., 2/32/261, p. 10, and interview 8.

their *ṭarīqa*. This was presumably because several of their practices and beliefs were considered by many Muslims as heretical.[78]

With the coming of the Mahdiyya, al-Huday swore allegiance to Muḥammad al-Khayr, the Mahdi's representative in Berber. Al-Huday was also appointed as *ᶜāmil* of Dongola province in the place of Muṣṭafā Yāwar.[79] On his arrival as the Mahdi's representative, al-Huday appointed his relative Shaykh al-Ṭayyib al-Sawarābī as his agent in the Shāyqiyya region (see p. 96). Al-Huday and members of his family began to preach the Tijāniyya in the region and won many followers.[80] This happened at a time when the Sufi orders had already been banned by the Mahdi's proclamation of the middle of 1301/the beginning of 1884. This combination of the Tijāniyya and the Mahdiyya is clear from an undated letter deploring the practice which was issued by the Khalifa, in the lifetime of the Mahdi, to all the believers.[81] The Tijāniyya did not gain a great following in the main centres of the Khatmiyya within the Shāyqiyya region, such as Nūri, al-Zūma, Abū Rannāt and al-Jirayf. Its followers were found mainly in areas that were inhabited by the Sawarāb or their relatives - for instance, in Uslī, al-Bāsā, al-Dibayba, al-Kurū and al-Qurayr.[82]

Al-Huday declared a *jihād* against Muṣṭafā Yāwar Pasha and was joined by many Hawwāra and Ḥassāniyya. His army was also reinforced when Nuᶜmān w. Qamar, head of the Manāṣīr, joined him with his people.[83] Al-Huday is said to have forced many Shāyqiyya, including the local *khalīfas* of the Khatmiyya, to join his army.

Aḥmad al-Huday fought two unsuccessful battles against Yāwar at al-Dabba on 18 May and 29 June 1884. He realized that he would not be able to face his enemy without reinforcements, so he appealed to the Mahdi. The latter, then at al-Rahad in Kordofan and about to leave for Khartoum, sent a force under his relative Maḥmūd al-Ḥājj whom he appointed *ᶜāmil ᶜumūm* (general agent) of Dongola, ordering al-Huday to join him.

78 Trimingham (1949), 238, and Abun-Nasr (1965), 27.

79 R.C. Slatin, *Fire and Sword in the Sudan*, London 1896, 172, and Shuqayr (1903), iii, 234.

80 Interviews 6 and 8.

81 Abū Salīm (1970), 45-8.

82 Interviews 6 and 8.

83 The following is based on Shuqayr (1903), iii, 239-40.

The Mahdist army, however, was defeated for the third time in September 1884. Maḥmūd al-Ḥājj and al-Huday, together with many of their supporters and those forced to join them, were killed. The villages of al-Dabba and al-Karad were burnt to the ground by the Government forces. This indiscriminate sacking also included the town of Kūrtī, an important trading centre in the Shāyqiyya region.

The development of the Tijāniyya after the death of al-Huday is not clear. Apparently some of his relatives, especially those living at Wad Ḥāmid south of Shendi, continued his activities.[84] A follower of al-Huday, al-Faḍl al-Nabrī, a descendant of the Awlād Jābir, and his own sons remained loyal to their master's relatives and acted as representatives for the Tijāniyya in the Karafāb area of the Shāyqiyya region.[85]

84 Interview 8.
85 *K. fī dhikrat ... Ghulām Allāh*, ms., pp. 36-7.

6

STRUCTURE AND ORGANIZATION

The Shaykh and his Followers

We distinguished earlier between two types of *ṭarīqa* in the Sudan, the "ancient" and the "new" centralized ones. The ancient orders, namely the Qādiriyya and the Shādhiliyya, were autonomous units, being divided into geographically-defined areas. Each of these had its own independent shaykh and its distinctive chain of transmission of spiritual authority (*silsila* or *sanad*). The only meeting ground between these sometimes antagonistic units was the common homage they paid to the founder. None of these "units", however, seems to have established a proper hierarchy during the Funj period. A shaykh of a *ṭarīqa* unit, who was usually a religious teacher, had no barrier between him and his students and followers. As Dr. Mahmoud Abdalla Ibrahim notes:

> His [the shaykh's] relationship with them [the followers] was direct, face-to-face and personal.[1]

It seems, however, that these autonomous units of the ancient *ṭarīqas* began to adopt a hierarchical structure after the Turco-Egyptian invasion of 1821, which put an end to the Funj Sultanate and imposed a centralized administration.[2] The Turkiyya, despite its limitations and shortcomings, created a form of infrastructure which facilitated the efforts of the various *ṭarīqas* to consolidate their position and to establish an effective administration.

In contrast to the geographically-limited units of the ancient *ṭarīqas*, the new centralized ones, which were consciously missionary in spirit, were widespread. Again, unlike the ancient orders, their followers shared a common devotional life.

The structure of the orders varied, for example in the number of offices and in the names adopted for them. They, however, also had much in common. The heart of every *ṭarīqa* was its shaykh, who was believed

1 Ibrahim, thesis (1980), 134.
2 ᶜAbd al-Majīd (1949), i, 245.

to be divinely authorized to teach and guide people in their worldly life and in the hereafter. In return for his guidance, he received great respect and absolute authority.

All the *ṭarīqas* were agreed that an aspirant who desired a safe arrival at his goal (i.e. perfect knowledge of God) should put himself under the guidance of a shaykh. Muḥammad ᶜUthmān al-Mīrghanī I quotes one of the early Sufi teachers, Abū Yazīd al-Bisṭāmī (d. 260/874-5):

He who has no shaykh, his shaykh is Satan.[3]

Al-Mīrghanī distinguished between three grades (*marātib*, sing. *martaba*) of shaykh. The first and the most sublime was that of *shaykh al-taḥqīq*, namely one who had attained complete spiritual truth and was qualified to guide aspirants towards that goal. The *shaykh al-taḥqīq* had certain attributes, duties and rights (see p. 127). The second category was the *shaykh al-tabarruk*, a general title adopted by al-Mīrghanī for his representatives, who derived their position and *baraka* from him. Al-Mīrghanī stressed the fact that the *shaykh al-tabarruk* was not a true shaykh like the *shaykh al-taḥqīq*, but merely a representative who was to be called *khalīfa*, *nāʾib* or *naqīb*, according to his position in the *ṭarīqa*'s hierarchy. Al-Mīrghanī repeatedly reminded his representatives that they were not independent shaykhs and that they should repress any tendency on the part of the followers to call them such. The *shaykh al-tabarruk* was also expected to remind his adherents that he did not possess *madad* (divine assistance) and that that they were to seek it from the head of the order alone. Al-Mīrghanī concluded his instructions to the *shaykh al-tabarruk* that laxity in observing them would result in expulsion from the order.[4]

The last grade in al-Mīrghanī's category of shaykhs was that of *shaykh al-qirāʾa*, i.e. a teacher of the Quran or other Islamic sciences. Somewhat paradoxically, al-Mīrghanī stated that the *shaykh al-qirāʾa* was to confine his teaching only to the Quran and *ᶜilm* and not to instruct people in Sufism.[5]

Al-Shaykh al-ᶜUbayd w. Badr of the Qādiriyya also distinguished between those shaykhs responsible for teaching and those for spiritual

3 Muḥammad ᶜUthmān al-Mīrghanī, *al-Hibāt al-muqtabasa li-iẓhār al-masāʾil al-khamsa*, in *al-Rasāʾil al-Mīrghaniyya*, 23.

4 Al-Mīrghanī, *al-Zuhūr al-fāʾiqa*, in *al-Rasāʾil al-Mīrghaniyya*, 49-52.

5 *Ibid.*

guidance. Al-Shaykh al-ᶜUbayd referred to the former as *shuyūkh al-taᶜlīm* and to the latter as *shuyūkh al-ifāda wa'l-tarqiya.*[6]

Several titles, apart from shaykh, were used for the heads of *ṭarīqas*. Al-Mīrghanī in addition to *shaykh al-taḥqīq*, also used *murshid*, "spiritual guide", or *murabī*, "educator".[7]

According to al-Mīrghanī, the shaykh of a *ṭarīqa* was usually known for his righteousness and good will. He combined the Sharia with *ḥaqīqa* (Sufism) and was authorized by God and the Prophet to teach and guide people. Moreover:

> If he speaks, it is by God. If he grants supernatural help [*madad*], it is from God. And if he receives it, it is for God.[8]

The shaykh was believed to be divinely guided and incapable of sin. Whatever his actions, even if they were in open contravention of the Sharia, they had to be understood within the context of his infallibility. Thus the term *imām* appears in the biographies of, for example, Shaykh Idrīs w. al-Arbāb and Muḥammad ᶜUthmān al-Mīrghanī I, presumably in the same sense as the infallible *imām* of the Shīᶜa.[9]

The various *ṭarīqas* formulated sets of rules that defined the rights and duties of their members and regulated relations among themselves and with the outside world. These rules reflected the absolute authority of the shaykhs, who expected the total submission of their adherents. Aḥmad al-Ṭayyib and al-Mīrghanī warned the followers of all *ṭarīqas* against arguing with their spiritual masters, for:

> He who says to his shaykh "why?" will never succeed [*sc.* in any endeavour].[10]

The rules also authorized the shaykh to control his follower's private lives. Members were not expected, for example, to marry or travel without first obtaining their master's permission.[11] We saw earlier the

6 Muḥammad b. Aḥmad al-Shaykh al-ᶜUbayd Badr, *K. sirāj al-sālikīn*, Cairo 1920, 8.

7 Al-Mīrghanī, *al-Zuhūr al-fāʾiqa*, 49; *idem*, *al-Hibāt al-muqtabasa*, 28.

8 Al-Mīrghanī, *al-Hibāt al-muqtabasa*, 27.

9 Ibn Ḍayf Allāh (1974), 50; see also Muḥammad ᶜŪthmān b. ᶜAlī al-Mīrghanī, *Majallat al-Fatḥ*, no.1, Ramaḍān 1402/June-July 1982, 10-11.

10 Aḥmad al-Ṭayyib b. al-Bashīr, *al-Ḥikam al-musammā bi'l-nafas al-raḥmānī fī'l-ṭawr al-insānī*, Cairo 1955, 161; see also al-Mīrghanī, *al-Hibāt al-muqtabasa*, 24.

11 Aḥmad b. ᶜAbd al-Raḥmān al-Raṭbī, *Minḥat al-aṣḥāb* ... in *al-Rasāʾil al-Mīrghaniyya*, 66.

case of a Khatmiyya senior representative in the Shāyqiyya region, ᶜAbd al-Ḥalīm al-Naqīb, whose death upon his arrival in Egypt was attributed to his refusal to seek his master's permission to go there.

The adherent was required to show respect to his shaykh; he was enjoined to sit in his presence "as if he were performing the prayers",[12] that is, cross-legged with his hands on his knees. Furthermore, he was not to sit on his master's prayer-mat, to use his private *ibrīq* (water container for ablution), or to lean on his stick. The family of the shaykh was also entitled to respect from the adherents of the order. The belief in the equality of all the members of the Mīrghanī family made them (including those who were living outside the Sudan) beneficiaries of gifts, favours and respect.

Paradoxically, the title "shaykh" was never adopted for the founder of the Khatmiyya or for any member of his family. Al-Mīrghanī was, for instance, referred to as *al-sayyid, al-ustādh, al-imām* and *al-khatim.* Another example is his son al-Ḥasan, whose name was generally preceded by *al-sayyid* and, sometimes, *al-ustādh.*[13]

In the Ismāᶜīliyya *ṭarīqa,* "shaykh" was reserved exclusively to describe Ismāᶜīl al-Walī, the founder of the order. His successor was referred to as *khalīfat al-ustādh* or *al-khalīfa al-mutawalī,* i.e. the *khalīfa* in charge of the order.[14]

Succession to the Office of Shaykh

Eligibility for the office of shaykh was almost entirely by descent from the founder. Succession was almost exclusively in the male line, although it could be transmitted through females. The shaykh usually nominated his successor before his death. The system of succession in the Mikāshfiyya branch of the Qādiriyya in the Gezira was that if the former shaykh had been married to more than one wife, the right of the succession went first to the eldest son of the first wife and then to that of the second wife, and so on. However, heads of *ṭarīqas* were not al-

12 Al-Mīrghanī, *al-Hibāt al-muqtabasa,* 29.

13 For examples, see *Kitāb al-ibāna,* ms., ff. 1, 4, 73 and 77, and al-Mīrghanī, in *Majallat al-Fatḥ,* 2, 5 and 10.

14 Ibrahim, thesis (1980), 148.

ways succeeded by their eldest sons.[15] Several examples have been given of shaykhs who died without nominating their successors; these usually led to serious disputes among the followers.

In the Mahdist period, electing a successor was not simply an internal affair of the order. Upon al-Shaykh al-ᶜUbayd's death in January 1885, his family received a letter from the Mahdi in which he expressed his condolences and appointed Aḥmad, the eldest son of the deceased shaykh, as a successor.[16] Similarly the Mahdi wrote to the descendants of Shaykh Idrīs w. al-Arbāb on 17 Rabīᶜ II 1302/3 February 1885, nominating ᶜAlī Ḥamad Muḥammad Barakāt to succeed their previous shaykh.[17]

The new shaykh was believed to inherit the position, *baraka* and *sirr*, "secret [of the Path]", of his predecessor. This latter belief was further developed by al-Mīrghanī, who called himself *al-khatim*, (the "seal [of all the saints]", *khatim al-awliyāʾ*), and named his first son Muḥammad *sirr al-khatim*. This son is believed to have passed on the same "secret" to his own son, Muḥammad *sirr al-khatim* II.[18]

In the Qādiriyya the new shaykh inherited certain items known as *ālāt* (lit. "tools"), which were considered to be the physical symbols of continuity of authority.[19] The ᶜArakiyyūn branch of the Qādiriyya is an example: the successor usually inherited his predecessor's *sajjāda* or prayer-mat, *rakwa* or *ibrīq* (water container for ablution); a *sibḥa alfiyya*, a large rosary consisting of a thousand *lālōba* seeds from the *hijlīj* (*Balanites aegyptiaca*) tree, and a Y-shaped stick called *shiᶜba*. He also received the *jubba* or gown and *kūfiyya* (headdress) of Ḥabīb Allāh al-ᶜAjamī, al-ᶜArakī's Sufi master, together with the latter's own *jubba*. Furthermore, the new shaykh also inherited a short and thick iron spear known as *umm kraysha*, and wooden shoes or *karkab* to be used in the *dhikr* ritual. Other items included wooden stools (sing. *kakar*), the standards of the order (*rāyāt*), and, finally, the *karrāb* or waist-band.[20]

15 One interesting example of a female who succeeded a deceased shaykh is the daughter of Shaykh ᶜAlī Abū Dilayq. See Ibn Ḍayf Allāh (1974), 72.

16 Abū Salīm, mimeograph (1969), 264-5, no. 535.

17 *Sanad ... al-Muḥammadiyya*, ms., Bergen KH 322. 15/29.

18 NRO, Intel. 2/32/270, p. 15, and Osman, thesis (1978), 22.

19 Ibn Ḍayf Allāh (1974), 323-4, and ᶜAbd al-Majīd (1949), i, 248.

20 Ibn Ḍayf Allāh (1974), 208 and 324.

The Hierarchy

There is considerable variation in the titles adopted by the various orders for the office immediately below that of shaykh. The Khatmiyya used *nāʾib*, "deputy"; his office was considered to be the most important in the hierarchy in that he assisted the shaykh in administering the *ṭarīqa*.[21] The parallel official in the Ismāᶜīliyya was called *wazīr*; in the other *ṭarīqas*, however, he was simply called *khalīfa*.[22]

In the Khatmiyya, below the office of *nāʾib*, came that of *khalīfat al-khulafāʾ*, lit. "the *khalīfa* of the *khalīfas*" or senior *khalīfa*. This office, however, was also adopted by the Ismāᶜīliyya, who borrowed much from the Khatmiyya organizational structure, in the time of Muḥammad al-Makkī b. Ismāᶜīl al-Walī.[23] The *khalīfat al-khulafāʾ* was authorized to lead and supervise all religious and secular activities of the order in his locality. He was also required to hold regular meetings with the *khalīfas* under his jurisdiction and to consult them on the affairs of the *ṭarīqa*. In cases of disagreement, a vote would be taken. However, the *khalīfat al-khulafāʾ* had the casting vote. He also had the right to take decisions on urgent matters without seeking his *khalīfas*' counsel. Another office, which was also peculiar to the Khatmiyya, was *al-nāʾib al-ᶜāmm*, "the deputy-general", whose duty it was to take over in the *khalīfat al-khulafāʾ*s absence or illness.

Below the offices of *khalīfat al-khulafāʾ* and his deputy came the local *khalīfas* or representatives, who were known in the Khatmiyya as *khulafāʾ al-balad* or *al-nāḥiya*. Like other officials, these *khalīfas* were entitled to their followers' respect and obedience. If one of the adherents disobeyed his *khalīfa*, the matter would be raised with the *khalīfat al-khulafāʾ*, who was authorized to reprimand the adherent in the presence of a number of the *khalīfas*. The rest of the followers would be enjoined not to talk or associate with the disobedient follower. The errant adherent, however, would be given a chance to express his sorrow and to repent. If he continued to show no sign of regret, the *khalīfat al-khulafāʾ*

21 Al-Mīrghanī, *Minwāl al-ṭarīqa*, in *al-Rasāʾil al-Mīrghaniyya*, 94.
22 Ibrahim, thesis (1980), 148.
23 Al-Mīrghanī, *Minwāl al-ṭarīqa*, 94, and Ibrahim, thesis (1980), 94-5.

and his assistants would use their authority to expel him from the order.

Below the office of *khalīfa*, the Khatmiyya and the Ismāʿīliyya had the rank of *umanāʾ* (sing. *amīn*), "trustee". Although, in the Khatmiyya, this office came immediately after that of the *khalīfa*, they in fact enjoyed much greater religious prestige in the order. Their duties were limited to the religious affairs of the *ṭarīqa* and they were authorized to investigate the religious performance of all the officials, including the *khalīfat al-khulafāʾ*, and to report any laxity to the head of the order himself. The *umanāʾ* in the Ismāʿīliyya *ṭarīqa* comprised seven officials whose duty it was to inspect the daily performance of devotions. Unlike the *umanāʾ* of the Khatmiyya, those of the Ismāʿīliyya were not authorized to report cases of laxity to the head of the order, but to an official called *naqīb* or to his deputy, *wakīl al-naqīb*.

An office which existed in the hierarchies of all the *ṭarīqas* was that of *muqaddam*. This title, which was originally used by Islamic armies for the leader of a detachment, was borrowed by the Sufi orders. Its place in the different hierarchies, however, varied considerably. In the Tijāniyya, for instance, it ranked immediately below the office of *khalīfa* and the person invested with it was licensed to initiate followers.[24] By contrast, the *muqaddam* of the Khatmiyya was not authorized to preach and his function was administrative. He was required to receive the visitors of the order and to arrange for their food and accommodation.

Another office common to both the Khatmiyya and Ismāʿīliyya was the *naqīb*. Al-Mīrghanī created this office on the analogy with the twelve *naqībs* appointed by the Prophet among the *Anṣār* in Medina.[25] The main function of the *naqīb* was to arrange for the daily prayers and the *dhikr*. He was also expected to exhort the followers to observe the devotions of the order and the prescribed time for their performance. Furthermore, he had to work with the *khalīfat al-khulafāʾ* of his locality and act as a liaison between him and his *khalīfas*. The Ismāʿīliyya adopted the title *naqīb al-umanāʾ* for the head of the board of trustees mentioned earlier. He was assisted by a *wakīl* or deputy and his status was apparently higher than that of the *naqīb* of the Khatmiyya. The *naqīb al-umanāʾ* was not responsible for arranging prayers or sessions of

24 Abun-Nasr (1965), 18.
25 Al-Raṭbī, *Minḥat al-aṣḥāb*, 74-5.

dhikr; that duty was entrusted by Muḥammad al-Makkī to an official called *shaykh al-dhikr*.

The organization of the Khatmiyya included another office unique to it, namely that of the *ḥukkām* (sing. *ḥākim*, "judge"). The incumbents of this office were entrusted with the duty of advising members of the *ṭarīqa* on legal matters and were also authorized to intervene in disputes.

In the Ismāᶜīliyya, the office which came immediately below that of the *amīn* was the *wāᶜiẓ* or preacher. He was responsible for the sanctity of the mosque and for organizing the followers at times of prayers. Another office peculiar to the Ismāᶜīliyya was that of *al-rāᶜī* or protector of the rights or "etiquette" of the *ṭarīqa*. His main duty was to implement disciplinary measures against members found guilty of violating the order's rules.

Among the lower echelons of the organization of the *ṭarīqas* were the attendants of mosques and shrines, *khuddām al-jawāmiᶜ* and *ḥurrās al-aḍriḥa*. The former were required to sweep and clean the mosque in their locality and the latter had to guard the shrines of the order, clean them and be certain that visitors observed the rules of visitation (*ziyāra*). The Khatmiyya authorized its local *khalīfas* to appoint a number of followers as *khuddām hadāyā* (lit. "servants of gifts"), whose duty it was to collect offerings and gifts from the adherents and to make them ready for a personal representative of the head of the order known as *mandūb* or emissary. Female members could hand over their gifts to female voluntary officials known as *ḥuwārāt*. The *khalīfa* had the right to dismiss any of these officials in case of laxity and to replace him or her with a more responsible follower.[26]

The different *ṭarīqas* included some individuals with defined roles who had no fixed rank in the hierarchy. These included, for instance, the *mandūb*, "emissary"; the *mādiḥ*, "chanter of religious songs"; *munshid*, "chanter of canticles", who were also known in the Sammāniyya as *shuᶜār*. Others included the drummers and the bearers of the standards (*rayāt*) of the *ṭarīqas*.[27]

Below the formal hierarchies came the mass of the *murīdīn* or adherents. The titles adopted for these followers again vary considerably. The Qādiriyya, for instance, referred to them interchangeably as *ḥīrān* (sing. *ḥuwār*, lit. "a young camel") or *fuqarāʾ* (sing. *faqīr*, i.e. the one who is

26 Al-Mīrghanī, *Minwāl al-ṭarīqa*, 95, and interview 9.

27 *Kitāb al-ibāna*, ms., f. 27; Qarīb Allāh, thesis (1965), *jīm*, n. 1, and Ibrahim, thesis (1980), 148.

spiritually poor).[28] These titles were also employed for the students of religious schools, reflecting the inseparability of Sufism and orthodoxy in Sudanese Islam. The followers of the Khatmiyya, like those of all the new *ṭarīqas*, were known as *ikhwān* or "brethren".

The adherents of all *ṭarīqas* may be divided into two categories: the adepts and lay-members. The former constituted only a small group in each order. In the Khatmiyya, for example, they were divided into two groups, namely the "elect", *al-khawāṣṣ*, and "the elect of the elect", *khawāṣṣ al-khawāṣṣ*.[29] Some of the adepts lived almost permanently in the centres of the *ṭarīqas*. These were usually known as *mulāzimīn*, a term that implies constant attendance and personal service by these followers for their shaykhs.[30] As we noted elsewhere, the *mulāzimīn* of the Khatmiyya included voluntary attendants called *awlād al-bayt*. The various orders formulated disciplinary rules for their followers. These regulations, as we have seen, defined the relationship between the adherents and their spiritual masters. Our concern here is to discuss how these rules regulated the common life of the followers of a particular *ṭarīqa* and defined their relations with outsiders. This, however, requires an account of the social constituency of the *ṭarīqas*.

The Social Constituency of the Order

Sufism and orthodoxy cannot be divorced from each other in Sudanese Islam. In this sense, the hypotheses of Geertz and Gellner of dividing Islam in Morocco into two opposing models of "orthodox urban" and "mystic rural" are inapplicable to the Sudan.[31] The Sufi brotherhoods, which dominated the Sudanese religious landscape, drew their members from all walks of life, from both town and countryside. These members included sultans and rulers (in the case of Qādiriyya during the Funj period), religious teachers, *qāḍis*, tribal chiefs, merchants, farmers,

28 Ibn Ḍayf Allāh (1974), 283-4, and Osman, thesis (1978), 37.

29 Al-Mīrghanī, *al-Zuhūr al-fā'iqa*, 52-3.

30 *Ibid.*, and Osman, thesis (1978), 32.

31 See further C. Geertz, *Islam Observed. Religious Development in Morocco and Indonesia*, Chicago 1971, and E. Gellner, *Saints of the Atlas*, London 1969; for a critique of their model, see V.J. Cornell, "The logic of analogy and the role of the Sufi Shaykh in post-Marinid Morocco", *IJMES*, xv (1983), 67-93.

nomads, and finally, government officials. Women, children and slaves could also be members; the latter were also frequently given to religious men as an endowment in the Sudan. Women did not participate in the ceremonies of their *ṭarīqa*, but demonstrated their allegiance by attending the rituals as observers and making gifts to the head of the order and members of his family. The adherence of fathers to the *ṭarīqas* often determined that of their children; many families in the Sudan have been loyal to their *ṭarīqas* for generations.[32]

Most of the senior representatives in the *ṭarīqas* were drawn from families and individuals of superior religious and social status. Occasionally, people of humble origin were also appointed. On one occasion the founder of the Khatmiyya invested a slave owned by a woman with the office of *khalīfa*.[33]

Sufi *ṭarīqas* in the Sudan and elsewhere in the Muslim world played significant unifying roles by cutting across the social backgrounds of their followers and bringing them together into associations of mutual help. A follower, by virtue of his initiation, could seek advice, hospitality and assistance from his fellows, especially in cases of hardship.[34] Muḥammad ᶜUthmān al-Mīrghanī I, exhorted his adherents to live together as brothers:

> the brotherhood of the *ṭarīqa* is similar to that of kinship.[35]

He also urged his followers to visit each other frequently and to exchange letters with their fellows in other areas. Furthermore, all the followers were expected to be present at the centres of the order on the last Friday of every month, to meet and participate in a communal recital of the *rātib*, a collection of devotions composed by the founder.[36]

The *ṭarīqas* may be divided on the basis of their attitudes towards outsiders into two categories, tolerant and intolerant. Thus the founder of the Khatmiyya asserts:

32 Trimingham (1949), 206, and Osman, thesis (1978), 45.

33 *Kitāb al-ibāna*, ms., ff. 13-14.

34 Al-Mīrghanī, *al-Hibāt al-muqtasaba*, 32; Trimingham (1971), 225-6; M. Gilsenan, *Saints and Sufis in Modern Egypt. An Essay in the Sociology of Religion*, Oxford 1973, 88, and Osman, thesis (1978), 47.

35 Al-Mīrghanī, *al-Hibāt al-muqtabasa*, 32.

36 Al-Mīrghanī, *Minwāl al-ṭarīqa*, 94.

I remind you, O community of aspirants, that our *ṭarīqa* is the greatest of all *ṭarīqas* and the closest to God.[37]

Despite this, he recognized the spiritual validity of other orders and permitted his followers to combine their devotions with those of his own. He repeatedly reproached all those who did not acknowledge *ṭarīqas* other than their own. Al-Mīrghanī also allowed his adherents to venerate and visit living and dead shaykhs of other orders and urged them to behave with modesty and respect towards their followers.[38] We have already seen how the adherents of the Khatmiyya endeavoured to put these instructions into practice (see, for instance, pp. 80-1).

By contrast, an intolerant *ṭarīqa* such as the Tijāniyya considered its followers as an exclusive and superior class of Muslims and its shaykh, Aḥmad al-Tijānī, the seal of the whole body of saints. It did not permit pluralism of allegiance nor did it allow its devotions to be combined with others; disobedience would lead to a state of disbelief (*kufr*). Again in contrast to other *ṭarīqas*, the Tijāniyya insisted that its followers should not visit non-Tijāniyya shaykhs living or dead.[39]

The *ṭarīqas*, as part of their disciplinary code, also regulated the dress of their affiliates. Certain ways of dress became associated with particular orders. The Qādiriyya, for instance, usually wore patched *jubbas* and coarse garments. Shaykh Khōjalī, however, who combined the Qādiriyya with the Shādhiliyya, used to dress, following the example of Abū'l-Ḥasan al-Shādhilī, in fine clothes. The *Ṭabaqāt* states that when it was remarked to Shaykh Khōjalī that the Qādiris only wore *jubbas* and patched clothes, he replied,

My clothes proclaim to all human beings "We are in no need of you" but their clothes say, "We are in need of you".[40]

The founder of the Khatmiyya expressed his dislike of the patched *jubbas* and the dress of the dervishes. He frequently urged his followers to appear decently dressed. He also established the tradition of bestow-

37 Al-Mīrghanī, *al-Hibāt al-muqtabasa*, 26.

38 Ibid., 33, and al-Raṭbī, *Minḥat al-aṣḥāb*, 73.

39 *Shurūṭ al-ṭarīqa al-Tijāniyya*, ms., NRO, Misc., 1/22/246. See also Abun-Nasr (1965), 39; C.E. Farah, "Social implications of a Sufi disciple's etiquette", in *Proceedings, VIth. Congress of Arabic and Islamic Studies*, ed. F. Rundgren, Uppsala/Leiden 1972, 52, and K. Dwyer, *Moroccan Dialogues. Anthropology in Question*, London 1982, 45.

40 Ibn Ḍayf Allāh (1974), 193-4.

ing a special dress upon his senior representatives. Currently, the followers of the Khatmiyya prefer to wear turbans and *jallābiyyas* with special collars. There is a general belief among the Khatmiyya that this type of *jallābiyya* was introduced from the Ḥijāz and that it was first worn by al-Ḥasan al-Mīrghanī, hence his nickname Abū Jallābiyya.[41] Another example is the followers of the Aḥmadiyya Idrīsiyya, who in a slight variant of the practice of the *Anṣār* of the Sudanese Mahdi, usually leave the loose ends of their turbans, known as *ᶜadhabāt* (sing. *ᶜadhaba*), hanging down behind their heads.[42]

Each *ṭarīqa* had its own standard or flag, *rāya*, which, as was shown in the previous chapter, was prominently displayed in the internal and public ceremonies of the orders. The shapes, colours and inscriptions written on the flags of the different *ṭarīqas* vary considerably. These flags, however, shared some common characteristics. For example, they usually bore the *shahāda*, or the formula "There is no God but God; Muḥammad is the messenger of God", the name of the *ṭarīqa* and that of its founder.[43]

The flag of the Khatmiyya is, however, very elaborate. It consists of four colours: red, black, white and green. These different colours apparently demonstrate the all-embracing nature of the order's doctrinal position. When this flag came into use is not easy to establish. Some informants claimed it was introduced by the founder. Others stated it was made by his son and successor al-Ḥasan al-Mīrghanī and it bears the formula:

Lā ilāh illā Allāh; al-amān al-amān
Muḥammad rasūl Allāh al-sulṭān al-sulṭān;

which is an extract from one of his famous devotional works.[44]

41 *Kitāb al-ibāna*, ms., f. 67, and interview 11.

42 Al-Aḥmadī, *Kitāb al-Īḍāḥ*, ms., f. 3, and interview 22, and al-Tuhāmī, *Risālat al-Dīn al-naṣīḥa*, ms., ff. 83-7.

43 NRO, Intel., 2/32/270, p. 53; SAD, Durham, 195/7/2, *The Magzub Tarika in the Sudan*, by Naum Shukeir (Naᶜūm Shuqayr); see NRO, Intel., 2/32/263, and Barclay (1964), 186.

44 Interviews 10 and 11.

Institutions Linked to the Orders

The *ṭarīqas* drew their local representatives mainly from among established religious teachers. Consequently, the different religious centres of these holy men, *khalwas, zāwiyas, masīd* and *masjīds*, came to be integrated into these *ṭarīqas*. The *Ṭabaqāt*, as Professor Yūsuf Faḍl Ḥasan has noted, fails to make clear the difference in function of these various institutions.[45] This is presumably due to considerable functional overlapping.

Because it was widespread and because of the social role of its central figure, the *faqīh*, the most important *ṭarīqa*-linked institution was the *khalwa* or Quranic school.[46]

Although the usual meaning of *khalwa* is the place where the Sufi mystic goes into retreat, in the Sudan it describes the place where the Quran and Islamic sciences were taught. The origin of this usage lies in the nature of Islam in the Sudan. The holy man who propagated Islam in most of the country combined *ᶜilm* or the esoteric Islamic sciences with Sufism and naturally used the same place to teach both.

Teaching in a *khalwa* was at two levels: the first, known as *nār al-Qurʾān*, "the fire of the Quran", was devoted to the memorization of the Quran; the second, *nār al-ᶜilm*. They were so called because the students studied by the light of a fire.[47] The *faqīh*, who was, of course, the central figure, was assisted in teaching the students of the first level by several *ᶜurafāʾ* (sing. *ᶜarīf*). These were students who had finished the first level but did not intend to proceed to the second.[48] There was no age limit for admission to the *khalwa*. The pupils, irrespective of their age, were divided into the seniors, *al-ḥīran al-kibār*, and juniors, *al-ḥīran al-ṣighār*. Moreover, no fees were paid by these students to their teacher.[49]

45 Ḥasan (1975), 83.

46 Trimingham (1949), 117, and Mohammed Omer Beshir, *Educational Development in the Sudan, 1898-1956*, Oxford 1969, 6.

47 Ibn Ḍayf Allāh (1974), 282 and 460, and Muṣṭafā, thesis (1977), 103.

48 ᶜAbd al-Majīd (1949), ii, 35.

49 Ibn Ḍayf Allāh (1974), 308-9, for the adult Shaykh ᶜAbd al-Qādir b. Idrīs (who was illiterate) joining the *khalwa* of Shaykh al-Aᶜsar of Nūrī. See

The physical structure may be illustrated by the *khalwa* of al-Ghurayba, just south of Kūrtī.[50] This *khalwa* was attached to the mosque of the village which has been in existence since as far back as 888/1483-4. It consists of the *faqīh*'s private room, a row of cells for the pupils, two classrooms called respectively *Qurʾāniyya*, where the Quran was taught, and *ʿalāmiyya*, where *ʿilm* was taught. The former is, however, known in the Gezira as *al-jāmiʿa*, a term that denotes congregation.

Outside the *khalwa* there was an open area known as *al-buqʿa* (lit. "the spot"), where the early morning and evening lessons were taught. The *khalwa* has a special room with a shelf hanging from the ceiling known as *al-kabas* (*al-rōshān* in the Gezira) for keeping the wooden tablets (sing. *lawḥ*) of the students at the end of their lessons. Because of its social function, the *khalwa* also has rooms for visitors and travellers.

Some *khalwas* - as, for instance, those of Ḥasan Muḥammad Balōl in Qarrī, al-Ḥasan al-Mīrghanī at Qubbat Khōjalī and Aḥmad al-Jaʿalī at Kadabas - had grottos (sing. *ghār*) built by these holy men for individual worship.

The *khalwas* in the Sudan have never had a standard curriculum. It was the individual *faqīh* who made up the syllabus and chose those texts that appealed or were accessible to him. Most of the books derived from the curriculum of al-Azhar in Cairo, although a number of Sudanese scholars wrote and taught their own commentaries. In addition to the Quran, *tajwīd*, *tawḥīd*, *fiqh* and Sufism were also taught.[51]

The *khalwa* of al-Ghurayba possessed a considerable number of printed books and manuscripts. The latter included *Sharḥ al-Tatāʾī ʿalā Khalīl*, a commentary on the *Mukhtaṣar* of Khalīl b. Isḥāq by

---

also Abdalla al-Tayyib, "The changing customs of the riverain Sudan", *SNR*., iii, 1964, 13; Beshir (1969), 7; Aḥmad al-Bīlī, *al-Taʿlīm fī'l-khalwa fī'l-Sūdān*, Khartoum 1974, 3; Ḥasan (1975), i, 84, and Ibrahim, thesis (1980), 54.

50 The following description is based on a visit to al-Ghurayba in September 1982. See also al-Bīlī (1974), 12, and al-Muʿtaṣim Aḥmad al-Ḥājj, "*al-Khalāwī fī'l-Sūdān, nuẓumuhā wa-rusūmuhā ḥattā nihāyat al-qarn al-tāsiʿ ʿashar*", MA thesis, Omdurman Islamic University 1982, 112.

51 Ibn Ḍayf Allāh (1974), 283-4, 351-2 and 360. See also Qarīb Allāh, thesis (1965), 277-86, and Ḥasan (1975), i, 135-40. For the curriculum of al-Azhar, see Manṣūr ʿAlī Rajab, *al-Azhar bayn al-māḍī wa'l-ḥāḍir*, Cairo 1946, 46-9.

Muḥammad Ibrāhīm al-Tatāʾī; *Sharḥ al-kabīr ᶜalā Khalīl*, one of two commentaries on the *Mukhtaṣar* by Tāj al-Dīn Bahrām al-Damīrī (d. 1402); and, finally, *Sharḥ ᶜalā Khalīl* by ᶜAlī Muḥammad al-Ajhūrī (d. 1560). The *Sharḥ al-Tatāʾī* was, according to its colophon, copied for the *khalwa* in 963/1555-6 by a certain Aḥmad b. Ibrāhīm b. al-Ṭayyib al-Maṭarāwī; the *Sharḥ Bahrām* was copied by Muḥammad Sirāj al-Dīn b. ᶜAlī al-Ḥājj Bilāl, (a son of the founder of the *khalwa* and a great-grandfather of al-Naqīb, a senior representative of the founder of the Khatmiyya in the Shāyqiyya region) in 971/1563-4, and the *Sharḥ al-Ajhūrī* by Muḥammad b. ᶜĀmir al-Dalḥamūnī in 1122/1710-11.[52]

Despite these books, the *faqīh* at al-Ghurayba usually taught from memory, dictating the syllabus, lesson by lesson, to the students who wrote it down on their wooden tablets. After they had memorized the lesson, the tablets were wiped clean.[53]

The ties of the *khalwa* of al-Ghurayba with the Khatmiyya were established when Muḥammad ᶜUthmān al-Mīrghanī I visited al-Dabba in 1814-15 (see above p. 59). Because of its position as a centre for the *ṭarīqa*, the latter's ceremonies and rituals were held at the *buqᶜa* and the students were taught its devotions. Thus the famous *mawlid* (see Glossary) of the founder, *al-Asrār al-rabbāniyya*, commonly known as *al-mawlid al-ᶜUthmānī*; his poem in praise of the Prophet, *al-Nūr al-barrāq fī madḥ al-nabī al-miṣdāq*; and his collection of prayers, the *rātib*, known as *al-Anwār al-mutarākima*, were taught to the students, who had finished the first memorization of the Quran, in exactly the same way as the other works.[54]

The *khalwa* had and has other functions in addition to its religious and educational ones. It played a social role by serving as a centre of hospitality with a resthouse for visitors, travellers and traders. The *Ṭabaqāt* gives several names of holy men in the Shāyqiyya region who were famous for their hospitality. These included Muḥammad w.

52 The mss. are in the possession of the current (1982) *faqīh* and *khalīfa*, Aḥmad ᶜAbd al-Raḥmān Muḥammad Khayr, known as al-Ṣayyādī.

53 Interview 6. Compare the Ḥamadtūiyāb *khalwa* at Nūrī, see Ibn Ḍayf Allāh (1974), 284. On the significance of memory in Islamic education, see further D. Eickelman, "The art of memory: Islamic education and its social reproduction", *Comparative Studies in Society and History*, xx/4, (1978), 485-516, and *idem*, *The Middle East. An Anthropological Approach*, New York 1981, 240 and *passim*.

54 Interviews 9, 11 and 20.

ᶜAdlān al-Shāyqī of Tanqāsī and two members of the Ḥamadtūiyāb holy family of Nūrī, namely ᶜAbd al-Raḥmān b. Madanī, known as Abū Nīrān, and Madanī b. Muḥammad al-Nāṭiq.[55] The *Ṭabaqāt*, however, gives greater information on the *khalwas* in the central Sudan. The *khalwas* of Shaykh Idrīs w. al-Arbab and his son Ḥamad, for example, used to serve respectively 60 and 120 plates of food every day. The same source also gives a striking description of how food was served at the *khalwa* of Ḥasan w. Ḥassūna at the end of a day in Ramadān. The process of having the food served by 240 slave girls and women, who were well-dressed and adorned with gold and ivory, shows the wealth of this holy man and also demonstrates his well-organized system.[56]

The *khalwa* was a place of refuge or sanctuary too; the community of Dabbat al-Fuqarāʾ, for instance, enjoyed such a status during the Funj regime.[57] It also functioned as a place for settling disputes, hearing complaints, and issuing *fatwas* or legal opinions. The *khalwa* was moreover a medical centre where people with physical and psychological illnesses could come for treatment. The various means adopted for curing these illnesses included writing amulets, preparing *miḥāya* (i.e. water used for washing some Quranic verses off a wooden tablet and then given to the sick person to drink) and the making of incantations (sing. *ᶜazīma*).[58]

The account above shows the multi-functional character of the *khalwa*. However, it also raises the question of how the institution was financed. Since this matter is discussed in detail below (pp.146-8) it is sufficient to mention here that the *khalwa*'s financial and other support derived from several sources. These included, for example, gifts from the pupils' parents, grants of land from the community, grants from political authorities, pious endowments from well-to-do families and individuals, *zakāh* and, finally, offerings in fulfilment of vows (*nadhr*).

55 Ibn Ḍayf Allāh (1974), 286, 354 and 360.

56 *Ibid.*, 57, 142-3 and 158.

57 T. Krump, *Hoher und Fruchtbarer Palm-Baum des Heiligen Evangelij*, Augsburg, 1710 (translation by Jay Spaulding), typescript, 254.

58 Ibn Ḍayf Allāh (1974), 283-4. For examples of prescriptions for curing illnesses, see Bergen NO 145. 7/1 to 7/3, *waṣfas* for the cure of semi-paralysis or hemiplegia, wind and migraine. See also Trimingham (1949), 119-20; Osman, thesis (1978), 90, and Abdullahi el Tom, "Religious men and literacy in Berti society", Ph.D. thesis, St. Andrews University 1983, 59-111.

Another *ṭarīqa*-linked institution in the Sudan and elsewhere in the Muslim world is the *zāwiya*. The original meaning of this term is the corner of a building where a Christian monk used to have a cell for his private worship. The term, however, was adopted by Muslims for a *ṭarīqa* centre where prayers and religious activities were performed. But the *zāwiya*, which is smaller and distinct from the mosque could not house the congregation for the Friday prayers, which had to be held in a Friday mosque (*jāmiᶜ*).[59]

Physically, a *zāwiya* could be no more than a single room or, as in the case of the Sanūsiyya's *zāwiyas* in the Libyan desert, a very elaborate group of buildings.[60] In addition to their religious function, the *zāwiyas*, like the *khalwa* in the Sudan and the *khanqāh* elsewhere, had social and educational functions.[61]

These roles may be illustrated by the *zāwiyas* of the Khatmiyya, especially in the eastern Sudan. Al-Mīrghanī expressed his concern about the ignorance of the people of the Tāka region and felt it was his mission to educate them.[62] He thus established several *zāwiyas* in the region and taught in them himself.[63] Trimingham argues that the *zāwiyas* of the eastern Sudan were used as centres for advanced Islamic sciences where students were provided with lodgings. He reserves the term *khalwa* for the schools where young children memorized the Quran.[64]

The various *ṭarīqas* also operated within the framework of the mosque. This religious institution has been in the Sudan and elsewhere in the Muslim world not only a place of worship but also a centre for teaching *ᶜilm*.[65] The combination of Sufism and *ᶜilm* by a number of

59 *Shorter Encyclopedia of Islam*, 658-8; *ERE*, x, 717-20; M. Lings, *A Moslem Saint of the Twentieth Century. Shaikh Ahmad Al-ᶜAlawi*, London 1961, 13, argues that "To translate *zāwiyah* by 'monastery' would no doubt lead to misunderstanding, none the less the monastic orders are the nearest equivalent in Christianity to the Sufi brotherhoods in Islam, although the Sufis are not celibates". See also Trimingham (1971), 18.

60 Evans-Pritchard (1949), 16-7, and N.A. Ziadeh, *Sanūsiyyah. A Study of a Revivalist Movement in Islam*, Leiden 1958, 69.

61 Trimingham (1971), 18.

62 Al-Mīrghanī, *al-Zuhūr al-fāʾiqa*, 48, and Voll, thesis (1969), 123.

63 *Kitāb al-ibāna*, ms., ff. 33-4.

64 Trimingham (1949), 118.

65 *Shorter Encyclopedia of Islam*, 330-53, and Aḥmad Shalabi), *History of Muslim Education*, Beirut 1954, 48.

Sufi teachers led many mosques to be automatically integrated into the orders. The mosque of the Ḥamadtūiyāb of Nūrī, for instance, functioned as an important Qādiriyya and, at a later stage, Khatmiyya centre in the region. Other examples are the mosques of the ᶜIrāqāb and Kawārīr religious clans of Nūrī which became significant local centres of the Khatmiyya.[66] Further examples are the mosques of al-Kurū and Duwaym wad Ḥājj, which were instrumental in propagating the teachings of Ibn Idrīs through his student, Ibrāhīm al-Rashīd.[67]

The *ṭarīqas* generally tended to operate within a number of institutions apart from the mosque. In contradistinction, the sons and descendants of Ibn Idrīs used the latter as their main centre for teaching. In this they were probably maintaining Aḥmad's practice, since, according to Ibrāhim al-Rashīd, he used the mosque as his centre.[68]

The *ṭarīqas* also made use of another centre of learning, namely the *masīd*. This term, which denotes the place where *ᶜilm* was taught, is merely a dialectical variant of the classical word *masjid*, "mosque"; the term is not unique to the Sudan but was also common in Morocco and Sicily.[69]

The most celebrated *masīds* in the Sudan were those of Aḥmad w. ᶜĪsā and his son Ibrāhīm, in the Gezira. The former was integrated into the Khatmiyya at the time of al-Mīrghanī's visit to the Gezira in 1817-18. Another example is the *masīd* of al-Shaykh al-ᶜUbayd w. Badr of Umm Ḍubbān which propagated the Qādiriyya. This *masīd*, like that of Kutrānj, was a comprehensive religious centre with *khalwas*, lodgings and a kitchen. Physically and functionally, the Sudanese *masīd* echoes the Egyptian *khānqāh*.[70]

No *masīds* comparable to these of the Gezira existed in the Shāyqiyya region. This is also true for Dār Fūr, where the *masīd* was a

66 Bergen NO 163.8/6; *Manāqib al-sayyid ᶜAlī al-Mīrghanī* (1390/1970), 10, and interviews 7, 19 and 20.

67 *K. fī dhikrat al-sayyid Ghulām Allāh*, ms., f. 43, and interview 2.

68 Al-Hajrasī (1314/1915-6), 91, and Karrār, thesis (1977), 94.

69 ᶜAbd al-Majīd (1949), i, 82, n. 1; al-Amīn (1395/1975), 14 n. 3, and al-Ḥājj, thesis (1982), 123.

70 ᶜAbd al-Majīd (1949), iii, 23-5; al-Amīn (1395/1975), 23; Idris Salim El-Hassan, "On Ideology. The Case of Religion in Northern Sudan", Ph.D. thesis, University of Connecticut 1980, 119. On the Egyptian *khanqāh*, see Tawfīq al-Ṭawīl, *al-Taṣawwuf fī Miṣr ibbān al-ᶜaṣr al-ᶜŪthmānī*, Cairo 1946, 39-40, and Trimingham (1971), 18.

simple physical structure, often no more than a small shed (*rākūba*) or a shady tree.[71] In some areas, its function was more social than religious.[72]

A holy man, whether a member of a *ṭarīqa* or not, plays a number of different roles within his community. His sanctity and its value to the community is, however, believed to survive or transcend his death. His *baraka* is believed to emanate from his grave and the places where he lived.[73] It is presumably because of the belief in *baraka* and its transcendence of death that each *ṭarīqa* developed its own cult of saints. The tombs or *qubbas* (lit. "dome"), of these holy men were and still are a conspicuous feature of the Sudanese religious landscape. According to a recent study, the region of Dongola alone has more than ninety-nine such tombs.[74] After the saint's death his tomb became an integral component of his community's life.[75] Some saints, however, enjoyed religious prestige over a wide geographical area. Although al-Ḥasan al-Mīrghanī was buried in Kasala, his name was invoked for help in places as far away as Nūrī in the Shāyqiyya country.[76]

The tombs were usually built by sons or followers; the tomb of Ibrāhīm al-Rashīd was built by Muḥammad al-Dandarāwī, one of his students, although it was renovated several times by other followers of al-Rashīd or through votive offerings from ordinary people.[77] It also used to receive a costly covering for the grave (*kiswa*) from Ibrāhīm al-Rashīd's nephew, Shaykh Muḥammad Ṣāliḥ, in Mecca.[78]

The *Kitāb al-ibāna* notes that the Khatmiyya, for instance, had a number of lesser shrines known as *baniyyāt* (sing. *baniyya*, lit. "a small building"). These were usually rectangular buildings of mud, with or without a roof. An example of such a shrine is that of Umm Kalthūm, a daughter of al-Mīrghanī, in Shendi.[79]

71 O'Fahey (1980), 120, and al-Ḥājj, thesis (1982), 125.
72 El Tom, thesis (1983), 25.
73 Trimingham (1949), 144-5.
74 ᶜAbd Allāh (1978) mimeograph, 40.
75 J.S. Trimingham, *Islam in Ethiopia*, London 1952, 247-8.
76 Aḥmad ᶜUthmān Ibrāhīm, *Min ashᶜār al-Shāyqiyya*, Khartoum 1965, 14-5, 52-3 and 66.
77 Interview 2.
78 Bergen NO 155. 7/11.
79 *Kitāb al-ibāna*, ms., f. 17; see also ff. 12 and 18.

The *ṭarīqas* also had another type of shrine known as *bayān* (lit. "revealing"), meaning where a particular holy man had revealed himself. Such shrines were usually enclosed with flags (*rāyāt* or *bayāriq*) and became places of local pilgrimage.[80]

The *qubbas* and other shrines, like all religious centres, were honoured as places of refuge and sanctuary. People also used them as places where they could deposit their goods for safekeeping.[81]

The tombs of famous holy men and women had caretakers to clean them, to take charge of visitors and to collect gifts and offerings. Muḥammad ᶜUthmān al-Mīrghanī I exhorted his followers to visit tombs frequently because that would remind them of the Day of Judgement. He also urged them to help the *ḥāris* of the shrine by observing the rules of "visitation", *ziyāra*. Obviously, the visitor should avoid laughing or sitting on the grave.[82] He should also recite the *Fātiḥa* for the soul of the deceased holy man. He should then make his petition and conclude his visit by making a gift in cash or in kind (known as *zuwāra*) to the saint.[83] The tombs and shrines also served as places where ceremonies for the anniversaries of the birth (*mawlid*) and death (*ḥawliyya*) of the holy man were held.

Hierarchy: The Naḍīfāb Community of Abū Rannāt Island, a Case Study

The Naḍīfāb were a holy clan who lived on Abū Rannāt Island in the Shāyqiyya region from about the beginning of the seventeenth century until 1917, when the encroachment of the Nile forced them and the inhabitants of the island to desert it and move to live at Tanqāsī al-Ruways, just opposite on the eastern (locally known as the west) bank. The island, and indeed the new settlement at Tanqāsī al-Ruways, occupied a strategic position, being just north of the famous Shāyqiyya region trading-centre of Tanqāsī, commonly known as Tanqāsī al-Sūq.[84]

80 Trimingham (1949), 143, and Ibrāhīm (1965), 56.

81 MacMichael (1922), ii, 287.

82 Al-Mīrghanī, *al-Fatḥ al-mabrūk*, 41.

83 J.W. Crowfoot, "Wedding customs in the northern Sudan", *SNR*, v, 1922, 15; Trimingham (1949), 144, and Ibrahim, thesis (1980), 119.

84 Shuqayr (1903), i, 86.

The pedigree of the Naḍīfāb shows that they were of Ṣawārda origin and that their ancestor Ṣārid was a brother of ᶜAbd al-ᶜAzīz, the "founding father" of the Maḥas.[85] According to oral tradition, as part of the general Maḥas diaspora, which began in the sixteenth century, members of the Ṣawārda began to migrate to the Shāyqiyya region which, apart from the fertility of its soil, was known for its hospitality to men of learning. These immigrants included Shaykh Ḥidirbī, who settled at Abū Dōm near modern Marawī, and *al-ḥājj* ᶜAmāra, who chose to live at al-Kurū. Both of these holy men married locally and received gifts of land and date-palms.[86] The descendants of these two religious teachers were to become the prominent representatives of the Khatmiyya in the Shāyqiyya area.[87]

Our main concern here is with the descendants of *al-ḥājj* ᶜAmāra, who lived, died and was buried at al-Kurū. Six of his great-grandsons, known as the Awlād Fāṭima, played a considerable religious role in the area. Among these was Ibrāhīm, nicknamed al-Naẓīf, "the clean", known colloquially as al-Naḍīf, the "founding father" of the Naḍīfāb. His cousin Shaykh Jiqaydī was the founder of the Awlād Jiqaydī, who, like several other religious families on Abū Rannāt Island, operated under the umbrella of the Naḍīfāb.

The Naḍīfāb used the mosque as their religious centre. It was not until about the latter half of the seventeenth century that Muhammad b. Ibrāhīm al-Naḍīf established the *khalwa* of the Naḍīfāb on the island. He was famous for his mastery of the seven alternative readings(*riwāyāt*) of the Quran, hence his title *qārī al-riwāyāt al-sabᶜa*.[88] *Al-ḥājj* Muḥammad established at his *khalwa* the tradition of issuing *ijāzas* (certificates) to the students who had successfully completed the memorization of the Quran and had mastered the rules and methods of its intonation. For instance, he issued an *ijāza*, dated Rajab 1160/July-

85 *Nasab al-Naḍīfāb*, ms., Bergen NO 130. 6/5, and MacMichael (1922), ii, 24.

86 Interviews 5 and 10.

87 *Ibid.*; see also NRO, Misc., 1/27/283, Endowment (*waqf*) of land by *faqīh* Ibrāhīm b. *al-ḥājj* Muḥammad, for his sons and their issue, and 1/27/460, *Ṣulḥ*, concerning the appointment of Muḥammad Ṣāliḥ al-Naḍīf as *khalīfa* of the Naḍīfāb, 4 Muḥarram 1265/30 November 1848.

88 NRO, Misc., 1/27/314, Marriage contract (*ṣadāq*) for Fāṭima bt. Ḥamad b. Muḥammad, from her husband, Muḥammad b. Muḥammad Ṣāliḥ al-Naḍīf, 10 *Rabī*ᶜ I 1279/ 5 September 1862. and interview 5.

DIAGRAM 7. *The Naḍīfāb*

Muḥammad al-Ṣāridī
|
Khamīs
|
Ḥammād
|
Idrīs
|
Faraj
|
al-ḥājj ᶜAmāra
|
Ibrāhīm (al-Naḍīf)
|
al-ḥājj Muḥammad
|
Ibrāhīm

al-Shaykh	Muḥammad Khayr (d. Muḥarram 1265/ October 1848)	Muḥammad Ṣāliḥ (d. Shawwāl 1289/ December 1872)
	al-Naḍīf	

August 1747, to his son, *faqīh* Ibrāhīm, certifying that he had memorized the Quran perfectly.[89]

It was in the time of Ibrāhīm's grandsons, Muḥammad Khayr and Muḥammad Ṣāliḥ, and their cousin Muḥammad Hammād w. Jiqaydī, that the ties of the Naḍīfāb with the Khatmiyya were established. The founder of the Khatmiyya sent them *ijāza*s from al-Dabba in 1814-15, appointing them *khalīfas* without actually meeting them (see p. 59). The community of Abū Rannāt elected Muḥammad Khayr as the senior *khalīfa* of the order.[90] He also acted as the leader of the Naḍīfāb clan. As a *ṭarīqa* representative, however, he was under the jurisdiction of the ᶜIrāqāb of Nūrī.

89 Bergen NO 139.6/14, *Ijāza;* from Muḥammad b. *al-faqīh* Ibrāhīm, *nasl al-ḥājj* ᶜAmāra, for his son, Ibrāhīm, *Rajab* 1160/July-August 1747.

90 Interviews 5 and 10.

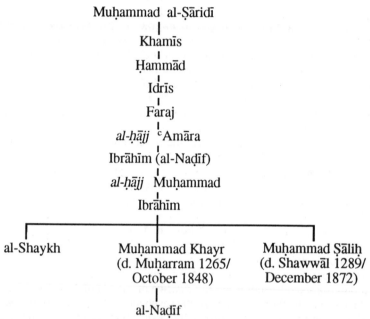

Muḥammad Khayr al-Naḍīf continued as the supreme *khalīfa* for about thirty-three years, until his death on 3 Muḥarram 1265/ 29 October 1848. When the news of his death reached the Khatmiyya regional headquarters at Nūrī, a delegation headed by *khalīfat al-khulafāʾ* ᶜAbd al-Ḥamīd Muḥammad Ṣāliḥ al-ᶜIrāqī and consisting of his brother *khalīfa* ᶜAbd al-Raḥmān and his uncle *khalīfa* al-Ṣādiq ᶜAbd al-Ḥamīd al-Aḥmar al-ᶜIrāqī, travelled to Abū Rannāt to offer their condolences to the Naḍīfāb.[91] On the following day, *khalīfat al-khulafāʾ* ᶜAbd al-Ḥamīd al-ᶜIrāqī and his companions held a meeting with the Naḍīfāb to discuss the question of electing a successor to the deceased *khalīfa*.

The discussion, however, grew long and, like all succession disputes, culminated in the division of the Naḍīfāb into two factions. One of these declared that the *khalīfa* had to be al-Naḍīf, a son of the deceased *khalīfa*. The other, however, supported Muḥammad Ṣāliḥ, a brother of the late *khalīfa*. Al-ᶜIrāqī, his companions and a number of mediators (*ajāwīd*) suggested that the successor should be Muḥammad Ṣāliḥ. This was because the late *khalīfa* used to entrust him with the affairs of the mosque and the Friday prayers, as well as those of the two *ᶜīds*. The *khalīfat al-khulafāʾ* and their mediators concluded their argument by saying that al-Naḍīf was not Muḥammad Ṣāliḥ's equal in that respect. The two groups, finally, agreed to the proposal, and Muḥammad Ṣāliḥ al-Naḍīf was acknowledged as the *khalīfa* of the order and head of the Naḍīfāb.

According to oral sources, the civil administration of Abū Rannāt in the time of Muḥammad Ṣāliḥ was under the village head (*shaykh al-balad*) Ṭāḥa w. Muḥārī, who was a follower of the Khatmiyya and connected by marriage with the ᶜIrāqāb of Nūrī.[92]

Muḥammad Ṣāliḥ al-Naḍīf, was, apart from his duties as a Khatmiyya representative and head of the Naḍīfāb, the *maʾdhūn* (the official authorized to perform marriages) of the island.[93]

Ṣāliḥ al-Naḍīf's period of office saw al-Ḥasan al-Mīrghanī's visit to Abū Rannāt. The Naḍīfāb, like other followers of the Khatmiyya, showed their loyalty to the order by granting estates and date-palms to members of the Mīrghanī family. They also used to collect gifts to send to the headquarters of the order in the eastern Sudan.

91 The following is based on NRO, Misc., 1/27/460.
92 Interviews 10 and 19.
93 NRO, Misc., 1/27/381, Marriage contract.

The Naḍīfāb also performed the traditional role of holy men in their community. They were leaders in prayer, teachers, mediators, healers and they issued legal opinions.[94] For their role as religious teachers, the Naḍīfāb received gifts from their pupils' parents. These, according to the economic and social status of the donors, usually consisted of date-palms or the produce of a *hōḍ* (see Glossary) or more from the *sāqiya*-land. The *khalwa* (Quranic school) and the mosque were also endowed with charitable gifts (*waqf*). The people of Abū Rannāt, like those of other communities in the region, used to endow the *khalwa* and mosque with a collective *waqf* of land known as *ᶜurāḍa*. This was a strip of fertile land extending along the bank of the Nile and lying immediately above the *jarf* land (the slope of the Nile bank down to the main water course).[95]

As Spaulding notes, holy men usually possessed landed properties that were scattered outside their own localities. This is further illustrated by the example of Muḥammad Ṣāliḥ al-Naḍīf, who possessed estates in al-Zūma, al-Kuray and Abū Dōm.[96]

The Naḍīfāb, like other holy men, also possessed a number of slaves.[97] The *Ṭabaqāt* too provides several examples of holy men and religious institutions that received *waqf*s of slaves. *Al-ḥājj* Saᶜīd, a grandson of Dāʾūd b. ᶜAbd al-Jalīl who invited the Qādirī Shaykh Tāj al-Dīn al-Bahārī to visit the Sudan (see pp. 21-2), had a dream in which the Prophet ordered him to build a mosque for Dafᶜ Allāh, a nephew of ᶜAbd Allāh al-ᶜArakī. *Al-ḥājj* Saᶜīd shipped stone from the village of Bānkiyū, built the mosque and endowed it with twelve slaves, male and female, and five *faddāns*.[98] It was usually slaves and students who worked the agricultural land of religious teachers.[99]

The holy man was also entitled to a portion (usually a *ḥod*) of the produce of the *sāqiya*-land. This was because of the belief that he could protect the *sāqiya* and oxen that pulled it against the evil eye or evil

94 NRO, Misc., 1/27/413, Settlement of a dispute concerning the inheritance of the property of Muḥammad Ṣālih al-Naḍīf, 26 *Jumādā* I 1291/11 July 1874.

95 Interviews 10 and 11.

96 Jay Spaulding, *The Heroic Age of Sinnār*, East Lansing 1985, 254, and NRO, Misc., 1/27/413.

97 NRO, Misc., 1/27/413.

98 Ibn Ḍayf Allāh (1974), 209.

99 *Ibid.*, 283.

underworld spirits.[100] In the Maḥas area, however, the share of the holy man in the produce of the *sāqiya* was called in the Nubian language *atī mashī*. A farmer who had, for instance, one ox was expected to give one eighth of the sorghum, wheat and barley that his *sāqiya* had produced.[101] Moreover, holy men also received the *zakāh* (Islamic tax) on livestock and that on the produce of agricultural land.[102]

According to Spaulding, the wealth of the Naḍīfāb may be seen in the fact that Muḥammad Ṣāliḥ al-Naḍīf offered his wife bridewealth of 1,000 *riyāls* at a time when the average among well-to-do families was 700.[103] It is presumably because of their wealth and their gifts that ᶜAbd Allāh al-Maḥjūb al-Mīrghanī, in a letter of 29 Dhū'l-Qaᶜda 1324/14 January 1907, addressed the Naḍīfāb as "the people of pious endowments" (*ahālī al-awqāf*).[104]

On 24 Shawwāl 1280/3 April 1864, Muḥammad Ṣāliḥ wrote his will, in which he entrusted his son Muḥammad with the affairs of the mosque, leading the five daily prayers, the *dhikr* and the teaching of the Quran. He also authorized his son to lead Friday prayers and those of the two *ᶜīds*. This, however, had to be done in consultation with his other brothers and the notables of the community, to avoid unnecessary disputes. Muḥammad Ṣāliḥ also in the same document transferred the rights to his share in a considerable number of date-palms scattered among different *sāqiyas* (agricultural units) in the region in order to use their produce to meet some of the expenses of accommodating guests and students. He continued by endowing the mosque with a number of date-palms, "for the sake of God and his Prophet".[105]

The Naḍīfāb maintained close relations with a number of religious families in the region with whom they also shared property. These families included the ᶜIrāqāb and the Ḥamadtūiyāb of Nūri, the family of

100 Muḥammad Ibrāhīm Abū Salīm, *al-Sāqiya*, Khartoum 1980, 188-9 and 191.

101 *Ibid.*, 169.

102 Ibn Ḍayf Allāh (1974), 58-60, and Abū Salīm (1980), 170.

103 See Spaulding (1985), 254-8. He refers to NRO, Misc., 1/27/428.

104 NRO, Misc., 1/27/396, Letter from ᶜAbd Allāh Maḥjūb al-Mīrghanī, to *khalīfa* Muḥammad ᶜAlī al-Naḍīf, 29 *Dhū'l-Qaᶜda* 1324/14 January 1907.

105 NRO, Misc., 1/27/413.

Ḥidirbī at Abū Dōm near modern Marawī and the Misaykāb family of religious men and traders of Tanqāsī al-Ruways.[106]

The Naḍīfāb also maintained a famous scholar of the ᶜIrāqāb who lived on Tulbunāb Island (now part of Tanqāsī), namely Muḥammad al-Ḥasan al-Tuḥāmī. An adherent of a *ṭarīqa* was expected to seek his shaykh's permission before performing certain acts. A letter from Muḥammad Ṣāliḥ al-Naḍīf to al-Tuḥāmī dated 21 Rabīᶜ I 1283/3 August 1866 shows how the latter's failure to seek permission when he intended to travel to Egypt resulted in misunderstanding. Al-Tuḥāmī, however, wrote back to the Naḍīfāb apologizing for what had happened, saying that he had abandoned the idea of travelling. He concluded by affirming that he would not undertake any act in the future without seeking their consent.[107]

Muḥammad Ṣāliḥ's period in office saw the death of al-Ḥasan al-Mīrghanī and the transfer of the headship of the order to Muhammad ᶜUthmān II. The Naḍīfāb loyalty to the Khatmiyya did not wane; the new head, like his predecessor, received great respect and gifts.[108] Shortly afterwards, on 21 Shawwāl 1289/22 December 1872, Muḥammad Ṣāliḥ died and was succeeded as a *khalīfa* by his son, Muḥammad, who remained in office until his death on 7 Dhū'l-Qaᶜda 1295/2 November 1878. His period saw the death of the Khatmiyya senior representative in the Shāyqiyya region, ᶜAbd al-Ḥamīd b. Muḥammad Ṣāliḥ al-ᶜIrāqī, and the transfer of office of *khalīfat al-khulafā'* to his nephew Muḥammad ᶜUthmān b. Muḥammad Khayr b. Muḥammad Ṣāliḥ al-ᶜIrāqī.[109]

Muḥammad b. Muḥammad Ṣāliḥ was succeeded by his brother al-Shaykh. It was during his tenure in office that the Mahdist revolution broke out in 1881. He survived the upheavals that followed, dying on 5 Ṣafar 1319/13 July 1901, shortly after the beginning of Condominium rule in the Sudan.[110]

106 NRO, Misc., 1/27/383; 1/27/392, Letter from Aḥmad Muḥammad ᶜUthman al-ᶜIrāqī, to *khalīfa* (Aḥmad) Muḥammad Ṣāliḥ al-Naḍīf and others, 24 Rajab 1321/16 October 1903, and 1/27/460.

107 NRO, Misc., 1/27/374, Letter from Muḥammad Ṣāliḥ al-Naḍīf and his sons to al-Ḥasan b. *al-khalīfa* al-Tuhāmī Bān al-Naqā, 21 *Rabiᶜ* I 1283/3 August 1866.

108 Interview 10.

109 Interview 19.

110 NRO, Misc., 1/27/413.

7

INITIATION AND RITUAL

The Stages of Initiation

Doctrinal differences between the orders were minimal; most of their teachings were based on the Quran and the *sunna*.[1] What makes a *ṭarīqa* distinctive is the form and method of its rituals and practices, such as initiation and *dhikr*, or remembrance of God.

Since it is impossible to treat here all the rituals and practices of the various orders in detail, a comparison between those of the Qādiriyya, the dominant order in the central Sudan, and the Khatmiyya, the main *ṭarīqa* in the Shāyqiyya region, is attempted instead.

This section begins with an account of the rituals of initiation and investiture. It then gives an analytical description of both the private and communal *dhikrs*. The section, however, also discusses other rituals and practices such as the "spiritual retreat" (*khalwa*) and *ḥawliya*, the celebration of the anniversaries of the deaths of shaykhs and members of their families.

The initiation or, as it is variously called, *akhdh al-ᶜahd*, "the taking of the compact"; *akhdh al-wird*, "the taking of the litany"; *akhdh al-ṭarīq* or *al-ṭarīqa*, "the taking of the order"; and, finally, *akhdh al-bayᶜa*, "the taking of the oath of allegiance", was in theory obligatory for all those who wished to join the orders.[2]

The formulae of initiation for the different *ṭarīqas* show slight variations in wording and structure. In the Qādiriyya, the neophyte and his shaykh would perform the ablutions and sit facing Mecca, as if they were about to pray. The shaykh would then ask the neophyte to repent of all his previous sins, in accordance with the Quranic verse (60:12). The neophyte would then perform two *rakᶜas* and kneel before his shaykh resting his knees against the latter's. The shaykh, holding the neophyte's right thumb, would ask him to repeat after him the

1 Karrār, thesis (1977), 21-44.
2 Trimingham (1971), 81-2.

ta^cawwudh, i.e. the formula, *a^cūdhu bi-llāh min al-shayṭān al-rajīm*, "I take refuge in God from the Devil, the cursed"; the *basmala*, and the *Fātiḥa*. Having completed these, they continued by reciting the formula of *al-istighfār*, i.e. "I ask forgiveness of the Mighty God"; and then said "May God bless our master Muḥammad", twice.

The shaykh would then ask the aspirant to close his eyes and open "the eyes of his heart" and concentrate on the meaning of the litanies which he was about to dictate to him (*yulaqin*). Having received the litanies, the aspirant would declare his acceptance of the act of initiation by saying,

> I have accepted Allah as my God, Islam as my religion, Muḥammad as the Prophet and Messenger and our shaykh as a guide.

He then would recite the *āyat al-mubāya^ca* (Quran 48:10) and kiss his shaykh's hand.

The initiation would conclude with a joint recital of the *Fātiḥa* by the shaykh and his *murīd*; the aspirant had now become an adherent.[3]

In the Khatmiyya, however, the aspirant was required to perform a ritual ablution on a Wednesday and perform two *rak^cas*. While performing the first, he was to recite the *Fātiḥa* and the *Kāfirūn* (Quran:109) and during the second the *Fātiḥa* and *al-Naṣr* (Quran:110).

The aspirant would then, as in the Qādiriyya, sit before his shaykh and they would clasp their right hands. The shaykh would ask the aspirant to repeat after him the following formula:

> In the name of God, the Compassionate, the Merciful. May God bless our master Muḥammad, his family and companions and grant him salvation. O God, I have repented before you and have accepted my master, sayyid Muḥammad ^cUthmān al-Mīrghanī, as a shaykh in this life and in the hereafter. O God, confirm my love for him and his order in this life and the one to come, by the right [*ḥaqq*] of our master Muḥammad and the right of the *Basmala* and the *Fātiḥa*.

The aspirant then recited *al-^cAṣr* (Quran:103).

The shaykh repeated silently,

> May God confirm upon you righteousness, patience and the Muḥammadiyya order,

3 Nūr al-Dā'im (1954), 103.

and declared to the aspirant that he had been accepted as an adherent of the Khatmiyya.[4]

The *murīd* would then be instructed by word of mouth (*talqīn*) in the *dhikr* of the order. The process of receiving the *dhikr* was, however, a gradual one. The new initiate would receive only a simple form of *dhikr* and a minor version of the basic litanies of the order known as *al-asās al-ṣaghīr*.[5] This latter is a collection of prayers and invocations based almost entirely on the Quran and the sayings of the Prophet.

The *murīd* who demonstrated his seriousness would be allowed to receive an advanced form of *dhikr* known as the *dhikr* of the *khawāṣṣ*, or the "chosen". This required the same rituals as in the first initiation. The *murīd* performed his ritual ablution on a Wednesday and the two *rakᶜas*, reciting the same Quranic chapters as in the initiation. He would then read the oath of allegiance (*bayᶜa*) to the founder of the order and recite the *Fātiḥa* silently. This having been completed, the *murīd* repeated the *tahlīl*, i.e. the formula of "There is no God but God", 7,000 times.

According to the same source, the *murīd* was to wash himself ritually again and recite the *Ikhlāṣ* (Quran:112) 100,000 times. On the following Wednesday, he would perform a ritual ablution and repeat the *basmala* 12,000 times.

Having completed these introductory rituals (*muqaddimāt*), the *murīd* would go to his shaykh, who would dictate the *dhikr* and instruct him in the major basic litanies of the Khatmiyya known as *al-asās al-kabīr*.[6]

Another ritual which, like initiation, entailed the swearing of an oath of allegiance to the head of the order was the investiture, *tanṣīb* or

4 Muḥammad ᶜUthmān al-Mīrghanī, *Majmūᶜ al-awrād al-kabīr*, Cairo (1358/1939), 125.

5 Muḥammad ᶜUthmān al-Mīrghanī I composed two collections of litanies and invocations known as *al-Asās al-ṣaghīr* and *al-Asās al-kabīr*. The term *asās* (lit. "foundations") means the basic litanies of the order. The minor version, *al-Asās al-ṣaghīr*, was intended for all who joined the order. The other version, *al-Asās al-kabīr* or the major basic litanies, is a very elaborate version of the former. It consists of three phases (*awjuh*, lit. "faces"): *ṣughrā*, *wusṭā* and *kubrā* and was intended for the chosen adherents (*al-khawāṣṣ*); see *K.al-ibāna*, ms., f. 91, and *al-Nafaḥāt al-Makkiyya*, in *Majmūᶜat al-nafaḥāt al-rabbāniyya*, 43.

6 Al-Mīrghanī (1358/1939), 62-3.

takhlīf. This ceremony took place when a *murīd* who had attained advanced knowledge in the affairs of the order was invested with an office within its hierarchy.

The investiture rituals were more elaborate in the Qādiriyya than in other orders. The *Ṭabaqāt* confirms that the Qādiriyya used to invest their new *khalīfas* with the *khirqa* (frock) or the *jubba.*[7] Moreover, the Yaᶜqūbāb branch of the Qādiriyya made use of some of the Funj symbols of royal authority, such as the horned-cap (*al-ṭāqiyya umm qiraynāt*) and the *kakar* (or wooden stools) in the ceremony of investiture.[8]

Although Tāj al-Dīn al-Bahārī, who introduced the Qādiriyya into the Sudan, did not issue written *ijāzas* to his initiates, this practice was later introduced by some Sudanese Sufi shaykhs. ᶜAbd Allāh al-ᶜArakī, for instance, appointed his brother Muḥammad, known as Abū Idrīs, as a *khalīfa*, invested him with the *khirqa* and issued him an *ijāza* certifying that he was authorized to initiate people into the Qādiriyya.[9]

By contrast, the ritual of investiture in the Khatmiyya order was simple. The Khatmiyya, like all the new *ṭarīqas*, did not adopt the custom of investiture with the frock or the *jubba*; indeed the founder of the order had expressed his distaste for the *jubba* or patched clothes. The *murīd* elected to an office in the hierarchy would simply sit before his shaykh as in the normal initiation ceremony and read the oath of allegiance (*bayᶜa*) described above and then receive his *ijāza.*[10]

However, al-Mīrghanī did appoint a number of *khalīfas* and issued them *ijāzas* without even without meeting them. He relied entirely on the reputation of these religious figures for learning and righteousness.

7 Ibn Ḍayf Allāh (1974), 66-7.

8 A.J. Arkell, "Fung origins", *SNR*, xv/2, 1932, 201-250; Trimingham (1949), 219, and al-Shāṭir Buṣaylī ᶜAbd al-Jalīl, *Maᶜālim taʾrīkh Sūdān Wādī'l-Nīl,* Cairo 1955, 119.

9 Ibn Ḍayf Allāh (1974), 66-7.

10 Interview 11; see Appendix B for an *ijāza* issued by Muḥammad ᶜUthmān al-Mīrghanī.

The Ritual Life

The most important ritual in the *ṭarīqas*, however, was, and still is, the *dhikr*. The original meaning of this term as it appears in the Quran[11] is "remembrance" (of God). In the *ṭarīqas*, however, the term has acquired a specialized meaning, namely the repetition of God's names and attributes in a variety of special ways.

Each *ṭarīqa* had, and has, two types of *dhikr*: the *dhikr al-waqt*, "the *dhikr* of the time", which was performed after the regular five daily prayers, and a communal one known variously as the *dhikr* of the circle (*al-ḥalqa*), the *ḥaḍra*, "presence", or *layliyya* (sessions of *dhikr* on specified nights).

Sufi shaykhs repeatedly stressed the significance of *dhikr* and exhorted their adherents to observe it. One example is Ibn Idrīs, who says of the *dhikr*:

> The supreme nourishment of my soul is the remembrance [*dhikr*] of God. Even to give it up for a moment, is impossible for me.

As an analogy, Ibn Idrīs cites the fishes which must live in water and die if they leave it.[12] His student al-Mirghanī equally urged his followers to perform the *dhikr* and quoted a number of Prophetic sayings that praise its practice, especially within the "circle" or *ḥalqa*.[13]

As we have seen, the Qādiriyya in the Sudan and elsewhere in the Muslim world was a widely-diffused order and its various branches did not share a common devotional life. For this reason, we shall use the Kabbāshī branch of the Qādiriyya, which had and has a number of followers in the Shāyqiyya region, as an example to illustrate the role of *dhikr* among one Qādiriyya branch.

Ibrāhīm al-Kabbāshī, who was a prolific Sufi writer and poet, composed a number of prayers and invocations to be repeated a prescribed number of times by his followers, individually or collectively, after the

11 For example, Quran, verses 18:24; 33:41; 73:8, and 76:25. See also Abū ᶜAbd Allāh Muḥammad al-Ghazālī, *Iḥyāʾ ᶜulūm al-dīn*, Cairo (n.d.), iv, 595-8, and L. Gardet, "Dhikr", *EI*², ii, 223.

12 Ibn Idrīs, *al-ᶜIqd al-nafīs*, 22-3.

13 Al-Mīrghanī, *al-Hibāt al-muqtabasa*, 35. See also al-Raṭbī, *Minḥat al-aṣḥāb*, 76.

regular daily prayers. These included, for instance, three prayers for the Prophet, entitled *Fatḥ al-futūḥ*, *Sirr al-asrār* and *Ṣalāt al-irshād*. He also composed five litanies (*aḥzāb*) based on the Quran and the sunna:

1) *Ḥizb al-jallāl,*
2) *Ḥizb al-anwār,*
3) *Ḥizb al-dāʾira,*
4) *Ḥizb al-ḥamd,* and
5) *Ḥizb al-salām.*[14]

However, he used to urge his followers to repeat the following form of *dhikr* after the morning and sunset prayers:

1) *al-Istighfār* (asking for God's forgiveness): 7 times.
2) *Bismillāh al-karīm wa-lā ḥawla wa-lā quwwa ilā biʾllah*: 3 times.

Al-Kabbāshī, like other Qādirī shaykhs, also had longer litanies that were repeated with the aid of a thousand-bead rosary, *misbaḥa alfiyya.* These included, for example, the following:

1) the *basmala,* to be repeated 1,500 times.
2) the *Tahlīl* (the formula of, "There is no God but God"). This formula could be repeated any number of times between 12,000 and 71,000, depending mainly on the capacity of the adherent.
3) a prayer for the Prophet known as *al-Ṣalāt al-ummiya* (lit. "the illiterate prayer"), to be repeated 1,000 times.[15]

By contrast to the Qādiriyya, the Khatmiyya like other new *ṭarīqas,* shared a common devotional life. The founder of the order and several of his sons and descendants were prolific writers on a wide range of Islamic subjects. These works included collections of devotions known as *musabbaʿāt.* They were so called because they were divided according to the seven days of the week. These *musabbaʿāt* were further divided into five sections in accordance with the five daily prayers.[16]

It has to be noted, however, that this order of devotional prayer was not unique to the Khatmiyya. It is likely that al-Mīrghanī borrowed it

14 Al-Kabbāshī, *Inshiqāq al-qamar,* 32-3. These devotional works are preserved in ms. in possession of al-Kabbāshī's family at the village of al-Kabbāshī.

15 This prayer was widely used in the Sudan. It is called *al-ummiyya* because the adjective *ummī,* "illiterate", appears in its formula, which reads as follows, "O God, bless our lord Muḥammad, the illiterate (*ummī*) Prophet". See Ibn Ḍayf Allāh (1974), 292, and interview 21.

16 Al-Mīrghanī (1358/1939), 77-96.

from his master, Ibn Idrīs.[17] The same system was also copied by Ismāʿīl al-Walī, al-Mīrghanī's former student.[18] Al-Mīrghanī I, like other Sufi shaykhs,[19] stated that half of the *dhikr* of this *ṭarīqa* was "remembrance in the heart", *dhikr bi'l-qalb*, and the other half, "upon the tongue", *bi'l-lisān*. He added that he had based his *dhikr* on "the remembrance in the heart" of the Naqshbandiyya and that "upon the tongue" of the Qādiriyya and Shādhiliyya.[20]

It is clear in the literature of the Khatmiyya that the minor *asās* (*ṣaghīr*) constituted a common factor in all litanies that were repeated after the five daily prayers.[21] Unlike other orders in the Sudan, the Khatmiyya had a wide range of *dhikr al-waqt*. These may be divided into three categories. The first includes the works of the founder, his sons and descendants.[22] The second comprises the devotions which the founder had received from his teacher, Ibn Idrīs. These latter included the formula:

> There is no God but God, Muḥammad is the Messenger of God in every glance and breath as much as the knowledge of God can contain.[23]

We stated earlier that Ibn Idrīs claimed that, of all saints, God had bestowed the above *dhikr* upon him alone. Ibn Idrīs also urged his student al-Mīrghanī, when in the Sudan, to teach it to those he initiated. Al-Mīrghanī also kept up the tradition of reciting and teaching his teacher's litanies, known as *aḥzāb al-tajalliyāt al-ilāhiyya*, after he had divided them into sections (sing. *subʿ*).[24]

The third category of the Khatmiyya's devotions included works by other Sufis which were universally used. We have already seen the example of the *Dalāʾil al-khayrāt*. Other examples are the two famous litanies of al-Shādhilī known as the *Ḥizb al-baḥr*, "litany of the sea", and the *Ḥizb al-barr*, "litany of the land",[25] and a prayer for the Prophet

17 Karrār, thesis (1977), 21-8.

18 Ibrāhīm, thesis (1980), 155-6.

19 Nūr al-Dāʾim (1954), 84-6 and 90.

20 *al-Nafaḥāt al-Makkiyya*, in *Majmūʿat al-nafaḥāt*, 7.

21 *Kitāb al-ibāna*, ms., f. 91, and al-Mīrghanī (1358/1939), 126.

22 Voll, thesis (1969), 153-61 and *passim*; Ḥasan (1975), i, 138-40, and Karrār, thesis (1977), 143-54.

23 *Sanad al-ṭarīqa al-Khatmiyya*, ms, Bergen, No 126. 6/1.

24 *Kitāb al-ibāna*, ms., f. 98.

25 Muḥammad ʿUthmān al-Mīrghanī, *Majmūʿat fatḥ al-rasūl*, Cairo 1367/1948, 213-26.

commonly known as the *Ṣalāt Ibn Mashīsh.*[26] Further, the Khatmiyya, like both the Qādiriyya and the Idrīsiyya, recited a litany known as *al-Ḥizb al-sayfī*, "the litany of the sword", which is attributed to ᶜAlī, the Prophet's cousin.[27] Finally, although the Khatmiyya had its own *mawlid* or litany for the birth of the Prophet, its followers also used to recite that of al-Barzanjī (d. 1766) at the celebration of the Prophet's birthday (*mawlid al-nabī* or *al-mawlid al-nabawī*).[28]

Since it is impossible to describe all of these devotions in detail, a set of those repeated after the sunset prayers (*al-maghrib*) may serve as an example. This set consisted of the repetition of the following formulae:

1) "There is no God but God. Alone and has no associate. He is the Kingdom and His is the Praise; and He has power over all things": 10 times.

2) the minor *asās*.

3) the *rātib*, known as *al-Anwār al-mutarakima*.

4) the prayer for the Prophet, known as *al-Ṣālat al-ummiyya*: 10 times.

5) the *Istighfār*: 100 times.

6) the *Tahlīl*: 2,000 times.

The *murīd*, however, had to say after every 100 times the *tahlīl* in the form, "Muḥammad is the Messenger of God in every glance and breath as much as the knowledge of God can contain."

Having completed the litanies listed above, the *murīd* then had to recite the *Ikhlāṣ* (Quran:112) a 1,000 times, followed by the formula: *Ḥayy, Qayyūm*, ("Living, Eternal"; names of God), the same number of times. The *murīd* concluded by repeating another prayer for the Prophet, known as *al-ṣalāh al-dhātiyya*, a 100 times.[29]

26 This was a famous prayer for the Prophet written by Muḥammad ᶜAbd al-Salām b. Mashīsh al-Maghribī (d. 625/1228), (see Trimingham (1971, 47-8 and 87) on which ᶜAbd Allāh al-Maḥjūb, a grandfather of the founder of the Khatmiyya, wrote a commentary (*sharḥ*) entitled *al-Nafaḥāt al-qudsiyya min al-ḥaḍra al-ᶜAbbāsiyya fī sharḥ al-ṣalāt al-mashīshiyya* (see GAL, ii, 386, S II 523), *Majmūᶜat al-nafaḥāt al-Makkiyya*, 129.

27 ᶜAbd al-Majīd (1949), i, 147, and Karrār, thesis (1977), 27.

28 Interview 10. This *mawlid* of al-Barzānjī was widely used in the Muslim world, see Trimingham (1971), 206 and 208.

29 Al-Mīrghanī (1358/1939), 48-9.

The founder of the Khatmiyya also composed litanies and supplications to be recited by individuals or collectively during the five holy months (*al-ashhur al-ḥurm*), i.e. Muḥarram, Rajab, Shaᶜbān, Ramaḍān and Dhū'l-ḥijja. These litanies were short formulae built upon a pattern of phrases, each to be repeated a 1,000 times.[30]

The doctrines of the various Sufi orders were directly or indirectly influenced by Shīᶜī ideas and practices. This may be illustrated by the fact that the *ṭarīqas*, like the Shīᶜa, used to hold a special ceremony on the anniversary of the death of al-Ḥusayn b. ᶜAlī, the grandson of the Prophet, on the tenth Muḥarram (ᶜĀshūra).[31] Thus the founder of the Khatmiyya formulated a number of supplications known as *adhkār ᶜāshūra*, each to be repeated thirty-three times after the sunset prayers.[32] The Khatmiyya also had a specific set of invocations to be said after the *ṣalāt al-tarāwīḥ* (prayers performed during the nights of Ramaḍān).[33]

Each *ṭarīqa* had two types of *dhikr*, the *dhikr al-waqt* and the *dhikr al-ḥalqa*. In both the Qādiriyya and the Khatmiyya, the latter was said aloud. The *dhikr* sessions of the Qādiriyya were generally known as *layliyya* rather than *ḥaḍra*, and were, like those of the Khatmiyya and other orders, held on Sunday and Thursday evenings.[34]

The *layliyya* of the Qādiriyya was usually held at the order's local centre; the participants performed their ablutions and sat in a circle in the middle of which the flag of the order had been raised. The *muqaddam* opened the *layliyya* which began with the recitation of the *mawlid*. Since the Qādiriyya did not possess their own *mawlid*, they recited that of al-Barzanjī.[35] The participants then stood up to perform the *dhikr*, which consisted of seven short formulae each of which formed a phase or "round" of *dhikr*, *martaba* or *ṭabaqa*.

30 *Ibid.*, 130.

31 Interviews 11 and 22.

32 Al-Mīrghanī (1358/1939), 71-1.

33 *Ibid.*, 72-4.

34 Trimingham (1971), 206, and interview 21. Although the *layliyyas* and *ḥaḍras* were, and are, actually held on Sunday and Thursday evenings they are called *laylat al-Ithnayn* (Monday night) and *laylat al-Jumᶜa* (Friday night) meetings because the Muslim day starts immediately after sunset; see Trimingham (1949), 215.

35 Trimingham (1971), 206 and 208, and interview 21. This *mawlid* is also used by another order that does not possess its own *mawlid*, namely the Aḥmadiyya Idrīsiyya; interview 22.

Having completed one *ṭabaqa*, a group of four or five *munshids* (chanters) would enter the circle and begin to perform various other types of *dhikr*, the most famous of which was the *dhikr al-ṣayḥa* (literally "shout") a cry for God's succour. The way this *dhikr* was performed is interesting; the *munshids*, standing at a distance from each other, chanted with a special intonation the verses of a particular religious ode (*qaṣīda*).[36] According to one source, the *dhikr al-ṣayḥa* originated among the Yaᶜqūbāb branch of the Qādiriyya, which later changed its spiritual allegiance to the Sammāniyya under the influence of Aḥmad al-Ṭayyib (see p. 46).[37] This is presumably why this type of *dhikr* was also adopted by the Sammāniyya, where those who performed it were commonly known as *Shuᶜār*.[38]

The followers of the Kabbāshī-ᶜArakī branch of the Qādiriyya among the Shāyqiyya used to recite, during the intervals between the different phases (*ḍarb*) of the *dhikr*, some religious poems composed by, for example, al-Busīrī and ᶜAbd al-Raḥīm al-Burᶜī, whose works were widely used throughout the Muslim world.[39] The adherents of this Qādirī branch also used to read the poems of a number of Sudanese Sufi poets. These included the works of Ibrāhīm al-Kabbāshī, who composed a number of songs of praise (*madāʾiḥ*) to the Prophet. He also wrote a *madīḥ* in which he devoted a considerable section to an account of the Prophet's ascent to Heaven (*al-miᶜrāj*). This poem was (and still is) recited by the followers at the annual celebration of the Prophet's ascent on the eve of 27 Rajab (*laylat al-miᶜrāj*).[40]

Other poems that were used by this branch included those of Abū Nafīsa and al-ᶜUbayd Muḥammad Ṣāliḥ.[41]

One of the main characteristics of the Qādirī *dhikr* was the employment of musical instruments. It is not clear when this custom, which provoked criticism from the *ᶜulamāʾ*,[42] became established in the Sudan. According to one source, musical instruments were introduced during the Funj period by a Qādirī shaykh, one Salmān al-Ṭawwālī,

36 Qarīb Allāh, thesis (1965), p. *jīm*; Ḥasan (1972), 39.

37 Al-Bashīr (1976), 25.

38 Qarīb Allāh, thesis (1965), p. *jīm*.

39 NRO, 7/1/10, p. 12, Abū Salīm; see also Trimingham (1971), 24 and 44, and interview 21.

40 Al-Kabbāshī, *Inshiqāq al-qamar* (1971), 24-6; interview 21.

41 Interview 21.

42 Trimingham (1971), 195.

known as al-Zaghrāt (standard Ar. *al-ẓaghrād*, meaning the one who utters trilling sounds).[43]

The same source, however, states that it was in fact shaykh ᶜAbd al-Qādir Abū Kisāwī (1818-81), a student of the Qādirī shaykh al-ᶜUbayd w. Badr, who consolidated the use of musical instruments in the *dhikr*. He, for instance, employed African drums (*nōba*) and tambourines (*ṭār*), whose use was eventually borrowed not only by other Qādirī branches but also by other orders such as the Ismāᶜīliyya.[44]

It is clear from a study of the Mikāshfiyya branch of the Qādiriyya in the Gezira that another African musical instrument, namely the *ṣājāt* (flat pieces of iron), was utilized in the *dhikr* of the Qādiriyya.[45] These instruments were presumably adopted by the Qādiriyya, the oldest order in the Sudan, to attract followers who were used to drums and rythmic music.

It is evident from the *Ṭabaqāt* that the Qādiriyya had two types of communal *dhikr* that differed in the method of ejaculating the names of God, the *karīr* and the *razīm*. The former was a heavy type of *dhikr* with a special method of intonation known as *karīr*, or the sound made by a pigeon; by contrast, the *razīm* was a lighter and quieter form of *dhikr*.[46]

The *dhikr* sessions of the Qādiriyya, like those of the Khatmiyya (and indeed all *ṭarīqas*), apart from the regular *layliyya*, were also held on a number of religious occasions. These included, for example, the *ḥōliyyas* (cl. Ar. *ḥawliyya*) or anniversaries of the deaths of the head of the branch and of famous members of his family. On such occasions, the *dhikr* was usually held near the tomb of the deceased holy man or woman. Other occasions were the eve of the 27 Rajab (*laylat al-miᶜrāj*), commemorating the Prophet's ascent to Heaven; the eves of the two *ᶜīds* (Ramaḍān Bayram and Kurban Bayram); and the *mawlid* or the anniversary of the birth of the Prophet, 12 Rabīᶜ I.[47]

The congregational *dhikr* of the Khatmiyya, the *layliyya* or more commonly the *ḥaḍra*, like that of the Qādiriyya, was held twice a week, on Sunday and Thursday evenings.[48] Each of these sessions was called

43 Al-Bashīr (1976), 26. On the *zaghrāt*, see Ibn Ḍayf Allāh (1974), 219-22.

44 Al-Bashīr (1976), 26, and Ibrahim, thesis (1980), 156-7.

45 Osman, thesis (1978) ,130.

46 Ibn Ḍayf Allāh (1974), 328.

47 Interview 21.

48 Al-Mīrghanī (1358/1939), 74.

ḥaḍra, because of the belief that the Prophet would be present whenever it was held.

The Khatmiyya used to hold their *dhikr* at the *buqᶜa* of the Quranic school (*khalwa*), in the *zāwiya* or in the mosque. The participants would form a circle or a number of rows according to the space available.[49] It was the *naqīb*'s task to arrange the *dhikr* and to ensure the observance of its rules by the followers. These rules, known as *ādāb al-dhikr*, required that those who wished to participate were, as we have seen with the Qādiriyya, in a state of complete ritual cleanness. They also had to keep their eyes closed and bear their shaykh's image in their mind throughout the different phases of the *dhikr*.

The same source shows that the participant was also expected to perfume himself. Further, the place of the *ḥaḍra* was to be fumigated with incense and the flag of the order, as in the Qādiriyya, was to be raised in the middle.[50]

Since Trimingham has given a detailed description of the *layliyya* of the Khatmiyya our description here is intended only to complement his. The structure of the *ḥaḍra* of the Khatmiyya was similar to that of the Qādiriyya. A fundamental difference is that the Khatmiyya recited their own *mawlid*, commonly known as *al-mawlid al-ᶜUthmānī*. The founder of the order states in the introduction to his *mawlid* that he saw a vision in which the Prophet ordered him to compose a *mawlid* rhyming in *hāʾ* and *nūn*. Al-Mīrghanī adds that the Prophet promised to be present whenever it was recited and that invocations would be answered by God when the section on the Prophet's birth and the conclusion of the *mawlid* were recited.[51]

After reciting the *mawlid*, the khalīfa would open the *dhikr*, which would begin while the participants were sitting on the floor. They would, however, stand up while repeating the names of God.[52]

The *Majmūᶜ al-awrād* lists several *dhikr* for the use of the Khatmiyya. The most frequently used, however, were those selected and arranged by al-Ḥasan al-Mīrghanī. These were:[53]

49 Al-Raṭbī, *Minḥat al-aṣḥāb*, 76, and interview 19.

50 Al-Raṭbī, *Minḥat al-aṣḥāb*, 75-7, and interview 19.

51 Muḥammad ᶜUthmān al-Mīrghanī, *Mawlid al-nabī, al-musammā al-asrār al-rabbāniyya*, Cairo 1350/1931, 7-8.

52 Interview 19.

53 Al-Mīrghanī (1358/1939), 74.

1)	*Lā Ilāh illā Allāh, al-amān al-amā Muḥammad rasūl Allāh, al-Sulṭān al-Sulṭān*	10	times
2)	the *Tahlīl*	50	"
3)	"There is no Adored save God"	50	"
4)	"There is no Ever-living save God"	50	"
5)	"He is God"	100	"
6)	"Allāh"	500	"
7)	"God is Eternal"	100	"
8)	"Living, Eternal"	154	"

As in the Qādiriyya, the Khatmiyya *dhikr* session was marked by series of intervals during which were recited songs of praise to the Prophet composed by al-Mīrghanī, members of his family or other adherents.[54] Songs of praise to the founder and members of his family were also chanted.

Having completed the repetition of the various formulas of *dhikr*, a group of chanters known as *musafinūn* entered the *ḥalqa* and walked around solemnly (*qadla*) chanting some poems commonly known as *safā'in* (sing. *safīna*, lit. "ship"). These were composed mainly by the founder and his son, Jaᶜfar.[55]

After the *safā'in*, the participants in the *ḥaḍra* sat on the floor and collectively chanted a poem of the founder.[56] The *ḥaḍra* would then conclude with a collective recital, "in the heart", of the *Fātiḥa*.[57]

Like the Qādiriyya, the *dhikr* of the Khatmiyya could be held on various occasions. On the eve of 27 Rajab, for example, the followers used to chant the story (*qiṣṣa*) of the *miᶜrāj* composed by Jaᶜfar al-Mīrghanī.[58] The *ḥaḍras* could also be arranged for private occasions such as the naming of a child (*simāya*) or circumcision or on return from pilgrimage.[59] The Khatmiyya, as Trimingham notes, usually kept

54 See for instance, Muḥammad ᶜUthmān al-Mīrghanī, *al-Nūr al-barrāq fī madḥ al-nabī al-miṣdāq*, and Jaᶜfar al-Ṣādiq al-Mīrghanī, *Dīwān Riyāḍ al-madīḥ fī madḥ al-nabī*.

55 Al-Mīrghanī, *al-Nūr al-barrāq*, 86-7; Trimingham (1949), 215, and interview 19.

56 Al-Mīrghanī, *al-Nūr al-barrāq*, 77.

57 Al-Shāhī, thesis (1971), 321.

58 Al-Mīrghanī, *al-Nūr al-barrāq*, 86-7.

59 Trimingham (1949), 215, and interview 19.

a tight hold on extravagances on the part of its followers during the performance of the *dhikr*.[60]

The Khatmiyya was and still is the only order that chants parts of the founder's poem of praise for the Prophet, *al-Nūr al-barrāq*, at the funerals of its followers.[61]

The Khatmiyya, like all the new orders and in contrast to the Qādiriyya, did not stress worship through strenuous physical effort. This may be illustrated by the practice of entering into spiritual retreat; the *Ṭabaqāt* gives several examples of Qādirīs who used to go on prolonged retreats, living only on a few dates and *qarād* seeds (the pods of the *Acacia adansonii*).[62] Ḥamad al-Naḥlān's retreat, for instance, lasted for thirty-two months.[63]

By contrast, the Khatmiyya discouraged prolonged retreats; its period of *khalwa* was very brief, between three to seven days. Again in contrast to the Qādiriyya, it was permissible for an adherent of the Khatmiyya during his retreat to eat bread, seed-oil, sugar and barley. He was, however, only to eat only vegetarian food during his retreat.[64]

60 Trimingham (1949), 212 and 217. See also al-Raṭbī, *Minḥat al-aṣḥāb*, 77.

61 Yūsuf al-Khalīfa ᶜAbd al-Raḥmān, *al-Jawāb al-kāfī fi'l-ijāba ᶜan asiʾlat fuhūm al-muslimīn ᶜāmmatan wa-ahl al-ṭuruq al-ṣūfiyya khāṣṣatan*, Cairo (n.d.), 24.

62 Ibn Ḍayf Allāh (1974), 163.

63 *Ibid.*, 61-3.

64 Al-Mīrghanī (1358/1939), 64 and 66.

CONCLUSION

The *ṭarīqas* in the Sudan operated on two different levels. They carried out their missionary activities among those who were already Muslim and converted them to Sufism. However, they also functioned in areas on the frontiers of Islam, in the western Sudan and the southern parts of the Gezira where they converted non-Muslims to Islam.

One example of those who undertook missionary work among non-Muslims is ᶜAbd Allāh al-Mawārzī, known as Abū'l-Maᶜālī, a Sudanese student of Ibn Idrīs. He converted a considerable number of pagan Nuba of southern Kordofan to Islam.[1] The Nuba mountains of Kordofan also saw the missionary activities of Ismāᶜīl al-Walī and his student, Badawī Abū Ṣafiyya. The latter, who was known for his hostility to the Turco-Egyptian Government, led a holy war against the Nuba, converting many to Islam.

The Sufi brotherhoods in the Sudan drew their followers from different social classes and ethnic groups in both the urban and rural areas. Thus the brotherhoods played a significant unifying role by cutting across the different social backgrounds of their followers and bringing them together into associations of mutual solidarity. The Khatmiyya *ṭarīqa* was to appeal to merchants such as Muḥammad Ṣāliḥ Shādūl, the Kawārta family and the Hawwāra *jallāba*; to learned groups and individuals such as Aḥmad w. ᶜĪsā, the ᶜIrāqāb, Ḥamadtūiyāb and the family of Suwār al-Dhahab; and to nomads such as the Banī ᶜĀmir and Shukriyya of the eastern Sudan.

Furthermore, the Shāyqiyya region, which is one of the main strongholds of the Khatmiyya in the Sudan, was, and still is, inhabited by people of different ethnic origins. The Khatmiyya, as indeed all the *ṭarīqas*, therefore functioned as an organization that transcended ethnic boundaries and so, directly or indirectly, paved the way for the first Sudanese quasi-national movement, the Mahdiyya.

In this context, the Mahdist revolution should not be seen as a break with what went before. In fact the Mahdiyya had, indeed, its roots within the Sudanese Sufi context. Muḥammad Aḥmad was a Sammānī Shaykh and a follower of the teachings of Ibn Idrīs before manifesting himself as the Mahdi.

1 See further Karrār, thesis (1977), 69-70.

Muḥammad Aḥmad made use of the Sufi network in the Sudan to mobilize people for his cause. Hence his earliest contacts in the early stages, that is before his public manifestation of his movement, were with influential Sufi figures in Kordofan, including members of the Khatmiyya. His first letter concerning the Mahdiyya was addressed to a Sufi Shaykh, namely Muḥammad al-Ṭayyib w. al-Baṣīr of the Sammāniyya.[2]

The Mahdi, like most Sufis, believed in *karāmāt*. It is presumably because of his awareness of their significance in Sudanese religious life that he made use of them in support of his claim to the Mahdiship.[3] The Mahdi also asserted that his Mahdiyya was unique and that it would not come again. It combined the ideas of the infallible (*maᶜṣūm*) *imām* of the Shīᶜa and the inspired (*mulham*) *imām* of the Sufis.[4]

With the spread of his movement, however, the Mahdi began to lay emphasis on the ideas of the Salafiyya movement. He abolished the *madhhabs* and called for a return to the origins (*uṣūl*) of the faith, the Quran and the *sunna*, as the basis of the Islamic community.[5]

The Mahdi, who was endeavouring to unite all Muslims, may have felt that loyalties to the numerous shaykhs of *ṭarīqas* would hamper his efforts. Thus the banning of the *ṭarīqas* in the middle of 1301/the beginning of 1884 was justified by the Mahdi on five grounds.

First, he had been authorized (*bi-tafwīd*, presumably by the Prophet) to abolish them. Furthermore, he added that the founders of the *ṭarīqas* and *madhhabs* had known that he would have the authority to do so upon his manifestation as the Mahdi. Thirdly, if the founders of these *ṭarīqas* and *madhhabs* had been alive in his time, they would have joined his cause. All are obliged to abandon the *ṭarīqas* and the *madhhabs* and join his "Way". Finally, his *madhhab* was the Quran and *sunna*.[6]

However, Mahdist policy towards the orders was complex. Although the present study has suggested that it should be understood within the framework of those who supported and those who opposed the Mahdiyya, further research is required.

2 Abū Salīm (1970), 18.

3 See, for example, Abū Salīm, mimeograph (1969), 28, no. 50.

4 Muḥammad Ibrāhīm Abū Salīm, *Mafhūm al-khilāfa wa'l-imāma fī'l-Mahdiyya*, mimeograph, Khartoum, n.d., 2.

5 Abū Salīm, ed. (1969a), 62.

6 Abū Salīm, mimeograph (1969), 207, no. 406.

The present monograph has shown that the *ṭarīqas* were, and still are, organizations of a multi-functional character. In addition to their religious, educational, political and socio-economic functions, they also played a cultural role. The coming of these *ṭarīqas* led to the flourishing of written and oral religious poetry. Even women, who did not participate in the ceremonies of their orders and usually demonstrated their allegiance by attending these rituals as observers and by making gifts, composed songs of praise to the head of the order and the members of his family.[7]

The cultural influence of the *ṭarīqas* may further be seen in the great number of Sufi technical terms that have found their way into popular sayings and secular songs.[8]

Although the *ṭarīqas*, especially the Khatmiyya, were overshadowed by the Mahdist revolution, they rapidly regained their vitality and importance in Sudanese religious and political life after the destruction of the Mahdist state by the Anglo-Egyptian forces in 1898.[9]

7 See further, for example, Muḥammad Ibrāhīm al-Shūsh, *al-Shiʿr al-ḥadīth fī'l-Sūdān*, vol. i, Cairo 1962, 9-35; Ibrāhīm (1965); Ṭaḥa, thesis (1967), 27 and 80-94, and Ḥasan (1972), *passim*.

8 Ṭāhā, thesis (1967), 104-22 and 201-35.

9 On the Sufi brotherhoods in the twentieth century, see, for example, Voll, thesis (1969); Warburg (1971), 89-119; Karrār, thesis (1977); El-Hassan, thesis (1980), and al-Shāhī (1981), 13-24.

APPENDIX A

MUḤAMMAD AL-MAJDHŪB, "THE YOUNGER"

Muḥammad b. Aḥmad Qamar al-Dīn b. Ḥamad al-Majdhūb, known as al-Ṣaghīr "the younger"[1] (1210/1795-6 to 1247/1831-2), was born and spent his early years at al-Matamma, where he memorized the Quran and learnt to read and write under Shaykh Aḥmad al-Rayyaḥ. Al-Majdhūb later moved to al-Dāmar, the Majādhīb centre, where he was initiated into the Shādhiliyya by his father Aḥmad Qamar al-Dīn. Al-Majdhūb then returned to al-Matamma where he rejoined his master Aḥmad al-Rayyaḥ. While in al-Matamma, he was initiated by al-Mīrghanī into the Khatmiyya *ṭarīqa*.[2] Afterwards al-Majdhūb returned to al-Dāmar, where he succeeded his father as *al-faqīh al-kabīr*, who, according to Burckhardt, who visited the area in 1814, was the effective ruler of al-Dāmar.[3] When al-Dāmar, together with most of the Jaᶜaliyyūn region, was destroyed in the harsh campaign by Muḥammad *al-daftardār* in 1823 in reprisal for the assassination of Ismāᶜīl Pasha, al-Majdhūb al-Ṣaghīr fled to Sawākin and thence to Mecca.[4] He stayed in Mecca for some seven years, during which he first joined Muḥammad al-Madanī who initiated him into the Shādhiliyya for a second time. Al-Majdhūb and his teacher joined Ibn Idrīs for a number of years. Ibn Idrīs is said to have been impressed by al-Majdhūb, saying to his students that al-Majdhūb received his *ᶜilm* directly from God.[5]

1 The author of the present book is aware of the fact that *Shaykh* al-Majdhūb was never called al-Ṣaghīr by his family. This nickname, however, is widely accepted in the Sudan.

2 *Kitāb al-Ibāna*, ms., f. 14.

3 Burckhardt (1822), 236.

4 SAD 195/7/2 and NRO, Intel., 2/32/263. According to the *Kitāb al-Ibāna*, ms., f. 4, and *Makhṭūṭa*, 111, he accompanied al-Mīrghanī to the Ḥijāz.

5 *Mukhtaṣar manāqib al-sayyid Muḥammad al-Majdhūb*, ms., f. 14, NRO, Misc., 1/67/1188 and 1/82/1315; al-Rashīd (1974), 63-4 & 97, and Karrār, thesis (1977), 57-9.

While in Medina, al-Majdhūb is said to have seen a vision in which he was ordered by the Prophet to abandon the Khatmiyya and return to the order of his grandfather, the Shādhiliyya.[6] In about 1830, he returned to Sawākin, where he established a *zāwiya* and preached the Shādhiliyya, which he revitalized in the light of the teachings of Ibn Idrīs. He called his *ṭarīqa* "*al-Muḥammadiyya al-Shādhiliyya al-Majdhūbiyya*". But the *ṭarīqa* is commonly known in the Sudan as *al-Majdhūbiyya al-Mujaddada* ("the renewed Majdhūbiyya") to distinguish it from the "ancient" Majdhūbiyya, the order of his grandfathers.

In 1831, after the Jaᶜaliyyūn were granted amnesty by the Turco-Egyptian authorities, al-Majdhūb returned to al-Dāmar, where he stayed until he died in 1832. After his death his nephew Shaykh Muḥammad al-Ṭāhir, to whom the *zāwiya* of Sawākin had passed in al-Majdhūb's lifetime, became the main representative of the Majdhūbiyya in the eastern Sudan. He was a rival to the Khatmiyya in the eastern Sudan and joined the Mahdist forces under the leadership of ᶜUthmān Diqna.

6 *Makhṭūṭa*, 111.

persevere in the unsullied remembrance [*dhikr*] of Him, [as I also charge him] to remember me in his righteous prayers, in his private retreats and his public worship. May God's blessings be upon our Lord Muḥammad to the extent of the glory of his essence.

APPENDIX B
A KHATMIYYA *IJĀZA*

Document A (Bergen NO 140. 6/15)

Translation

In the name of God, the Compassionate, the Merciful.

With Him is help in the beginning and the end, and God bless His Chosen One with His essence, attributes and names. Praise be to God Who has linked our spiritual descent [*sanad*] with His Chosen One; for the sublimity of every spiritual descent lies in its origin. And Thanks be to Him who has made the paths to His presence [*ḥaḍrātihi*] innumerable, and blessings and peace be upon him who is our support in our affairs and upon his family and all the diligent followers of his way.[1]

Hereafter: the one who has this name [*kunya*] from the chosen one, namely the father of Muḥammad, ᶜAbd Allāh, Jaᶜfar and Zaynab, Muḥammad ᶜUthmān al-Mīrghanī al-Makkī al-Khatim, may God lead him to the springs of purity.

This is a major and comprehensive *ijāza* in the most glorious path of the esoteric and exoteric. I say herewith, entering the fray with the help of God and His messenger, their sword, by God's might, being unsheathed against those who oppose me that I state I have named as my deputy and have given authority to my devoted chosen and bosom friend, my trustworthy and faithful companion, my sincere friend and close companion, my friend and devoted and obedient follower, the *khalīfa* Muḥammad Ṣāliḥ al-Naẓīf. We have granted him authority in my path and have given it to him along with those noble exoteric sciences in which I am qualified, as those whom I have mentioned and others granted me authority in the two paths. May God confirm me and him and you and all of my children, companions, and beloved friends in both disciplines. I charge him to fear God in all his breaths and to

1 *man ṭarīqahi jadd = man jadda fī ṭarīqihi.*

persevere in the unsullied remembrance [*dhikr*] of Him, [as I also charge him] to remember me in his righteous prayers, in his private retreats and his public worship. May God's blessings be upon our Lord Muḥammad to the extent of the glory of his essence.

GLOSSARY

abkār (sing. *bikr*)	lit. "first-born", "eldest"; the original followers (*sc.* of an order).
ādāb al-dhikr	the rules that regulate the *dhikr* (*q.v.*).
ᶜadhaba (pl. *ᶜadhabāt*)	tassel hanging down from turban.
ahālī al-awqāf	"the people of the pious endowments"; those who make pious endowments to the *ṭarīqas* (*q.v.*).
ahl Allāh	lit. "the people of God".
ahl al-ḥadīth	"people of the Tradition"; scholars who emphasized the Traditions of the Prophet in opposition to the schools of Law (*madhhab*, *q.v.*): *EI*[2], i, 258-9 (J. Schacht).
aḥwāl	see *ḥāl*.
aḥzāb al-tajalliyāt al-ilāhiyya	"the litanies of the divine manifestations"; two litanies written by Ibn Idrīs.
ajāwīd (sing. *jawād*)	mediators; elders who act as mediators in a dispute.
akhdh al-ᶜahd	the act of taking the compact, i.e. joining a *ṭarīqa* (*q.v.*).
akhdh al-bayᶜa	the act of taking the oath of allegiance.
akhdh al-ṭarīqa (or *al-ṭarīq*)	the act of joining a brotherhood; *cf. akhdh al-wird.*
akhdh al-wird	the act of taking the litany; synonymous with *akhdh al-ṭarīqa.*
al-ᶜalāmiyya	the place in the *khalwa* (*q.v.*) set aside for the teaching of *ᶜilm* (*q.v.*).
ālāt	lit. "tools"; the ritual instruments inherited by a Qādirī shaykh from his predecessor.

ᶜālim (pl. *ᶜulamāʾ*)	religious scholar.
ᶜamal	performance, action, or practice: cf. *EI²*, i, 426-9.
amān	safe-conduct; pardon: cf. *EI²*, i, 429-30.
ᶜāmil	administrative agent, representative, or commissioner: cf. *EI²*, i, 435-6.
ᶜāmil ᶜumūm	general agent.
amīn (pl. *umanāʾ*)	commissioner, trustee; office-holder in the Ismāᶜīliyya *ṭarīqa* (*q.v.*).
amīn bayt al-māl	the administrator of the treasury; a term used in the Mahdist state.
amīn khatm al-Mahdi	the keeper of the Mahdi's seal.
amīr maṭbaᶜat al-ḥajar	director of the lithograph press used by the Mahdist state.
amīr al-muʾminīn	the Commander of the Faithful; Caliph.
anṣār	"Companions"; a term originally used for the Medinan followers of the Prophet. The term was used by the Sudanese Mahdi in imitation of the Prophet.
al-aqrab	lit. "the nearer" (in terms of time); the second.
ardabb	a measure of capacity; approximately 180 litres.
al-ᶜarsh	the throne (*sc.* of God).
asās	lit. "foundation"; the basic litany of a *ṭarīqa* (*q.v.*).
al-Asās al-kabīr	the major version of the basic litanies of the Khatmiyya.
al-Asās al-ṣaghīr	the minor version of the basic litanies of the Khatmiyya.
al-ashhur al-ḥurum	the five Muslim holy months, namely Muḥarram, Rajab, Shaᶜbān, Ramaḍān and Dhū'l-ḥijja.

^{c}*Āshurā*$^{\prime}$	the tenth of Muḥarram (the first Islamic month); the anniversary of the death of al-Ḥusayn b. ^{c}Alī, nephew of the Prophet: EI^2, i, 705.
al-^{c}*aṣr*	the afternoon prayers; the name of Quran, 103.
awlād al-bayt	lit. "the boys of the house [*sc.* of the Mīrghanī]", who voluntarily offered their services as attendants to the male members of the Mīrghanī household.
awqāf	see *waqf.*
awrād	see *wird.*
āyat al-mubāya^{c}*a*	the Quranic verse of the pledge of allegiance: Quran, 48:10.
azīma (pl. *azā*$^{\prime}$*im*)	incantation.
banāt al-bayt	lit. "the girls of the house [*sc.* of the Mīrghanī]", who voluntarily offered their services as attendants to the female members of the Mīrghanī household.
baniyya (pl. *baniyyāt*)	a small rectangular building of mud usually without a roof.
baraka	this term has two main meanings: 1) heritable beneficent force of divine origin; 2) benediction or blessing.
bāshī-būzuq (Turkish)	irregular cavalry.
basmala	the formula "In the Name of God, the Merciful, the Compassionate".
bay^{c}*a*	oath of allegiance.
bayān (pl. *bayanāt*)	lit. "revealing, manifestation"; by extension, the place where a holy man has revealed himself in a dream or vision.
bayraq (pl. *bayāriq*)	flag; see also *rāya.*

buqᶜa	open space in the *khalwa* (*q.v.*), where the Quran is taught and *dhikr* (*q.v.*) sessions are held.
daftardār	"keeper of the records"; Mamluk title held by Muḥammad bey Khusraw.
Dalāʾil al-khayrāt	"the signs of the good [deeds]", the title of al-Jazūlī's famous religious poem: *EI²*, ii, 527-8.
dār (pl. *diyār*)	acknowledged territory of ethnic group.
al-daraja al-kawniyya	according to the *Ṭabaqāt*, 207, the creative powers attained by a saint of the middle rank.
ḍarb	see *martaba*.
al-dhākir	one who remembers (God).
dhikr	remembrance or invocation of God: *EI²*, ii, 223-7.
dhikr al-ḥalqa	the communal invocation of God in which the participants sit or stand in a circle (*ḥalqa*).
dhikr al-karīr	a type of Qādirī *dhikr* (*q.v.*) with a special method of forceful intonation resembling the sound made by a pigeon.
dhikr bi'l-lisān	remembrance (*sc.* of God), "upon the tongue", i.e. verbally.
dhikr bi'l-qalb	remembrance (*sc.* of God), "in the heart", i.e. silently.
dhikr al-ṣayḥa	lit. "the invocation of the shout"; it is practised by the Yaᶜqūbāb branch of the Qādiriyya and the Sammāniyya. It opens with a loud cry for God's succour.
dhikr al-waqt	lit. "the invocation [*sc.* of God] of the time". These are sets of invocations to be repeated a prescribed number of times after the five canonical daily prayers.
faddān	measurement of land, equalling 4,200.833 m^2.
fakī	Sudanese colloquial form of *faqīh*.

faqīh (pl. *fuqahāʾ*)	one who is versed in jurisprudence; a jurist; frequently used in the Sudan with the anomalous pl. of *fuqarāʾ*.
faqīr (pl. *fuqarāʾ*)	one who is poor in the presence of God. Although this term is generally confined to Sufis, in the Sudan it is frequently used for holy men in general.
faqīra	a female *faqīr*.
far^{c}	branch.
farajiyya	a kind of robe.
fatḥ	lit. "opening"; illumination of inspiration; see *kashf*.
Fātiḥa	lit. "opening"; the name of the first chapter in the Quran.
fijayja	small plot of cleared land.
fiqh	Islamic law, jurisprudence.
fitna	sedition.
fuqarāʾ	see *faqīr*.
ghār	"cave", retreat for personal devotions. Several holy men made artificial caves or grottos, in imitation of the Prophet who used a cave on Ḥirāʾ Mountain for religious devotions before the manifestation of his prophethood: *EI*^{2}, iii, 462.
al-ghawth	lit. "the succour"; a Sufi rank, being those who exist by virtue of the *quṭb al-aqṭāb* (*q.v.*).
ghawthiyya	the rank or state of *al-ghawth*.
ḥadīth	a tradition going back to the Prophet Muḥammad based upon a chain of transmission.

ḥaḍra (pl. *ḥaḍrāt*)	lit. "presence" (*sc.* of God or His Prophet, Muḥammad); a session of a communal *dhikr* (*q.v.*) or a recital of litanies by members of a Sufi brotherhood.
ḥaḍrāt al-rasūl	a gathering of the saints in the presence (*ḥaḍra*) of the Prophet.
al-ḥājj	pilgrim; title of one who has performed the pilgrimage to Mecca.
ḥākim (pl. *ḥukkām*)	"judge"; among the Khatmiyya the title of an official who was entrusted with the duty of advising members on legal matters and who was also authorized to intervene in disputes.
ḥāl (pl. *aḥwāl*)	state; spiritual state; a transitory state, as opposed to *maqām* (*q.v.*).
ḥalqa (pl. *ḥalaqāt*)	circle; synonym: *dāʾira.*
ḥāris (pl. *ḥurrās*)	keeper, guard, attendant.
ḥawliyya (Sud. Ar. *ḥōliyya*)	from *ḥawl* or "year", meaning the anniversary of the death of a holy man or woman.
Ḥayy, Qayyūm	"Living", "Eternal": two of the ninety-nine names of God.
al-ḥīrān al-kibār	senior students at a Quranic school.
al-ḥīrān al-ṣighār	junior students at a Quranic school.
ḥizb	"group"; "division": in the latter sense, one sixteenth of the Quran; in Sufism, "litany": *EI*[2], iii, 513-14.
Ḥizb al-anwār	"the litany of the lights [*sc.* of the Prophet]"; composed by Ibrāhīm al-Kabbāshī.
Ḥizb al-baḥr	"the litany of the sea", a famous litany composed by Abū'l-Ḥasan al-Shādhilī.
Ḥizb al-barr	"the litany of the land", a famous litany composed by Abū'l-Ḥasan al-Shādhilī.
Ḥizb al-dāʾira	"litany of the circle", composed by al-Kabbāshī.

Ḥizb al-ḥamd	"the litany of praise [*sc.* to God]", composed by al-Kabbāshī.
Ḥizb al-salām	"the litany of peace", composed by al-Kabbāshī.
al-Ḥizb al-sayfī	"the litany of the sword", attributed to ᶜAlī b. Abī Ṭālib, the Prophet's cousin.
ḥōḍ (cl. Ar. *ḥawḍ*)	small piece of agricultural land, usually rectangular in shape.
ḥuwār (cl. Ar. *ḥiwār*, pl. *ḥīrān*)	lit. "a young camel"; student at a Quranic school or a follower of a Sufi shaykh.
ḥuwāra (pl. *ḥuwārāt*)	a female member of the Khatmiyya who voluntarily offers her service as a link between the female members of the Mīrghanī family and the female followers of the order.
ᶜibāya (cl. Ar. *ᶜibāʾa*)	cloak-like woollen wrap.
ibrīq (also *rakwa*)	water container used for ritual ablutions.
ᶜīd	"festival"; the two main *ᶜīds*, namely *ᶜīd al-fiṭr* (1 Shawwāl) and *ᶜīd al-aḍḥā* (10 Dhu'l-ḥijja).
ᶜidda	legally prescribed period during which a woman is not allowed to remarry after being divorced or widowed.
idhn	permission.
idhn nabawī	Prophetic permission.
ijāza	licence or authorization to teach a specified text or to initiate followers into an order.
ijmāᶜ	consensus: *EI²*, iii, 1023-6.
ijtihād	the action of applying independent judgement in legal or theological matters: *EI²*, ii, 1026-7.
ikhlās	lit. "faithfulness"; the name of the Quranic chapter 112.
ikhwān	"brethren"; fellow members of a brotherhood.

ᶜilm (pl. *ᶜulūm*)	knowledge; Islamic sciences.
ᶜilm rabbānī	"divine knowledge"; knowledge or learning that is inspired directly by God. A synonymous phrase is *ᶜilm ladunī.*
imām	leader; leader of a public prayer; spiritual and temporal leader in Shīᶜa Islam: *EI²*, iii, 1163-9.
indhār (pl. *indhārāt*)	"warning"; letters sent by the Sudanese Mahdi to those who did not freely support his cause.
ism Allāh al-aᶜẓam	the most exalted name of God. This name is believed to be more sublime than the ninety-nine names of God. The Shīᶜa believe that God made use of this name when he created the world. Although this name is generally considered to be known only to the prophets, knowledge of it was claimed by holy men as proof of their claim to the *wilāya* (*q.v.*).
istighfār	the act of asking God for forgiveness.
istiqāma	righteousness.
jāh	"rank, dignity"; a term used in the Sudan to denote the privileged or tax-exempt status granted by rulers to holy men.
jallāba (sing. *jallābī*)	itinerant merchants.
jallābiyya	a long shirtlike garment, usually made of cotton.
jāmiᶜ (pl. *jawāmiᶜ*)	mosque where the public prayer is performed on Fridays.
jarf	the slope on the river bank down to the river.
jibba or *jubba*	a long outer garment with long wide sleeves.
jihād	a) *jihād al-nafs*; struggle against one's carnal self, otherwise *jihād akbar*: "greater *jihād*"; b) *jihād*; holy war as a religious duty against non-believers, otherwise *jihād aṣghar*: "minor *jihād*".

jihādiyya	troops usually of slave origin, employed by both the Turco-Egyptian and Mahdist regimes.
al-kabas (or *al-rōshan*)	a shelf hanging from the ceiling of a room at the Quranic school set aside for storing the wooden tablets (Sud. Ar. *lōḥ*) of the students at the end of their lessons.
kakar	wooden stool.
karāma (pl. *karamāt*)	charisma; miracle, especially of a saint.
karkab	wooden shoes.
karrāb	a piece of cloth or leather tied around the waist to secure the *jibba* (*q.v.*) during the *dhikr* (*q.v.*).
kashf	"uncovering", illumination in mystical sense.
khalīfa	lit. "successor"; deputy or representative of the head of an order.
khalifāt al-khulafā'	the head of the *khalīfas*; a senior representative of an order.
khalīfa mustawalī	the *khalīfa* actually in charge of an order.
khalq	people, mankind.
khalwa	has several meanings: a) spiritual retreat or seclusion; b) the place of spiritual retreat; c) and in the Sudan, it is used of a Quranic school.
khanqāh (*khānqāh*)	Sufi centre.
khatim al-awliyā'	"the seal [i.e. the last] of the saints"; the title of Muḥammad ʿUthmān al-Mīrghanī.
khatm (also *khatim* and *khātim*)	the last, the seal, the final.
khaṭwa	lit. "step"; the ability of a holy man to cover vast distances in an instant.
al-khawāṣṣ	the chosen, the privileged.

khawāṣṣ al-khawāṣṣ	the elect of the elect, the most privileged among the chosen.
khuddām (sing. *khādim*)	servant or attendant.
khuddām al-hadāya	lit. "the servants of the gifts"; adherents of the Khatmiyya whose duty it was to collect gifts for the order.
*khuddām al-jawāmi*ᶜ	the servants of the mosque.
khuṭṭ	sub-district.
kiswa	a) the covering of the holy Kaᶜba in Mecca; b) covering for the grave of a holy man or woman.
kūfiyya	headdress.
kufr	unbelief, blasphemy.
lawḥ (Sud.Ar. *lōḥ*; pl. *alwāḥ*)	a) writing wooden tablet; b) chapter.
al-lawḥ al-maḥfūz	"the Guarded Tablet", which is believed to be preserved beneath the Throne of God.
laylat al-miᶜrāj	see *al-miᶜrāj*.
layliyya	*dhikr* (*q.v.*) session held on specified nights.
madad	supernatural help, divine assistance.
madāʾiḥ (sing. *madīḥ* or *madḥa*)	eulogies; religious songs of praise.
madḥ	commendation, praise, glorification.
madhhab (pl. *madhāhib*)	school of law in Islam; sometimes used in the phrase, *madhhab al-taṣawwuf.*
maʾdhūn	a Muslim authorized to perform marriages.
mādiḥ	eulogist; chanter of religious songs of praise.
madrasa	school.

al-Mahdī	"the divinely guided"; the person who will appear before the end of time to re-establish justice on earth.
al-Mahdī al-muntaẓar	"the expected Mahdī".
majlis	council, assembly, gathering.
al-Majlis al-ṣūfī al-aᶜlā	the High Sufi Council in Cairo.
majlis ᶜumanāʾ al-Mahdī	the council of the Mahdi's commissioners.
makk (pl. *mukūk*)	ruler.
malāmatiyya	lit. "the blameworthy"; those who held an antinomian position in Islam, "who combined virtue with vice".
malik	king, sovereign.
manāqib	lit. "virtues"; hagiography.
mandūb (pl. *manādib*)	emissary.
maqām (pl. *maqāmāt*)	place; rank; permanent spiritual status in the Sufi hierarchy; the opposite of *ḥāl.*
maqdūm (pl. *maqādīm*)	commissioner appointed for a fixed term or purpose by the Dār Fūr Sultan.
martaba (pl. *marātib*)	grade; a stage or phase in the communal *dhikr* (*q.v.*); its synonyms are *ḍarb* and *ṭabaqa.*
masīd	a dialectical variant of the cl. *masjid*, "mosque"; used also for a Quranic school. In some parts of the Sudan, however, its function is more social than religious or educational.
maᶜṣūm	"infallible, sinless".
mawlā	master.

mawlid (col. *mūlid*; pl. *mawālid*) — birthday of:
a) the Prophet on 12 Rabīᶜ I, known as *mawlid al-nabī* or *al-mawlid al-nabawī*; or of
b) a saint.
The term is also used of religious poems recounting the life of the Prophet.

midd (cl. Ar. *mudd*) — a measure of grain.

miḥāya — the water used for washing off Quranic verses written on wooden tablet (*lawḥ*); the water is considered to have medicinal value.

al-miᶜrāj, laylat al-miᶜrāj — the Prophet's ascent to Heaven, celebrated on 27 Rajab.

misbaḥa (or *sibḥa*) *alfiyya* — rosary of a thousand beads.

muftī — a scholar who delivers formal legal opinions (*fatwa*).

muḥāfaẓa — province.

muᶜjiza (pl. *muᶜjizāt*) — a miracle worked by a prophet, in contrast to *karāma* (*q.v.*).

mukhtaṣar — lit. "abridgement, synopsis"; in the Sudan, it almost invariably refers to the Mālikī lawbook, the *Mukhtaṣar* of Khalīl b. Isḥāq (d. 776/1374).

mulāzim (pl. *mulāzimūn*) — "attendant"; followers or adepts who lived almost permanently at the centre of their orders.

mulham — inspired.

munshid (pl. *munshidūn*) — chanter of religious poems or litanies.

muqaddam — leader of a local branch (*qism*) in the Qādiriyya; in the Khatmiyya, assistant to the *khalīfa* (*q.v.*).

muqaddima — lit. "introduction"; introductory rituals for initiation into the Khatmiyya.

murīd — aspirant, novice.

murshid	spiritual guide or director.
musabbaᶜāt	the term used to describe the devotions (litanies etc.), as divided for use during the seven days of the week.
musafin (pl. *musafinūn*)	chanter of *safīna* (*q.v.*) in the *dhikr* sessions of the Khatmiyya.
al-nabī ᶜĪsā	the Prophet Jesus.
nadhr (pl. *nudhūr*)	votive offering.
nāʾib	deputy.
al-nāʾib al-ᶜāmm	deputy to the head of the Khatmiyya.
naqīb (pl. *nuqabāʾ*)	guardian of the liturgy in a Sufi order.
naqīb al-umanāʾ	the head of the board of *umanāʾ* of the Ismāᶜīliyya *ṭarīqa* (*q.v.*).
nār al-ᶜilm	lit. "the fire of learning", referring to the second level, after *nār al-Qurʾān* (*q.v.*), of education in a religious school.
nār al-Qurʾān	lit. "the fire of the Quran", referring to the first level of education in a religious school which was devoted to the memorization of the Quran. It was so called because lessons were conducted by the light from a fire.
al-naṣr	lit. "victory, triumph"; name of Quran, Chapter 110.
nōba (cl. *nawba*)	drum.
nūn	the twenty-fifth letter of the Arabic alphabet.
qāḍī	judicial official; judge.
qāḍī al-Islām	senior judge.
qadla	walking in a solemn manner.
qalᶜa	"fort, citadel"; in the Sudan it can mean a high and open piece of land.

qāriʾ al-riwāyāt al-sabʿa	one who has mastered the seven alternative ways of reciting the Quran.
qaṣīda (pl. *qaṣāʾid*)	poem.
qāṭiʿ or *qāṭūʿa*	storeroom.
qawāʿid al-sulūk	the rules that regulate the aspirant's progress on the Sufi way.
qiṣṣa (pl. *qiṣas*)	story.
qiyās	inference by analogy.
qubba	domed tomb of a saint.
quftān	a long robe with long sleeves, usually made of silk or cotton.
al-Qurʾāniyya	the place where the Quran is taught in the *khalwa* (*q.v.*).
quṭb	lit. "pole or pivot"; head of the hierarchy of saints.
quṭb al-aqṭāb	lit. "the pole of the poles"; head of the hierarchy of saints.
quṭb al-shamāl	lit. "the pole of the north"; its meaning is obscure, but it was used of Shaykh al-Qurashī w. al-Zayn of the Sammāniyya.
quṭbiyya	the state of being a *quṭb*; a term used in the Sudan to denote those who had attained an advanced level of Islamic learning.
al-rāʿī	office-holder in the Ismāʿīliyya; his duty was to protect the rights of the order.
rakʿa	the words and acts that comprise a prostration in ritual prayers.
rākūba	small shelter.
rakwa	see *ibrīq*.
Ramaḍān	the ninth month of the Muslim calendar, which is the month of fasting.

rāya (pl. *rāyāt*)	flag or standard.
razīm	a quiet form of Qādirī *dhikr* (*q.v.*).
ribāṭ	frontier-post; a religious centre.
Risāla	lit. "letter, treatise"; in the Sudan, it almost invariably refers to the *Risāla* of Ibn Abī Zayd al-Qayrawānī (d. 389/996).
al-rōshān	see *al-kabas*.
ruʾyā	dream or vision.
safīna (pl. *safāʾin*)	lit. "ship"; the name of that part of the Khatmiyya communal *dhikr* (*q.v.*), during which poems by Muḥammad ᶜUthmān al-Mīrghanī and his son, Jaᶜfar, are recited.
ṣaḥāba	the Prophet's companions.
ṣājat	flat pieces of iron used in the communal *dhikr* (*q.v.*) of the Qādiriyya.
Salafiyya	an Islamic movement of the nineteenth century, and before a call for a return to the sources of belief, i.e. the Quran and the *sunna* (*q.v.*).
ṣalāt al-tarāwīḥ	prayers performed during the nights of Ramaḍān.
sanad	chain of spiritual authority.
sāqiya	waterwheel; land so irrigated.
saray	palace.
shahāda	the testimony of faith in Islam; the formula "There is no God but God, and Muḥammad is the messenger of God."
shaqīqa	fractional share in *sāqiya* land.
sharḥ	commentary.
sharīfa (pl. *sharīfāt*)	females who claim to descend from the Prophet. A female member of the Mīrghanī family.

shaykh	lit. "old man"; also a) tribal chief; b) religious teacher; c) head of a Sufi order.
shaykh al-balad	community or village head.
shaykh al-dhikr	director of the *dhikr* (*q.v.*) in the Ismā^cīliyya order.
shaykh al-qirā'a	one who teaches the Quran or other Islamic sciences; a common synonym is *shaykh al-ta^cālīm*.
shaykh al-taḥqīq	the one who has attained the stage of realization of "Truth" (*ḥaqīqa*) and is qualified to guide aspirants towards that end.
shi^cba	Y-shaped stick.
shu^cār	a group of chanters who perform the *dhikr al-ṣayḥa* (*q.v.*) in the Sammāniyya *ṭarīqa* (*q.v.*).
sibḥa	see *misbaḥa*.
silsila	chain of spiritual descent.
simāya	naming of a child.
sirr al-khatim	"the secret of the seal [of the saints]"; honorific title used in the Mīrghanī family.
sub^c	one-seventh; section.
ṣulḥ	reconciliation; compromise.
sulṭān al-awliyā'	the ruler or head of all the saints.
sunna	custom, saying or act of the Prophet.
al-Ta^cawwudh	the formula "I take refuge in God from the Devil, the cursed."
ṭabaqa	see *martaba*.
tafsīr	Quranic exegesis.
al-Tahlīl	the formula "There is no God but God."
ṭā'ifa	"part, portion", religious group.

tajwīd	the art of reciting the Quran.
takiyya	centre belonging to a *ṭarīqa* providing food and accommodation.
takhlīf	investiture; the ceremony of investiture as a *khalīfa* (*q.v.*): synonym, *tanṣīb.*
talqīn	instruction by word of mouth in the litanies of a particular Sufi order.
tanṣīb	see *takhlīf.*
taqashhuf	asceticism.
taqlīd	the unquestioning acceptance of the teachings of one of the *madhhabs* (*q.v.*).
ṭār	tambourines.
ṭarīqa	"path or way"; Sufi order or brotherhood.
tarjama (pl. *tarājim*)	lit. "translation"; a form of biography.
taṣawwuf fardī	personal form of Sufism.
tawḥīd	profession of the unity of God; theology.
tilmīdh	pupil or student.
ᶜulamāʾ	see *ᶜālim.*
ᶜulūm al-ḥaqīqa	lit. "the sciences of the [divine] Reality"; a term adopted by the Sufis to denote Sufism. A synonym is *ᶜulūm al-bātin*: "the esoteric sciences".
al-ᶜulūm al-laduniyya	see *ᶜilm rabbānī.*
ᶜulūm al-ẓāhir	the exoteric sciences.
umanāʾ	see *amīn.*
ᶜumra	minor pilgrimage.
ᶜurāḍa	strip of fertile land extending along the bank of the Nile and lying immediately above the *jarf* (*q.v.*) land.

ustādh teacher, master.

uṣūl "origins, foundations", specifically the Quran and *sunna* (*q.v.*).

wāᶜiẓ preacher.

wakīl al-nāᵓib assistant to the deputy.

walī (pl. *awliyāᵓ*) saint.

waqf (pl. *awqāf*) pious endowment or charitable gift.

al-wasīla one who acts as an intermediary with God; originally used of the Prophet.

wazīr minister.

wilāya the state of being a *walī* or saint; sanctity.

wird "litany"; it is sometimes used to mean a Sufi order or "way".

wird al-basmala the litany of the formula of "In the name of God the Merciful, the Compassionate".

yulaqin see *talqīn*.

al-zaghrāt (cl. Ar. *al-zaqhrād*) one who makes a shrill sound.

zakāh Islamic tax.

zāwiya lit. "corner"; a *ṭarīqa* centre.

ziyāra lit. "visit"; visitation to the tombs or shrines of holy men and women.

zuwāra gifts in kind or cash placed at the tombs and shrines of holy men.

SOURCES AND BIBLIOGRAPHY

The Sources

The present book is based on a combination of written and oral sources. These sources, which are complex and varied, fall into several categories, listed below. I, in fact, began to collect data in 1976. Part of the material I collected was incorporated into my MA thesis, entitled *The influence of the the Idrīsiyya teachings on the Sufī Orders in the Sudan*, University of Khartoum, 1977 (in Arabic).

The present study is also based on field research which I conducted in the Shāyqiyya region between August and September 1982. Armed with letters of introduction from some of my relatives and friends in Khartoum to some senior representatives (*khalīfas*) and followers in the Shāyqiyya region, I visited a number of villages and towns, among which the most important were Karīma, Nūrī, Duwaym Wad Ḥājj, al-Ghurayba and al-Zūma.

My choice of these places was based on information drawn from both non-Sudanese sources, that is to say the European travellers, as well as those of Sudanese origin, namely the *Ṭabaqāt* of Wad Ḍayf Allāh, and the *Kitāb al-ibāna* of Ibn al-Naṣayḥ (both discussed below), on the history of the founder of the Khatmiyya, together with the private archive of the Naḍīfāb family of Abū Rannāt Island, preserved in the NRO, Khartoum. Some informants also recommended to me other potential informants or owners of documents in other places within the region.

I always approached my informants both in my capacity as a researcher intending to write on the evolution of their orders, and as a member of the staff of the NRO in Khartoum. The willingness of the religious families to co-operate with the NRO by depositing or donating original or photographic copies of their private archives may be seen in the continuous growth of the NRO collections of religious documents.

The procedure which I adopted in the field was to photograph some of the relevant documents still in private hands, as well as recording the appropriate oral traditions. I photographed a number of documents concerning a variety of topics. These included, for example, the titles of some of the books used in the Quranic schools (sing. *khalwa*) of Abū Rannāt Island and al-Ghurayba during the period from the sixteenth to the eighteenth centuries.

The present study also used another set of documents which I photographed in the Shāyqiyya region. These are a number of formulas that were used by holy men in curing various illnesses such as wind, hemiplegia and migraine.

Anoher type of non-literary documents that I photographed during my field-trip were letters exchanged between the local representatives of the various brotherhoods and their headquarters, and at the local level between the *khalīfas*. The present study has also made use of some letters that I have photographed in Duwaym Wad Ḥājj and that were exchanged between the Duwayḥiyya holy clan in the Shāyqiyya region and their branch in Mecca.

A further category of non-literary material which I photographed in the Shāyqiyya region comprises the *ijāzāt* (sing. *ijāza*, certificate or authorization) that were issued by the heads of the different orders to their adherents. Valuable information has been gleaned from these documents. Thus the seal-dates of two *ijāzās*, issued by the founder of the Khatmiyya to two of his senior representatives in the Shāyqiyya area, enabled me to establish the date when al-Mīrghanī first arrived in the Sudan (see example in Appendix B). Furthermore, a number of pedigrees of holy families have also been photographed and used in the present study.

The Oral Sources

This study is also based in part on oral sources drawn from a number of formal interviews and informal discussions both in Khartoum and the Shāyqiyya region. All my informants, whose names are listed at the end of this study, are descendants of prominent holy men. I have, however, also interviewed many ordinary followers, including women, whose names do not appear in the list of informants. These secondary interviews were conducted in order to obtain a more generalized insight into the religious life of the region.

As to the form of the interviews, in most cases I put a question and let the informant answer without interruption; interviews were usually recorded. The same question was frequently directed to different informants in different localities. Most of the informants were willing to and interested in sharing their information with me. For their adherents, the religious figures who founded or propagated the brotherhoods still have the greatest significance.

During my field-trip I was able to use conversations with informants to confirm and amplify a number of aspects noted briefly in the written sources. One example of this is information on the careers of some of the local representatives of the Khatmiyya in the Shāyqiyya region referred to in the *Kitāb al-ibāna.* Another example is the preaching of the Tijāniyya among the Shāyqiyya by a Mahdist *amīr*, Aḥmad al-Huday al-Shāyqī al-Sawārabī, and his battles with the Governor of Dongola, Muṣṭafā Yāwar. Furthermore, my visit to the Naḍīfāb holy family of Abū Rannāt, who possess a large collection of nineteenth-century documents, enabled me to gain a better insight into their documents which give a clear picture of how the Khatmiyya functioned at the local level. They also throw light on the socio-economic status of members of the Naḍīfāb family who were (and still are) loyal adherents of the Khatmiyya.

The Literary Sources

This category comprises first, the *Kitāb al-Ṭabaqāt* by Ibn Ḍayf Allāh, commonly known as Wad Ḍayf Allāh, a member of a religious family living at Ḥalfāyat al-Mulūk, north of Khartoum North. In the present study, the edition by Professor Yūsuf Faḍl Ḥasan has been used. Since this valuable source has been analysed by a number of scholars, their conclusions need not be repeated here.[1] It is, however, worth noting that Wad Ḍayf Allāh shows a certain bias in favour of Sufis against jurists. Although several studies of Islam in the Sudan have made use of the *Ṭabaqāt*, this rich source has still to be fully exploited.

Another major source for the present thesis is the *Kitāb al-ibāna al-nūriyya fī shāʾn ṣāḥib al-ṭarīqa al-Khatmiyya, Khatm ahl al-ʿirfān sayyidinā wa-ustādhinā al-sayyid Muḥammad ʿUthmān al-Mīrghanī.*

The author of this indispensable source for any study of the Khatmiyya in the nineteenth century was Aḥmad, known as Ibn Idrīs,

1 See Ibn Ḍayf Allāh (1974), introduction by Yūsuf Faḍl Ḥasan; see also Hillelson (1923) 191-230, and Holt, "Traditional historical writing" (unpublished paper, 1969).

b. Muḥammad al-Naṣayḥ, a member of an old-established religious family at al-Dākhila, a section of Atbara town. He was a student and senior representative (*khalīfat al-khulafā'*) of Muḥammad al-Ḥasan al-Mīrghanī, son of the founder of the order. Al-Naṣayḥ was also a poet and a Sufi writer. The structure, language and style of the *Kitāb al-ibāna* reflect its author's learning.

The original manuscript of the work was composed and completed in Sawākin on 2 Rajab 1307/22 February 1890. Sawākin was still under Egyptian control, while the rest of the Sudan was under Mahdist rule (1885-1898). Al-Naṣayḥ describes how he came to write the *Kitāb al-ibāna*:

> Some Government administrators in the province [*muḥāfaẓa*] of Sawākin requested verbally, time and time again, information about the most noble *ustādh* and the most exalted refuge, *sayyid* Muḥammad ᶜUthmān, the seal [*khatm*] of all the perfect saints, al-Makkī al-Mīrghanī, the founder of the Khatmiyya order and the channel of all knowledge that comes from God [*al-ᶜulūm al-laduniyya*]. The inquiry was about his personal affairs, his brotherhood, descendants and suchlike. Their [i.e. the Government administrators] request was answered by a concise account which did not satisfy them. The same request was made again through the *qāḍī al-Islām* in Sawākin province, our master Shaykh Ibrāhīm ᶜAbd al-Samīᶜ. The request was first put to the senior representative of the eminent teacher [i.e. al-Mīrghanī] in Sawākin, Muḥammad al-Ṣāfī ("the pure") who had been given that epithet by the said teacher. The request was then brought before our masters, the Mīrghanī [family], the descendants of *al-ustādh al-khatim*, who were in the port of Sawākin at that time, namely *al-sayyid* ᶜUthmān Tāj al-Sirr b. Muḥammad Sirr al-Khatim and *sayyid* ᶜAlī b. Muḥammad ᶜUthmān, the son of the *ustādh*, my master, *sayyid* Muḥammad al-Ḥasan. These, in addition to some *khalīfas*, agreed that an answer to the request should be made.[2]

The original manuscript was widely copied by the senior followers of the Khatmiyya. The author of the present study knows of several copies kept in private hands. There are, however, three versions preserved in NRO, Khartoum under Miscellaneous 1/62/1110, *idem* 1/63/1126 and *amānāt* 1/14/59. References in the present study are given to another version, originally discovered in Eritrea, of which a

2 Aḥmad b. Idrīs b. al-Naṣayḥ, *Kitāb al-ibāna*. The passage cited here comes from the NRO ms., misc. 1/62/110, ff. 1-3 (the foliation of this ms. is inaccurate; f. 3 is numbered as f. 31).

copy has been deposited at the Department of History, University of Bergen.

Dr. Abū Salīm has published an analysis of the *Kitāb al-ibāna* based on the first two versions in the National Records Office.[3] He also intends to publish a critical edition of the same manuscript. This will be supplemented by a translation of the manuscript by Professor R.S. O'Fahey and myself.

The author of the *Kitāb al-ibāna* incorporated at the end some of the letters that Muḥammad ᶜUthmān al-Mīrghanī had received from his teacher, Aḥmad b. Idrīs al-Fāsī. Versions of the same letters, together with a number of others exchanged between Ibn Idrīs and some of his principal students, are available in Khartoum (NRO Misc. 1/22/247, and 1/81/1294) in a manuscript entitled *Majmūᶜ jawābāt al-sāda al-ᶜiẓām*, which is incorporated into an anonymous biography of Ibn Idrīs entitled *Tarjamat al-ustādh al-aᶜẓam wa'l-malādh al-afkham ṣāḥib al-ᶜIqd al-nafīs mawlāy al-Maghribī al-sharīf sayyidī al-sayyid Aḥmad b. Idrīs.* Some of these letters have been edited by an Azharī scholar, Ṣāliḥ Muḥammad al-Jaᶜfarī, and published at the end of a book entitled *Aᶜṭār azhār aghṣān ḥaẓīrat al-taqdīs*, which is devoted mainly to the miracles of Ibn Idrīs.[4]

Another category of sources used in this study are the *manāqib* (lit. "virtues", hagiography) and *tarājim* (sing. *tarjama*, a type of biography). As Moriah notes,

> The average *tardjamah* is not a biography in the European sense, nor is it a concise account of the *shaykh*'s life. Although it has some of the characteristics of a curriculum vitae, many important facts concerning the *shaykh*'s life are usually omitted.[5]

The *tarjama* usually retains some measure of objectivity in comparison with the *manāqib*, in its portrayal of its subject.

By contrast, the *manāqib* is much more hagiographical. The writers of these devotional accounts were not producing scientific biographies for the benefit of future historians, but works for the edification of their

3 Abū Salīm (1968), 36-43.

4 See al-Rashīd (1394/1974), 6-32. The texts and translations of all the extant letters of Ibn Idrīs will be published in *The Letters of Aḥmad ibn Idrīs*, ed. Einar Thomassen and Bernd Radtke (forthcoming).

5 G. Moriah, "The Social Structure of the Sufi Associations in Egypt in the 18th Century", Ph.D. thesis, University of London, 1963, 3.

contemporaries. Even in the case of the *Kitāb al-ibāna*, which may be considered as falling halfway between hagiography and biography there is a tendency to present a conventional picture of the holy men described, crediting them with the standard virtues and spiritual powers.

Common to all this devotional literature is the presentation of holy men as workers of miracles or *karāmāt* (sing. *karāma*), such as predicting the future, succouring in moments of distress, punishing those who oppose them, changing stones into silver and gold or resurrecting the dead; all acts establishing the sanctity (*wilāya*) of the holy men.

An adherent of a brotherhood would not question the validity of these *karāmāt*. This may be illustrated by the comment of the author of the *K. al-ibāna* on one of al-Ḥasan al-Mīrghanī's miracles:

> We were astonished at what he said, although we did not doubt its veracity; for such things often happen to holy men and women and are recorded in their writings and works about miracles.

The ability of holy men to perform *karāmāt* was widely acknowledged by both Sufis and jurists.[6] The significance of *karāmāt* in Sudanese religious life may be seen in the definition of the stages of *wilāya* given by an eighteenth century Sudanese religious notable, Idrīs w. al-Arbāb:

> There are three categories of saints, higher [*ᶜulya*], middle [*wuṣta*] and lower [*ṣughra*]. The lower entails that the saint can fly in the air, walk on the surface of the water, and has powers of clairvoyance. The middle is that God gives him creative powers [*al-daraja al-kawniyya*], which means that he says to a thing "Be" and it is, and this is the category to which my "son" Dafᶜ Allāh[7] belongs. The highest degree is the *quṭbāniyya*.[8]

The early Sufis were aware of the sensitivity of the issue of miracles. Several of them stated that a true saint should hide his supernatural deeds.[9] Furthermore, they distinguished between prophetic and saintly

6 Muḥammad b. ᶜAbd al-Wahhāb is one example of a non-Sufi who recognized *karāmāt*; see, Ibn Ḥajar (1395/1975-6), 59.

7 He is referring to Dafᶜ Allāh b. Muḥammad Abū Idrīs; see Ibn Ḍayf Allāh (1974), 206-7.

8 *Ibid*, 207.

9 One example of these early Sufis is al-Qushayrī. See Trimingham (1971), 26.

miracles by referring to the former as *muᶜjizāt* (sing. *muᶜjiza*, which is usually translated as "miracle") and the latter as *karāmāt*.[10]

Al-Kalābādhī (d. c.380/990) stated that a certain Sufi said,

> The miracles accorded to the saints come to them they know not whence, whereas the prophets know [the origin] of the marvels, and speak in confirmation of them. This difference is due to the fact that with saints there is a danger that they may be tempted [by their miracles] as they are not divinely preserved, whereas with prophets, in view of the fact that they are under God's protection this danger does not exist.[11]

Ibn Idrīs al-Fāsī is another example of a Sufi and scholar who expressed his distaste for *karāmāt* and also for having them recorded by his students.

> Righteousness [*al-istiqāma*] is the ultimate goal of the *karāma*, and we are, praise be to God, following the straight path which was followed by our example, the Messenger of God, may God's blessing and peace be upon him. As to these favours [*sc.* of God, i.e. miracles], they are like shadows that come and go. They are of no importance on the path to God except for those who are imperfect. For the perfect, his good fortune lies in having the Quran as his ethos [*khulquhu*], as had the Messenger of God, may God's blessing and peace be upon him.[12]

Muḥammad ᶜUthmān al-Mīrghanī II used to remind his followers that man was only a vehicle for these *karāmāt* and that it was God who actually performed them. It was the students who compiled and interpreted the deeds of their spiritual masters as *karāmāt*. Despite Ibn Idrīs' distaste for *karāmāt*, some of his students (for example, Ibrāhīm al-Rashīd) collected some of them in a manuscript.[13]

The performance of *karāmāt* is closely associated with the belief that all holy men are possessors of *baraka* ("blessing", or "spiritual charisma"). This belief in its turn is linked to the claim by most holy men to Sharifian origin, that is descent from the Prophet Muḥammad.

I am aware that other scholars may well interpret the *karāmāt* in an entirely different way from that of adherents of the brotherhoods. Nevertheless I have not presumed to pass judgement on the validity of

10 *Ibid*, 26.

11 Al-Kalābādhī (1400/1980), 89-90; the transl. is from Arberry (1935), 59-60.

12 *Tarjamat ... al-ustādh Aḥmad b. Idrīs*, ms., f. 11.

13 See al-Rashīd (1394/1974), 6-32.

such deeds, but rather have tried to present them as an integral part of the traditions and world-view of the orders under study.

The sources and bibliography are divided as follows:

A. Oral Sources
B. Written Sources

The latter are divided as follows:

B. 1 Manuscripts and letters in private hands
B. 2 Manuscripts in Public Collections
B. 3 Archives
B. 4 Theses, mimeographs, conference papers and forthcoming works
B. 5 Arabic printed primary sources
B. 6 European primary sources
B. 7 Secondary literature

In a number of instances, manuscripts and other documents are listed under sections B.1 and 2 that have been consulted but not directly cited in the thesis.

Where the name of the author is unknown, the work is listed alphabetically under its title.

A. *Oral Sources*[14]

1. ᶜAbd al-Ḥamīd Idrīs ᶜAbd Allāh: Maqal, north of Karīma, 6.9.1982.
2. ᶜAbd al-Raḥmān al-Rashīd, a descendant of Ibrāhīm al-Rashīd: Duwaym wad Ḥājj, al-Rijayla, 1.9.1982.
3. Abū'l-ᶜAbbās ᶜAlī ᶜĪsā al-Aḥmadī, Dandarāwī *khalīfa*: Karīma, 15.9.1982.
4. *al-khalīfa* Aḥmad Muḥammad al-Amīn Ṭāhā, a descendant of Shaykh Khōjalī: Khartoum North, 30.7.1982.
5. Aḥmad al-Ḥasan Aḥmad, a descendant of Muḥammad Ṣāliḥ al-Naḍīf: Abū Rannāt Island, 30.8.1982.
6. Aḥmad Muḥammad Khayr al-Tōm: al-Ghurayba, south of Kūrtī, 3 and 4.9.1982.
7. Aḥmad Muḥammad al-Ṣādiq al-Karūrī: Nūrī, 2.9.1982.

14 The interviews are referred to by their number in the footnotes.

8. Aḥmad Muḥammad Ṣāliḥ al-Amīn, *imām* of the mosque of al-Qurayr: al-Qurayr, 18.9.1982.
9. The late Dr. Aḥmad ᶜUthmān Ibrāhīm, a grandson of Shaykh Muḥammad w. Ibrāhīm of al-Arāk, north of Karīma: Department of History, Faculty of Education, University of Khartoum, 10.7.1982.
10. ᶜAlī Muḥammad al-Shaykh Jiqaydī, a member of the Naḍīfāb family of Abū Rannāt Island, Kobar: Khartoum North, 5.10.1982.
11. ᶜAwaḍ Muḥammad al-Darwīsh, a grandson of Shaykh Muḥammad al-Darwīsh: al-Zūma, north of Karīma, 9.9.1982.
12. Ḥasan ᶜUthmān Ibrāhīm, a grandson of Shaykh Muḥammad w. Ibrāhīm of al-Arāk, 6 and 7.9.1982.
13. *al-khalīfa* al-Ḥibr al-Kabbāshī, a grandson of Ibrāhīm al-Kabbāshī: al-Kabbāshī village, north of Khartoum North, 17.10.1982.
14. Dr. Ibrāhīm Karsanī, a descendant of Wad al-Karsanī of the Shāyqiyya region, Faculty of Economics, University of Khartoum. The interview took place in Bergen, 10.11.1983.
15. *shaykh* Idrīs Muḥammad ᶜAbd al-ᶜĀl al-Idrīsī, head of the Idrīsiyya *ṭarīqa* in the Sudan (d. 1982): Omdurman, May 1976.
16. Jaᶜfar Sālim Diᶜaymāwī: al-Jirayf, north of Nūrī, 27 and 29.9.1982.
17. al-Khaḍir Ḥusayn al-Malik: Kūrtī, 5.9.1982.
18. Dr. al-Mikāshifī Ṭāhā, a descendant of Shaykh Ibrāhīm w. al-Kabbāshī and editor of the latter's *Inshiqāq al-qamar*: hillat al-Kabbāshī, 27.10.1982.
19. *al-khalīfa* Muḥammad ᶜAbd al-Ḥamīd al-ᶜIrāqī: Nūrī, 26 to 29.8.1982 and 2.9.1982.
20. *ustādh* Muḥammad Aḥmad ᶜAbd al-Raḥmān al-Nāṭiq, a descendant of Shaykh Madanī al-Nāṭiq b. ᶜAbd al-Raḥmān w. Ḥamadtū, 27.8.1982.
21. Muḥammad and Aḥmad ᶜUbayd Allāh Karr, the present (1982) *khalīfa*s of the Qādiriyya *ṭarīqa* in Karīma: Karīma, 16.9.1982.
22. Muḥammad al-Tuhāmī al-Ḥasan, senior *khalīfa* of the Aḥmadiyya Muḥammadiyya Idrīsiyya *ṭarīqa*: Khartoum, 18 and 28.11.1982.

23. *khalīfa* Sahal ᶜAlī w. al-Tīkal: al-Zūma, north of Karīma, 8.9.1982.
24. Shaykh Sīd Aḥmad al-Rashīd Muḥammad Ṣāliḥ, a descendant of Shaykh Ibrāhīm al-Rashīd: Ḥalfāyat al-Mulūk, July 1977 (see Karrār (1977), 76).
25. Ṣiddīq Shaykh ᶜAbd al-Raḥmān, a descendant of ᶜAbd al-Raḥmān w. Ḥamadtū: Nūrī, 12.9.1982.
26. *Letter*, dated 20.7.1984 from ᶜAlī Muḥammad al-Shaykh Jiqaydī, a member of the Naḍīfāb clan of Abū Rannāt Island, presently (1982) living at Kobar in Khartoum North (see above no. 5).

B. *Written Sources*

B. 1. *Manuscripts and Letters in Private Hands*

1. al-Aḥmadī, ᶜAlī ᶜĪsā: *K. al-Īḍāḥ li-ahl al-falāḥ*, ms. in the possession of the author's son and successor, Abū'l-ᶜAbbās ᶜAlī ᶜĪsā, at Karīma.
2. *Manāqib al-ḥājj ᶜAbdullāhi al-Dufārī*, ms. in the possession of al-Dufārī's descendants at al-Sajjāna, Khartoum.
3. *Manāqīb al-shaykh Aḥmad al-Jaᶜalī*, ms. in the possession of al-Jaᶜalī's descendants at al-Kadabās (see *Sudanow*, vii/3, March 1982, 38).
4. *Nasab al-Bīliyāb*, ms. in the possession of Muḥammad al-Ḥasan Sīd Aḥmad al-Bīlī, Khartoum.
5. *Nasab al-Ḥamadtūiyāb*, ms. in the possession of Ṣiddīq Shaykh, a descendant of ᶜAbd al-Raḥmān w. Ḥamadtū, Nūrī.

B. 2. *Manuscripts in Public Collections*

Abū Bakr b. Abū'l-Maᶜālī: *Madīḥ*, in praise of *al-sayyid* Muḥammad al-Ḥasan al-Mīrghanī, Bergen NO 136. 6/11.

Abū Bakr w. al-Mutᶜāriḍ: *Madīḥ*, in praise of *al-sayyid* Muḥammad al-Ḥasan al-Mīrghanī, Bergen NO 137. 6/12.

Ibn al-Naṣayḥ, Aḥmad "b. Idrīs" b. Muḥammad: *al-Daᶜāwī al-munaẓẓaha li-rūḥ al-nabī ... wa-ahl baytihi Sādatinā al-Marāghina*. Bergen, NO 158. 8/1.

— *Kitāb al-ibāna al-nūriyya fī sha'n ṣāḥib al-ṭarīqa al-Khatmiyya.* NRO, misc., 1/63/1126; NRO, *Amānāt*, 1/14/59, and Bergen, accession number 240. Cited as *Kitāb al-ibāna*. Unless otherwise specified, references are given to the Bergen version; see Abū Salīm (1968), 36-44 for an analysis of the two NRO mss.

— *Manāqib al-sayyid Muḥammad al-Ḥasan al-Mīrghanī.* NRO, misc., 1/64/1159.

K. fī dhikrat al-sayyid Ghulām Allāh wa-dhikrat Awlād Jābir wa-dhikrat al-Sāda al-Rikābiyya wa-man tanasal minhum. NRO, misc., 1/18/208.

*Majmū*ᶜ *jawābāt al-sāda al-*ᶜ*iẓām*, incorporated in *Tarjamat al-ustādh Aḥmad b. Idrīs.* NRO, misc., 1/81/1294.

Makhṭūṭ ta'rīkh dukhūl al-ṭarā'iq li'l-Sūdān. NRO, Intel., 2/32/261.

Manāqib wa-karāmāt sayyidī al-shaykh Ibrāhīm al-Rashīdī, tilmīdh wa-khalīfat al-sayyid Aḥmad b. Idrīs. NRO, misc., 1/15/179.

Manāqib al-sayyid al-Ḥasan al-Mīrghanī. Bergen, NO 171. 11/1.

al-Mīrghanī, Jaᶜfar al-Ṣādiq b. Muḥammad ᶜUthmān: *Lu'lu'at al-ḥuṣn al-sāṭiᶜa fī baᶜd manāqib dhī 'l-asrār al-lāmiᶜa wa'l-fuyuḍāt al-wahbiyya al-nāfiᶜa sayyidī Muḥammad* ᶜ*Uthmān al-Mīrghanī.* Bergen, accession number 258.

Mukhtaṣar manāqib al-sayyid Muḥammad al-Majdhūb. NRO, misc., 1/67/1188 and 1/82/1315. There are several published versions: Cairo, n.d.; Cairo, 1319/1901-2, and Khartoum, n.d.

Nasab al-Naḍīfāb. Bergen, NO 130. 6/5.

Nisbat al-Duwayḥiyya. Bergen, NO 152. 7/8.

Nisbat al-shaykh ᶜ*Abd al-*ᶜ*Arakī.* NRO, misc., 1/15/83 [copy, Bergen].

Ṣādiq ᶜAbd al-Maḥmūd: *Qaṣīda*, in response to a letter from Shaykh al-Daqlāshī. Completed 12 Dhu'l-Qaᶜda 1249/23 March 1834. Bergen, NO 127. 6/2.

Sanad, Ismāᶜīl b. ᶜAbd Allāh (al-Walī). Bergen, KH 322. 15/29.

Sanad wa-ijāza kubrā, al-ṭarīqa al-Khatmiyya. 28 Rabīᶜ II 1310/19 November 1892. NRO, misc., 1/22/248.

Sanad al-ṭarīqa al-Aḥmadiyya al-Muḥammadiyya. Bergen, KH 228. 12/3.

Sanad al-ṭarīqa al-Khatmiyya. Bergen, NO 126. 6/1.

Sanad ṭariqāt ... al-sayyid Muḥammad ᶜ*Uthmān al-Mīrghanī.* Bergen, NO 128. 6/3.

Shurūṭ al-ṭarīqa al-Tijāniyya. NRO, misc., 1/22/246.

Ta'rīkh al-khulafā' (of al-Ghurayba). Bergen, NO 169. 9/3.

Tarjamāt al-sayyid Muḥammad ᶜUthmān al-Mīrghanī. NRO, misc., 1/63/1126.

Tarjamāt al-ustādh Aḥmad b. Idrīs. NRO, misc., 1/81/1294.

al-Tuhāmī, Muḥammad al-Ḥasan: *R. al-Dīn al-naṣīḥa aw al-Nūr al-ṣātiᶜ wa'l-hiṣām al-qātiᶜ*. Completed 20 Rabīᶜ II 1294/12 May 1874. Bergen, accession number 237.

al-Walī, Ismāᶜīl b. ᶜAbd Allāh: *Sanad*. Bergen, KH 322. 15/29.

--- *K. al-ᶜuhūd al-wāfiyya al-jaliyya fī kayfiyyat ṣifat al-ṭarīqa al-Ismāᶜīliyya*. NRO, misc., 1/82/1319.

B. 3. *Archives*

a. *Bergen: Photographic Collection, Department of History, University of Bergen, Norway*

a. 1. Northern Province (NO)

The following item was photographed by the author at Abū Rannāt Island, 1982:

NO 139. 6/14 *Ijāza*; from Muḥammad b. *al-faqīh* Ibrāhīm, *nasl al-ḥājj* ᶜAmāra, for his son, Ibrāhīm, that he has completed the memorization of the Quran. Rajab 1160/July-August 1747.

The following items were photographed at Duwaym wad Ḥājj, 1982:

NO 145. 7/1 *Waṣfa*; for the cure of semi-paralysis or hemiplegia (*fālij*). Undated.

NO 146. 7/2 *Waṣfa*; for the cure of wind (*rīḥ*). Undated.

NO 147. 7/3 *Waṣfa*; for the cure of migraine (*shaqīqa*). Undated.

NO 155. 7/11 Letter from the Duwayḥiyya of Duwaym Wad Ḥājj to al-Shaykh b. Muḥammad Ṣāliḥ al-Rashīd in Mecca; 21 Ṣafar 1329/21 February 1911.

The following item was photographed by the author in Nūrī, 1982:

NO 163. 8/6 Letter from Muḥammad al-Ḥasan al-Mīrghanī, to the Ḥamadtūiyāb of Nūrī. 10 Rabīᶜ I 1283/23 July 1866.

The following item was photographed by the author at al-Ghurayba, 1982:

NO 167. 9/1 Letter from Muḥammad al-Ḥasan al-Mīrghanī, to the people of al-Ghurayba. Dhū'l-Ḥijja 1272/August-September 1856.

a. 2. Nile Province (NI)

The following items were photographed by Dr. Anders Bjørkelo in al-Matamma, 1980:

NI 298. 15/26 a+b Lithographed appeal from Muḥammad *sirr al-khatim* al-Mīrghanī to ᶜAbd Allāh Ḥamza and his brothers to support the Turco-Egyptian regime. Signed. 8 Dhū'l-Qaᶜda 1302/27 November 1885.

NI 369. 15/97 Letter from Jaᶜfar b. Muḥammad ᶜUthmān al-Mīrghanī to Muḥammad al-Ḥasan al-Mīrghanī. 10 Rabīᶜ II 1272/20 December 1855.

b. *Cairo: Egyptian National Archives (ENA).*

Case no. 265 copy of an Arabic dispatch, *ḥamrā'*, no. 154. Letter from Ismāᶜīl b. ᶜAbd Allāh al-Walī. 4 Dhū'l-Ḥijja 1254/18 February 1838. (ᶜAbd al-Majīd [1949], ii, 19).

daftar, no. 1282 *ṣādir ᶜarḍuḥālāt turkī*. Dispatch from *nāẓir al-dākhliyya* to *kātib al-dīwān al-khidawiyya*. 16 Rajab 1286/22 October 1869. (ᶜAbd al-Majīd [1949], iii, 176).

daftar, no. 1864 *maᶜiyya*, p. 23. From the *mudīriyya* of Dongola to *al-maᶜiyya al-saniyya*. 19 Rajab 1289/22 September 1872. (ᶜAbd al-Majīd [1949], iii, 184).

daftar, no. 1886 *Awāmir ᶜArabī*, p. 16. A noble order from Cairo to the province of Kordofan concerning al-Walī, his sons and students. 13 Shawwāl 1273/8 June 1856.

maᶜiyya turkī, case *Ḥā'*/2, p. 42 (old number, case 46). A letter from Jaᶜfar Pasha Mazhar to the Khedive Ismāᶜīl concerning a monthly subvention to the sons of al-Ḥasan al-Mīrghanī. 8 Ramaḍān 1268/12 December 1869. (ᶜAbd al-Majīd [1949], iii, 178).

sijill (formerly *daftar*), no. 583, p. 16, doc. no. 12, 21 Shaᶜbān 1286/26 November 1869. *Irāda* to *nāẓir al-dākhliyya*. (ᶜAbd al-Majīd [1949], iii, 172).

c. *Sudan Archive, School of Oriental Studies, University of Durham, England (SAD)*

SAD 195/7/2 The Magzub Tarika in the Sudan, by Naum Shukeir (Na^c^ūm Shuqayr); see NRO, Intel., 2/32/263.

d. *National Records Office, Khartoum (NRO)*

Departmental Reports 11/1/4, C.A. Willis, "The Religious Confraternities". A shortened version of this report was published as Willis (1921), 175-94.
Intelligence (Intel.) 2/32/261, English title, "A general note on Tarikas in the Sudan"; contains Ar. ms. *Makhṭūṭ taʾrīkh dukhūl al-ṭarāʾiq li'l-Sūdān.*
Intel. 2/32/262 H.A. MacMichael, "Notes on the Tijania Tarika".
Intel. 2/32/263 "The Magzub Tarika in the Sudan (Na^c^ūm Shuqayr)"; see SAD 195/7/2.
Intel., 2/32/266 "The Kadria Tarika-Dongola."
Intel., 2/32/270 "Tarikas in the Sudan."
Intel., 6/7/22 "A short history of the Idrisia Tarika and its connection with Senussia."
Kassala, 2/124/523 "Religion- Tarikas."
Northern Province, 1/19/127 "Abu el-Hasan Abd el-Mutaal".
Northern Province, 1/25/259 "The Idrisia Tarika."
Northern Province, 1/25/263 "Religion-Tarigas".
Majmū^c^at Abī Salīm, 7/1/10, Abū Salīm, Muḥammad Ibrāhīm, *al-Ṭāʾifiyya fi'l-Sūdān,* typescript.
Miscellaneous (Misc.) 1/27/361 to 1/27/468 constitute an archive of 107 nineteenth-century legal and private documents concerning the affairs of the Naḍīfāb family of Abū Rannāt Island.
Misc. 1/27/371 Letter from Muḥammad al-Ḥasan al-Mīrghanī, to various members of the Naḍīfāb community; undated.
Misc. 1/27/374 Letter from Muḥammad Ṣāliḥ al-Naḍīf and his sons to al-Ḥasan b. *al-khalīfa* al-Tuhāmī Bān al-Naqā. 21 Rabī^c^ I 1283/3 August 1866.
Misc. 1/27/376 Letter from *al-ḥājj* Muḥammad b. Waḥ ... to *al-khalīfa* Muḥammad b. al-Ṣādiq; undated.

Misc. 1/27/381 Marriage contract (*ṣadāq*) for Fāṭima bt. Muḥammad b. ᶜAbd al-Ḥamīd, from her husband, Ḥājj Ḥasan b. ᶜAwḍa. 1269/1852-3.

Misc. 1/27/383 Endowment (*waqf*) of land by *faqīh* Ibrāhīm b. *al-ḥājj* Muḥammad, for his sons and their issue. Undated; incomplete.

Misc. 1/27/386 Letter to Muḥammad Āghā, *ḥākim khuṭṭ al-Shāyqiyya*, 1298/1880-1.

Misc. 1/27/392 Letter from Aḥmad Muḥammad ᶜUthmān al-ᶜIrāqī to *khalīfa* [Aḥmad] Muḥammad Ṣāliḥ al-Naḍīf and others. 24 Rajab 1321/16 October 1903.

Misc. 1/27/396 Letter from ᶜAbd Allāh Maḥjūb al-Mīrghanī to *khalīfa* Muḥammad ᶜAlī al-Naḍīf. 29 Dhū'l-Qaᶜda 1324/14 January 1907.

Misc. 1/27/413 r. & v. Settlement of a dispute concerning the inheritance of the property of Muḥammad Ṣāliḥ al-Naḍīf. 26 Jumādā I 1291/11 July 1874.

Misc. 1/27/314 Marriage contract (*ṣadāq*) for Fāṭima bt. Ḥamad b. Muḥammad, from her husband, Muḥammad b. Muḥammad Ṣāliḥ al-Naḍīf. 10 Rabīᶜ I 1279/5 September 1862.

Misc. 1/27/460 *Sulḥ*, concerning the appointment of Muḥammad Ṣāliḥ al-Naḍīf as *khalīfa* of the Naḍīfāb. 4 Muḥarram 1265/30 November 1848.

B. 4 *Theses, Mimeographs, Conference Papers and Forthcoming Works*

ᶜAbd Allāh, Muḥammad Saᶜīd Aḥmad, "*Min taʾrīkh manṭaqa Dunqulā*", mimeograph, Khartoum, 1978.

ᶜAbd al-Raḥmān, Kamāl Bābikr, "*al-Ṭarīqa al-Sammāniyya fī'l-Sūdān*", BA Honours dissertation, University of Khartoum, 1976.

ᶜAbd al-Sīd, Antūnī Sūrīyāl, "*Juhūd Miṣr al-thaqāfiyya fī'l-Sūdān, 1820-1879*", MA thesis, Department of History, Centre of African Studies, University of Cairo, 1972.

Abū Salīm, Muḥammad Ibrāhīm, "*al-Murshīd īlā wathāʾiq al-Mahdī*", mimeograph, Khartoum: NRO, 1969.

--- "*Dawr al-ᶜulamāʾ fī nashr al-Islām fī'l-Sūdān*", Conference paper, Khartoum, 27-30 November 1982.

--- "*Mafhūm al-khilāfa wa'l-imāma fī'l-Mahdiyya*", Khartoum, n.d.

Badri, Yusuf, "A Survey of Islamic Learning in the Funj State, 1505-1820 AD.", B. Litt. thesis, Oxford University, 1970.

al-Fātih, So'ad, "The Teachings of Muhammad Ahmad, the Sudanese Mahdi", MA thesis, University of London, 1961.

al-Ḥājj, al-Muᶜtaṣim Aḥmad, "*al-Khalāwī fī'l-Sūdān, nuẓumuhā wa-rusūmuhā ḥattā nihāyat al-qarn al-tāsiᶜ ᶜashar*", MA thesis, Omdurman Islamic University, 1982.

El-Ḥassan, Idrīs Sālim, "On Ideology. The Case of Religion in Northern Sudan", Ph.D. thesis, University of Connecticut, 1980.

Holt, P.M., "Traditional historical writing of the Nilotic Sudan", Paper presented to the seminar, "Islamic influences on the literary cultures of Africa", School of Oriental and African Studies, London, January 1969.

Ibrahim, Mahmoud Abdalla, "The history of the Ismāᶜīliyya Ṭarīqa in the Sudan: 1792-1914", Ph.D. thesis, University of London, 1980.

Ibrāhīm Yaḥyā Muḥammad, "*al-Taᶜālīm al-dīnī fī'l-Sūdān*", MA thesis, University of Cairo, Khartoum Branch, 1978.

al-Idrīsī, Ibn Idrīs al-Ḥasan, "*al-Ḥaraka al-Sanūsiyya wa-atharuhā al-thaqāfī fī shamāl Ifrīqiyya*", MA thesis, University of Cairo, 1976.

Karrār, ᶜAlī Ṣāliḥ, "*Athar al-taᶜālīm al-Idrīsiyya fī'l-ṭuruq al-ṣūfiyya fī'l-Sūdān*", MA thesis, Institute of African and Asian Studies, University of Khartoum, 1977.

The Letters of Aḥmad ibn Idrīs, ed. Einar Thomassen and Bernd Radtke (forthcoming).

Lobban, R.A., "Social Networks in the Urban Sudan", Ph.D. thesis, Northwestern University, 1973.

McHugh, N., "Holymen of the Blue Nile: Religious leadership and the genesis of an Arab Islamic society in the Nilotic Sudan, 1500-1850", Ph.D. thesis, Northwestern University, 1986.

Moriah, G., "The Social Structure of the Sufi Associations in Egypt in the 18th Century", Ph.D. thesis, University of London, 1963.

Mustafa, Awad al-Sid al-Saied, "The Majdhubiyya Ṭarīqa: its Doctrine, Organization and Politics", M.Sc. thesis, University of Khartoum, 1977.

O'Fahey, R.S., "A colonial servant. Al-Salāwī and the Sudan", *Der Islam* (forthcoming).

Osman, Abdullahi Mohamed, "The Mikashfiyya: a study of a Religious Ṭarīqa in the Sudan", MA thesis, University of Khartoum, 1978.

Osman, Khadiga Karrar, "Aspects of Sufism in the Sudan", MA thesis, University of Durham, 1975.

Qarīb Allāh, Ḥasan Muḥammad al-Fātiḥ, "*al-Taṣawwuf fī'l-Sūdān ilā nihāyat ᶜaṣr al-Funj*", MA thesis, University of Khartoum, 1965.

Al-Shahi, Ahmed, "An Anthropological Study of a Sudanese Shaigiyya Village", Ph.D. thesis, Oxford University, 1971.

Spaulding, J.L., "Kings of Sun and Shadow: a History of the ᶜAbdallāb Provinces of the Northern Sinnār Sultanate, 1500-1800 AD.", Ph.D. thesis, Columbia University, 1971.
Ṭāhā, Muṣṭafā Ibrāhīm, "*al-Adab al-shaᶜbī ᶜinda'l-Shāyqiyya*", MA thesis, University of Khartoum, 1967.
El Tom, Abdullahi Osman, "Religious men and literacy in Berti society", Ph.D. thesis, St. Andrews University, 1983.
Voll, J.O., "A History of the Khatmiyya Tariqah in the Sudan", Ph.D. thesis, Harvard University, 1969.

B. 5. *Arabic Printed Primary Sources*

This section includes works of a primary or quasi-primary nature, and works of reference.

a) *General*

al-Aᶜlām, al-Ziriklī, Khayr al-Dīn n.d. (*c.* 1979), *al-Aᶜlām Qāmūs tarājim li-ashhar al-rijāl wa'l-nisāʾ min al-ᶜarab wa'l-mustaᶜribīn wa'l-mustashriqīn*. 12 vols., n.p. (Beirut?).
al-Ghazālī, Abū ᶜAbd Allāh Muḥammad (1967), *Tuḥfat al-nuẓẓār fī gharāʾib al-amṣār wa-ᶜajāʾib al-aṣfār*, Cairo.
--- *Iḥyaʾ ᶜulūm al-dīn* (n.d.); Cairo.
Ibn Baṭṭūṭa, Abū ᶜAbd Allāh Muḥammad (n.d.), *Tuḥfat al-nuẓẓār fī gharāʾib al-amṣār wa-ᶜajāʾib al-asfār*, Cairo.
Ibn Khaldūn, ᶜAbd al-Raḥmān b. Muḥammad (1958), *al-ᶜIbar wa-dīwān al-mubtadāʾ wa'l-Khabar*, 7 vols., Beirut.
al-Jabartī, ᶜAbd al-Raḥmān (n.d.), *Taʾrīkh ᶜajāʾib al-athār fī'l-tarājim wa'l-akhbār*, 3 vols., Beirut.
Kaḥḥāla, ᶜUmar Riḍā (1957-61), *Muᶜjam al-muʾallifīn, tarājim muṣannifī al-kutub al-ᶜarabiyya*, 15 vols., Damascus.
al-Kalābādhī, Abū Bakr Muḥammad (1400/1980), *al-Taᶜarruf li-madhhab ahl al-taṣawwuf*, Cairo.
al-Nabhānī, Yūsuf b. Ismāᶜīl (n.d.), *Jāmiᶜ karāmāt al-awliyāʾ*, 2 vols., Cairo.
al-Shādhilī, al-Ḥasan b. *al-ḥājj* Muḥammad (1347/1928-9), *K. Ṭabaqāt al-Shādhiliyya al-kubrā, al-musammā Jāmiᶜ al-karāmāt al-ᶜaliyya fī ṭabaqāt al-sādāt al-Shādhiliyya*, Cairo.

b) *Works relating to the ṭarīqas or to the Sudan*

ᶜAbd al-Karīm, ᶜAydarūs (n.d.), *Manāqib al-quṭb al-ḥājj ᶜAbd Allāh al-Dufārī*, n.p.

ᶜAbd al-Mutaᶜāl, Shams al-Dīn (1358/1939), *Kanz al-saᶜād wa'l-rashād*; pp. 9-10 contain a biography of Aḥmad b. Idrīs. Khartoum.

ᶜAbd al-Raḥīm, Muḥammad (1953), *al-Nidāʾ fī dafᶜ al-iftirāʾ*, Cairo.

ᶜAbd al-Raḥmān, Yūsuf al-Khalīfa (n.d.), *al-Jawwāb al-kāfī fi'l-ijāba ᶜan asiʾla fuhūm al-muslimīn ᶜāmmatan wa-ahl al-ṭuruq al-ṣūfiyya khāṣṣatan*, Cairo.

Abū Salīm, Muḥammad Ibrāhīm, ed. (1969a), *Manshūrāt al-Mahdiyya*, Beirut.

--- ed. (1974), *Mudhakkirāt ᶜUthmān Diqna*, Khartoum.

al-Aḥmadī, Kāmil Muḥammad Ḥasan (n.d.), *Dumūᶜ al-wafāʾ ᶜalā imām al-aṣfiyāʾ [al-sayyid Muḥammad al-Sharīf b. ᶜAbd al-Mutaᶜāl al-Idrīsī]*, Khartoum.

Badr, Muḥammad b. Aḥmad al-Shaykh al-ᶜUbayd (1920), *K. sirāj al-sālikīn al-maʾkhūdh min kalām al-Shaykh Muḥammad b. Aḥmad Badr al-mashhūr bi'l-ᶜUbayd, wa-qad rattabahu tilmīdhuhu Aḥmad b. Ibrāhīm al-Jibayl*. Published together with Muḥammad b. *al-ḥājj* Nūr, *Kitāb miftāḥ al-baṣāʾir*. Cairo.

al-Bashīr, ᶜAbd Allāh al-Shaykh, ed. (1976), *Dīwān al-shāᶜir al-ṣūfī, Wad Nafīsa*, Khartoum.

al-Bayyādī, ᶜUmar ᶜAbd al-Azīz (1979), *Nasab al-sayyid Aḥmad b. Idrīs*. Al-Zayniyya/al-Uqṣur: published privately by the sons of al-sayyid Muṣṭafā b. ᶜAbd al-ᶜĀl al-Idrīsī.

al-Faḥl, al-Fakī al-Ṭāhir (n.d.), *Taʾrīkh wa-uṣūl al-ᶜArab bi'l-Sūdān*, Khartoum.

al-Hajrasī, Muḥamma Khalīl (1314/1915-6), *al-Qaṣr al-mushīd fi'l-tawḥīd wa-fī ṭarīqa sayyidī Ibrāhīm al-Rashīd*, Cairo.

Ibn al-Bashīr, Aḥmad al-Ṭayyib (1955), *al-Ḥikam al-musammā bi'l-Nafas al-raḥmānī fi'l-ṭawr al-insānī*. Cairo: M. al-Miṣrī.

Ibn Ḍayf Allāh, Muḥammad al-Nūr (1974), *K. al-ṭabaqāt fī khuṣūṣ al-awliyāʾ wa'l-ṣāliḥīn wa'l-ᶜulamāʾ wa'l-shuᶜarāʾ fi'l-Sūdān*, ed. Yūsuf Faḍl Ḥasan, 2nd edn, Khartoum.

Ibn Idrīs, Aḥmad (1372/1953), *al-ᶜIqd al-nafīs fī naẓm jawāhir al-tadrīs ... al-sayyid Aḥmad b. Idrīs*, Cairo. A compilation by an Indian scholar, Ismāᶜīl al-Nawwāb, based on Ibn Idrīs' lectures as recounted

by one of his Sudanese students, Abū'l-Maᶜālī ᶜAbd Allāh al-Mawārzī. *al-ᶜIqd* contains a brief biography (pp. 3-6).
--- (1359/1940), *Majmūᶜat awrād aḥzāb wa-rasāʾil*, Cairo.
Ibrāhīm, Aḥmad ᶜUthmān (1965), *Min ashᶜār al-Shāyqiyya*, Khartoum.
al-Kabbāshī, Ibrāhīm (1971), *Inshiqāq al-qamar li'l-rasūl sayyid al-bashar*, ed. al-Mikāshfī Ṭāhā al-Shaykh Muḥammad ᶜAlī, Khartoum.
al-Lībī,ᶜAbd al-Malik b. ᶜAbd al-Qādir b. ᶜAlī (1966), *al-Fawāʾid al-jaliyya fī taʾrīkh al-ᶜāʾila al-Sanūsiyya al-ḥākima fī Lībīyā*. Damascus, Dār al-jazāʾir al-ᶜArabiyya.
al-Madanī, Ṣāliḥ b. *al-ḥājj* Muḥammad b. Ṣāliḥ al-Jaᶜfarī (1380/1960), *al-Muntaqā al-nafīs fī manāqib quṭb dāʾira al-taqdīs sayyidinā wa-mawlānā al-Sayyid Aḥmad b. Idrīs*, Cairo.
Majmūᶜat al-nafaḥāt al-rabbāniyya al-mushtamila ᶜalā sabᶜa rasāʾil Mīrghaniyya (1370/1950), Cairo.
Makhṭūṭa Kātib al-Shūna fī taʾrīkh al-salṭana al-Sinnāriyya wa'l-idāra al-Miṣriyya n.d. (1963), ed. al-Shāṭir Buṣaylī ᶜAbd al-Jalīl, Cairo.
Manāqib al-sayyid ᶜAlī al-Mīrghanī, Khartoum, 1390/1970.
al-Mīrghanī, Jaᶜfar al-Ṣādiq b. Muḥammad ᶜUthmān (1936), *Dīwān Riyāḍ madīḥ wa-jalāʾ kull dhī wudd ṣaḥīḥ wa-shifāʾ kull qalb jarīḥ fī madḥ al-nabī al-malīḥ*, Cairo.
al-Mīrghanī, Muḥammad ᶜUthmān, *al-Fatḥ al-mabrūk fī kathīr min ādāb al-sulūk*, in *al-Rasāʾil al-Mīrghaniyya*, 37-46.
--- *al-Hibāt al-muqtabasa li-iẓhār al-masāʾil al-khamsa*, in *al-Rasāʾil al-Mīrghaniyya*, 19-36.
--- (1358/1939), *Majmūᶜ al-awrād al-kabīr*, Cairo.
--- (1367/1948), *Majmūᶜ fatḥ al-rasūl*, Cairo
--- (1391/1971), *Manāqib ... al-Sayyid Aḥmad b. Idrīs*, Wad Madanī.
--- (1350/1931), *Mawlid al-nabī al-musammā al-asrār al-rabbāniyya*, Cairo.
--- *Minwāl al-ṭarīqa al-ṭāhira al-nūrāniyya*, in *al-Rasāʾil al-Mīrghaniyya*, 93-96.
--- *al-Nūr al-barrāq fī madḥ al-nabī al-miṣdāq*, several editions.
--- (1375/1955-6), *Tāj al-tafāsīr li-kalām al-malik al-kabīr*, also called *Khitām al-tafāsīr*, ed. *al-ḥājj* ᶜAbd al-Salām b. Muḥammad b. Shaqrūn, 2 vols., Cairo.
--- *al-Zuhūr al-fāʾiqa fī ḥuqūq al-ṭarīqa al-ṣādiqa*, in *al-Rasāʾil al-Mīrghaniyya*, 47-54.
al-Mīrghanī, Muḥammad ᶜUthmān b. ᶜAlī, Interview in, *Majallat al-fatḥ*, Ramaḍān 1402/June-July 1982, no. 1. Journal published by

Jamā^cat fatḥ al-rasūl of the mosque of *al-sayyid* ᶜAlī al-Mīrghanī, Khartoum North.
Nūr al-Dāʾim, ᶜAbd al-Maḥmūd (1954), *Azāhīr al-riyāḍ fī manāqib al-ᶜārif bi-llāh al-shaykh Aḥmad al-Ṭayyib*, Khartoum.
--- (1955), *al-ᶜUrf al-fāʾiḥ wa'l-ḍiyāʾ al-lāʾiḥ fī manāqib al-quṭb al-rājiḥ wa'l-ghawth al-wāḍiḥ sayyidī al-ustādh al-shaykh Aḥmad al-Ṭayyib b. al-Bashīr*, Omdurman.
al-Rasāᶜil al-Mīrghaniyya (1399/1979), *al-Rasāʾil al-Mīrghaniyya ... fī ādāb al-ṭarīqa al-Khatmiyya*, Cairo.
al-Rashīd, Ibrāhīm (1394/1974), *Aᶜṭār azhār aghṣān haẓīrat al-taqdīs fī karāmāt ... al-sayyid Aḥmad b. Idrīs*, Cairo.
al-Raṭbī, Aḥmad b. ᶜAbd al-Raḥmān, *Minḥat al-aṣḥāb li-man arāda sulūk ṭarīq al-aṣfiyāʾ wa'l-aḥbāb*, in *al-Rasāʾil al-Mīrghaniyya*, 61-86.
al-Sanūsī, Muḥammad b. ᶜAlī (1968), *al-Manhal al-rawī al-rāʾiq fī asānīd al-ᶜulūm wa-uṣūl al-ṭarāʾiq*, n.p.
al-Sarrāj, Muḥammad b. ᶜAbd al-Majīd (1374/1955), *al-Manāḥij al-ᶜaliyya fī tarājim al-sāda al-Mīrghaniyya*, Khartoum.
Shuqayr, Naᶜūm (1903), *Taʾrīkh al-Sūdān al-qadīm wa'l-ḥadīth wa-jughrāfiyatuhu*, 3 vols., Cairo.
Taʾrīkh mulūk al-Sūdān, ed. Makkī Shibayka. Khartoum 1947.
Tarjamat al-ᶜallāma al-sayyid Aḥmad ibn Idrīs (1315/1897-8), n.p.
al-Tijānī, Muḥammad al-Sayyid (n.d.), *Ghāyat al-amānī fī manāqib wa-karāmāt aṣḥāb al-shaykh sayyidī Aḥmad al-Tijānī*, Cairo.
al-Waṭanī, Zaghlūl Muḥammad (1953), *Abṭāl al-Khatmiyya*, vol. i (all published), Cairo.

B. 6. *European Primary Sources*

Budge, E.A.W. (1907), *The Egyptian Sudan*, 2 vols, London.
Burckhardt, J.L. (1822), *Travels in Nubia*, London.
English, G.B. (1822), *A Narrative of the Expedition to Dongola and Senaar*, London.
Hoskins, G.A. (1835), *Travels in Ethiopia*, London.
Krump, T. (1710), *Hoher und Fruchtbarer Palm-Baum des Heiligen Evangelij*, Augsburg, unpublished English translation by J.L. Spaulding; copy in the possession of R.S. O'Fahey.
Le Châtelier, A. (1887), *Les Confréries musulmanes du Hedjaz*, Paris.
Slatin, R.C. (1896), *Fire and Sword in the Sudan*, London.

Wingate, F.R. (1968), *Mahdiism and the Egyptian Sudan*, 2nd edn, London.
--- (1982), *Ten Years' Captivity in the Mahdi's Camp, 1882-1892, from the original manuscript of Father Joseph Ohrwalder*, London.

B. 7. *Secondary Literature*

ᶜAbd al-Jalīl, al-Shāṭir Buṣaylī (1955), *Maᶜālim taʾrīkh Sūdān Wādī'l-Nīl*, Cairo.
ᶜAbd al-Majīd, ᶜAbd al-ᶜAzīz Amīn (1949), *al-Tarbiyya fī'l-Sūdān wa'l-usus al-nafsiyya wa'l-ijtimāᶜiyya allatī qāmat ᶜalayhā min awwal al-qarn al-sādis ᶜashar ilā nihāyat al-qarn al-thāmin ᶜashar*, 3 vols., Cairo.
ᶜAbd al-Raḥīm, ᶜAbd al-Raḥīm ᶜAbd al-Raḥmān (1979), *Min taʾrīkh shibh al-jazīra al-ᶜArabiyya fī'l-ᶜaṣr al-ḥadīth*. vol. 1. *al-Dawla al-Saᶜūdiyya al-ūlā*, 1158-1233/1745-1818, Cairo.
ᶜAbd al-Raḥīm, Muḥammad (1952), *Al-Nidāʾ fī dafᶜ al-iftirāʾ*, Cairo.
ᶜĀbdin, ᶜAbd al-Majīd (1967), *Taʾrīkh al-thaqāfa al-ᶜarabiyya fī'l-Sūdān*, 2nd edn, Beirut.
Abū Salīm, Muḥammad Ibrāhīm (1968), "Makhṭūṭ fī taʾrīkh muʾassis al-Khatmiyya", *MDS*, 36-43.
--- (1969b), "Ijāza Sammāniyya", *MDS*, 30-44.
--- (1970), *al-Ḥaraka al-fikriyya fī'l-Mahdiyya*, Khartoum.
--- (1980), *al-Sāqiya*, Khartoum.
Abun-Nasr, J.M. (1965), *The Tijaniyya. A Sufi Order in the Modern World*, London.
Adams, W.Y. (1977), *Nubia. Corridor to Africa*, Princeton.
ᶜAlī, al-Ṭāhir M. (1970), *al-Ādāb al-ṣūfī fī'l-Sūdān*, Khartoum.
ᶜAmār, ᶜAlī Sālim (1951), *Abū'l-Ḥasan al-Shādhilī*, Cairo.
al-Amawī, Muḥammad ᶜUthmān (1963), "Dhikrā al-Sayyid al-Ḥasan al-Mīrghanī", *Ṣawt al-Sūdān*, 8 February 1963.
al-Amīn, ᶜIzz al-Dīn (1395/1975), *Qariyat Kutrānj wa-āthāruhā al-ᶜilmī fī'l-Sūdān*, Khartoum.
Arberry, A.J. transl. (1935), *The Doctrines of the Ṣūfis* (transl. of al-Kalābādhī, *K. al-Taᶜarruf li-madhhab ahl al-taṣawwuf*), Cambridge.
--- (1950), *Sufism*, London.
Arkell, A.J. (1932), "Fung origins", *SNR*, xv/2, 201-50.
Arnold, T.W. (1913), *The Preaching of Islam. A History of the propagation of the Muslim faith*, 2nd edn, London.

al-ᶜAwaḍ, ᶜAwaḍ ᶜAbd al-Hādī (1971), "al-Shāyqiyya: taʾrīkhuhum wa-thaqāfatuhum ḥattā al-fatḥ al-Turkī", *MDS*, 5-36.

al-Bakrī, Muḥammad Tawfīq (1323/1905-6), *Bayt al-Ṣiddīq*, Cairo.

Barbour, K.N. (1961), *The Republic of the Sudan: A Regional Geography*, London.

Barclay, H.B. (1964), *Buuri al Lamaab*, Ithaca.

Bashīr, Bashīr Ibrāhīm (1979), "ᶜAydhāb, ḥayātuhā al-dīniyya wa'l-adabiyya", *MDS*, 54-84.

Beshir, Mohammed Omer (1969), *Educational Development in the Sudan, 1898-1956*, Oxford.

al-Bīlī, Aḥmad (1974), *al-Taᶜlīm fī'l-khalwa fī'l-Sūdān*, Khartoum.

Bjørkelo, A. (1989), *Prelude to the Mahdiyya. Peasants and Traders in the Shendi Region, 1821-1885*, Cambridge.

Brett, M. ed. (1973), *Northern Africa: Islam and Modernization*, London.

Brockelmann, C. "al-Bakrī, Muḥammad b. ᶜAbd al-Raḥmān", *EI²*, i, 965.

Cornell, V.J. (1983), "The logic of analogy and the role of the Sufi Shaykh in post-Marinid Morocco", *IJMES*, xv, 67-93.

Crawford, O.G.S. (1951), *The Fung Kingdom of Sennar*, Gloucester.

Crowfoot, J.W. (1922), "Wedding customs in the northern Sudan", *SNR*, v, 1-28.

Douin, G. (1936), *Histoire du Règne du khédive Ismail.* Tome III (four parts): *L'Empire Africain*, Cairo.

--- (1944), *Histoire du Soudan Egyptien*, vol. i (all published), Cairo.

Dwyer, K. (1982), *Moroccan Dialogues. Anthropology in Question*, London.

Eickelman, D. (1978), "The art of memory: Islamic education and its social reproduction", *Comparative Studies in Society and History*, xx/4, 485-516.

--- (1981), *The Middle East. An Anthropological Approach*, New York.

Eustache, D. "Idris I", *EI²*, iii, 1031.

--- "Idrisids", *EI²*, iii, 1035-7.

Evans-Pritchard, E.E. (1949), *The Sanusi of Cyrenaica*, Oxford.

Farah, C.E. (1972), "Social implications of a Sufi disciple's etiquette", in *Proceedings, VIth Congress of Arabic and Islamic Studies*, ed. F. Rundgren, Uppsala/Leiden, pp. 45-57.

Fleming, G.J. (1922), "Kasala", *SNR*, v, 65-77.

Gardet, L. "Dhikr", *EI²*, ii, 223-7.

Geertz, C. (1971), *Islam Observed. Religious Developments in Morocco and Indonesia*, Chicago.

Gellner, E. (1969), *Saints of the Atlas*, London.

--- (1981), *Muslim Society*, Cambridge.

Gibb, H.A.R. "ᶜAydhāb", *EI²*, i, 782.

Gilsenan, M. (1973), *Saints and Sufi in Modern Egypt. An Essay in the Sociology of Religion*, Oxford.

Gleichen, A.E.W., Count, ed. (1905), *The Anglo-Egyptian Sudan*, 2 vols, London.

Hamilton, J.A. de C., ed. (1935), *The Anglo-Egyptian Sudan from Within*, London.

Ḥasan, Qurashī Muḥammad (1972), *Maᶜa shuᶜarāʾ al-madāʾiḥ*, 2nd edn, Khartoum.

Ḥasan, Yūsuf Faḍl (1967), *The Arabs and the Sudan*, Edinburgh.

--- ed. (1971), *Sudan in Africa*, Khartoum.

--- (1971a), "External Islamic influences and the progress of Islamization in the Eastern Sudan between the fifteenth and the nineteenth centuries", in Ḥasan, ed., *Sudan in Africa*, 73-86.

--- (1971b), *Muqaddima fī taʾrīkh al-mamālik al-Islāmiyya fī'l-Sūdān al-sharqī*, 1450-1821, Cairo.

--- (1975), *Dirāsāt fī taʾrīkh al-Sūdān*, vol. i, Khartoum.

Hill, R. (1959), *Egypt in the Sudan*, London.

--- (1967), *A Biographical Dictionary of the Sudan*, 2nd edn, London.

--- (1970), *On the Frontiers of Islam*, Oxford.

--- ed. (1984), *The Sudan Memoirs of Carl Christian Giegler Pasha, 1873-83*, London.

Hillelson, S. (1918), "The people of Abu Jarid", *SNR*, i, 175-93.

--- (1923), "Tabaqat Wad Dayf Allah: studies in the lives of the scholars and saints", *SNR*, vi/2, 191-230.

--- (1935), *Sudan Arabic Texts*, Cambridge.

Hiskett, M. (1973), "The Development of Islam in Hausaland", in M. Brett, ed., *Northern Africa*, London, 57-64.

Holt, P.M. "Djaᶜaliyyūn", *EI²*, ii, 351-2.

--- "Fundj", *EI²*, ii, 943-5.

--- (1963), *A Modern History of the Sudan*, 2nd edn, London.

--- (1970), *The Mahdist State in the Sudan, 1881-1898*, 2nd. ed., Oxford.

--- (1973a), "Islamization of the Sudan", in M. Brett, ed., *Northern Africa*, London, 13-22.

--- (1973b), *Studies in the History of the Near East*, London.

--- and Daly, M. (1979), *The History of the Sudan. From the coming of Islam to the present day*, London.

Hourani, A. (1967), *Arabic Thought in the Liberal Age, 1798-1939*, London.

Hughes, T.P. (1885), *A Dictionary of Islam*, London.

Hunwick, J.O. (1984), "Ṣāliḥ al-Fullānī (1752/3-1803): the career and teachings of a West African ᶜ*ālim* in Medina", in *In Quest of an Islamic Humanism*, ed. A.H. Green, 139-5, American University, Cairo.

Ibn Ḥajar, Aḥmad (1395/1975-6), *Muḥammad b. ᶜAbd al-Wahhāb*, Mecca

Ibrāhīm, Aḥmad ᶜUthmān (1965), *Min ashᶜār al-Shāyqiyya*, Khartoum.

Ibrāhīm, Ḥasan Aḥmad (n.d.), *Muḥammad ᶜAlī fī'l-Sūdān*, Khartoum.

Ibrahim, Hayder (1979), *The Shaiqiya. The cultural and social change of a Northern Sudanese riverain people*, Wiesbaden.

ᶜInayatulah, Sh., "Shaykh Aḥmad Sirhindī", *EI*², i, 297-8.

Jackson, H.C. (1919), "The Mahas of 'Eilafun'", *SNR*, ii, 285-92.

Jenkins, R.G. (1979), "The evolution of religious brotherhoods in North and Northwest Africa, 1523-1900", in J.R. Willis (ed.), *Studies in West African Islamic History*, i, 40-77.

Jong, F. de (1972), review of *The Sufi Orders in Islam*, by J. S. Trimingham, Oxford 1971, in *Journal of Semitic Studies*, vol. 17/2, 279-85.

--- (1978), *Ṭuruq and Ṭuruq-linked Institutions in Nineteenth Century Egypt*, Leiden.

--- "Khalwatiyya", *EI*², iv 991-3.

--- "al-Duwayḥī, Ibrāhīm", *EI*². supplement, 278-9.

Keddie, N.R., ed. (1972), *Scholars, Saints and Sufis. Muslim Religious Institutions in the Middle East Since 1500*, Berkeley.

Landolt, H. "Khalwa", *EI*²., iv, 990-1.

Laoust, H., "Ibn ᶜAbd al-Wahhāb",*EI*²., iii, 677-9.

Lewis, B. (1960), *The Arabs in History*, London.

Lewis, I.M. (1955), "Sufism in Somaliland", *BSOAS*, xvii, 581-602.

Lings, M. (1961), *A Moslem Saint of the Twentieth Century. Shaikh Ahmad Al-ᶜAlawi*, London.

MacMichael, H.A. (1912), *The Tribes of Northern and Central Kordofan*, Cambridge.

--- (1922), *A History of the Arabs in the Sudan*, 2 vols., Cambridge.

al-Maghribī, Muḥammad al-Fātih Maḥmūd (1982), "Taʾrīkh al-ṭuruq al-Ṣūfiyya fī'l-Sūdān. Al-ṭarīqa al-Qādiriyya", in *Majallat al-taṣawwuf al-Islāmī*, 56-7, Cairo.

Maḥmūd, ᶜAbd al-Qādir (1971), *al-Ṭawāʾif al-ṣūfiyya fī'l-Sūdān. Ansābuhum wa-uṣūl turāthihim wa-falsafatihim*, Khartoum.

Martin, B.G. (1972), "A Short History of the Khalwati Order of Dervishes", in Keddie, ed., *Scholars, Saints and Sufis*, 275-305.

--- (1976), *Muslim Brotherhoods in Nineteenth Century Africa*, Cambridge.

Montet, E. (1967), "Religious orders (Muslim)", *ERE*, x, 719-26.

al-Muftī, Ḥusayn Sīd Aḥmad (1378/1959), *Taṭawwur niẓām al-qaḍāʾ fī'l-Sūdan*, vol. i (all published), Khartoum.

Musᶜad, Muṣṭafā (1959), "The Downfall of the Christian Nubian Kingdoms", *SNR*, xl, 124-7.

Musᶜad, Muḥammad Muṣṭafā (1972), *al-Maktaba al-ᶜArabiyya al-Sūdāniyya*, Cairo.

al-Muṣṣawar (Cairo), no. 1277, 1 April 1949; no. 2988, 15 January 1982.

Nicholls, W. (1913), *The Shaikia*, Dublin.

O'Brien, D. Cruise (1971), *The Mourids of Senegal*, Oxford.

O'Fahey, R.S. (1980), *State and Society in Dār Fūr*, London.

--- (1982/3), "A history of the Awlād Hindī", *Bulletin of Information, Fontes Historiae Africanae*, 7/8, Evanston, 43-50.

--- (1990), *Enigmatic Saint. Aḥmad ibn Idrīs and the Idrīsī Tradition*, London.

--- and Spaulding, J.L. (1972), "Hāshim and the Musabbaᶜāt", *BSOAS*, xxxv/2, 316-333.

--- and Spaulding, J.L. (1974), *Kingdoms of the Sudan*, London.

Padwick, C. (1969), *Muslim Devotions. A Study of Prayer-Manuals in Common Use*, London.

Paul, A. (1955), "Aidhab: A Medieval Red Sea Port", *SNR*, xxxvi/1, 64-70.

Rajab, Manṣūr ᶜAlī (1946), *al-Azhar bayn al-māḍī wa'l-ḥāḍir*, Cairo.

Reid, J. (1935), *Tribes and Prominent Families in the Blue Nile Province*, Khartoum.

Samatar, Said (1982), *Oral Poetry and Somali Nationalism*, Cambridge.

Sāmī, Aḥmad ᶜAbd Allāh (1968), *al-Shāᶜir al-Sūdānī, Muḥammad Saᶜīd al-ᶜAbbāsī*, Khartoum.

al-Shahi, Ahmed (1981), "A Noah's Ark: the Continuity of the Khatmiyya Order in Northern Sudan", *Bulletin, British Society for Middle Eastern Studies*, viii/1, 13-29.

al-Shahi, Ahmed (1986), *Themes From Northern Sudan*, London.

Shalabi, Aḥmad (1954), *History of Muslim Education*, Beirut.

al-Shayyāl, Jamāl al-Dīn (1965), *Aᶜlām al-Iskandariyya fī'l-ᶜaṣr al-Islāmī*, Cairo.

Shinnie, P.L. (1971), "The culture of medieval Nubia and its impact on Africa", in Hasan (ed.), *Sudan in Africa*, Khartoum, 42-50.

al-Shūsh, Muḥammad Ibrāhīm (1962), *al-Shiᶜr al-ḥadīth fī'l-Sūdān*, vol. i (all published), Cairo.

Spaulding, J.L. (1982), "Slavery, land tenure and social class in the northern Turkish Sudan", *IJAHS*, xv/1, 1-20.

--- (1985), *The Heroic Age in Sinnār*, East Lansing.

Suban, J.A. (1970), *Sufism: its Saints and Shrines. An Introduction to the Study of Sufism with special reference to India*, New York.

Sudanow, 7/3, March 1982 (report on Kadabās).

al-Ṭawīl, Tawfīq (1946), *al-Taṣawwuf fī Miṣr ibbān al-ᶜaṣr al-ᶜUthmānī*, Cairo.

al-Tayyib, Abdalla (1964), "The changing customs of the riverain Sudan, III", *SNR*, xlv, 13-28.

al-Ṭayyib, al-Ṭayyib Muḥammad (1977), *Faraḥ wad Taktūk*, Khartoum.

Trimingham, J.S. (1949), *Islam in the Sudan*, London.

--- (1952), *Islam in Ethiopia*, London.

--- (1971), *The Sufi Orders in Islam*, Oxford.

ᶜUthmān, Sirr al-Khatim (1975), *Awlād Jābir*, Khartoum.

Voll, J.O. (1975), "Muḥammad Ḥayyā al-Sindī and Muḥammad ibn ᶜAbd al-Wahhāb: an analysis of an intellectual group in eighteenth-century Madīna", *BSOAS*, xxxviii, 32-39.

Wahba, Hāfiẓ (1946), *Jazīrat al-ᶜArab fī'l-qarn al-ᶜishrīn*, Cairo.

Warburg, G. (1971), "Religious policy in the northern Sudan: ᶜulamāʾ and Ṣūfism, 1899-1918", *Asian and African Studies* (Jerusalem), vii, 89-119.

Wensinck, A.J., "al-Khaḍir", *EI²*, iv, 902-5.

Willis, C.A. (1921), "Religious confraternities of the Sudan", *SNR*, iv/4, 175-94.

Willis, J.R., ed. (1979), *Studies in West African Islamic History*, i. The Cultivators of Islam, London.

Winter, M. (1982), *Society and Religion in Early Ottoman Egypt. Studies in the Writings of ᶜAbd al-Wahhāb al-Shaᶜrānī*, London.
Ziadeh, N.A. (1958), *Sanūsīyah. A Study of a Revivalist Movement in Islam*, Leiden.

INDEX OF PERSONS

GENERAL INDEX

Some of the most frequently recurring names, such as the Sudan and Shāyqiyya, have not been indexed